MY RED BLOOD

MY RED BLOOD

A Memoir of Growing Up Communist,
Coming onto the Greenwich Village Folk Scene,
and Coming Out in the Feminist Movement

ALIX DOBKIN

ALYSON books

My Red Blood
A Memoir of Growing up Communist, Coming onto the Greenwich Village Folk
Scene, and Coming Out in the Feminist Movement

© 2009 Alix Dobkin

Published by Alyson Books
245 West 17th Street, Suite 1200, New York, NY 10011
www.alyson.com

First Alyson Books edition: October 2009

Library of Congress Cataloging-in-Publication data are on file.

ISBN-10: 1-59350-107-2
ISBN-13: 978-1-59350- 107-5

10 9 8 7 6 5 4 3 2 1

Cover design by Victor Mingovits
Book interior by Maria E. Torres, Neuwirth & Associates, Inc.

Printed in the United States of America
Distributed by Consortium Book Sales and Distribution
Distribution in the United Kingdom by Turnaround Publisher Services Ltd

For my favorite migafnees,
Lucca, Marly & Sorella

The force that through the green fuse drives the flower . . .
Drives my red blood . . .

—DYLAN THOMAS

Contents

PREFACE
Why I Wrote This, or, As Pop Would Say,
    "Why Is a Cow? ix

PART ONE
1934–1952
Red Diaper on a White Horse 1

PART TWO
1952–1954
Philly... 47

PART THREE
1954–1956
Flat Kansas 75

PART FOUR
1956–1962
Driving My Red Blood... 95

PART FIVE
1962–1965
The Folk Biz... 149

PART SIX
1965–1971
Marriage.. 209

PART SEVEN
1971–1972
And Beyond 255

EPILOGUE 267
ACKNOWLEDGMENTS 271
SOURCES AND RESOURCES 273

Why I Wrote This, or, As Pop Would Say, "Why Is a Cow?"

WHAT NOTORIETY I have is due to more than three decades of work as an opinionated songwriter, entertainer, cultural organizer, and community activist. For those who expect to read about my adventures as a Professional Lesbian, I refer you to what I have documented in songs, liner notes, and my out-of-print songbook as well as articles and columns in the gay, lesbian, and women's press. This memoir, however, concerns my "pre-lesbian" life.

Several factors drove me forward, not the least of which was a desire to exploit the FBI dossier I'd requested under the Freedom of Information Act in 1983 in order to extract quotes to use for promotion. From the mostly blacked-out pages of my two-inch-thick file, I managed to find enough material to add the perspective of the Department of Justice to a narrative in which they play a role.

More important, this project has been a way to pass on the great stories Pop told about his times in a movement that significantly transformed our country, yet remains decidedly absent from popular history. Decisive moments and pivotal events are easily erased from collective memory, and I wanted to do my part to fill in some of the gaps through a conscious political/social/cultural lens.

It seems important to me to illustrate how differently life was lived during the time of the Brooklyn Dodgers, ten-cent ice cream cones, and doctors who made house calls. I wrote this memoir to document the days before common sense prevailed over rabid anti-Communism, and before peace, love, and folk music slipped off the charts. I wanted to convey the excitement that ignited my generation in the women's movement.

To those of us over sixty, the first three decades of our lives are ancient history: done, gone, and unimaginable to our children and grandchildren, yet they profoundly shaped the world we all currently inhabit. I want Adrian, Lucca, Marly, and Sorella to have access to what life in a disappeared world was like for "Grandma Alix" when she was growing up.

Retelling becomes a tricky business, but in sorting out my recollections I've been as faithful as possible to my early life while regretting the abandoned bits. Many favorite stories hit the dust in a five-year editing process along with a mountain of adjectives and adverbs, and the names of many people I have known and learned from, loved, and hated. What remains is what you get, and, I hope, will find worthwhile.

Alix Dobkin
Woodstock, NY
July 2009

Red Diaper on a White Horse

Once upon a time,
New York City was as delightful a place to live in as to visit.

—GORE VIDAL, New York Review of Books

PAUL ROBESON SAT in our Manhattan kitchen, his grand dimensions making the small room appear even smaller. He claimed to prefer the informal setting to our living room and tried to put my parents at ease with his unassuming manner. But how could anyone not be awestruck by his towering stature, or starstruck by his daunting reputation? At seven years old I was aware of the admiration my parents felt for him and for the songs he had made famous. Grandma knew Mr. Robeson through her Communist Party connections and had invited the great man to visit at our Manhattan apartment on West Eighty-third Street. She beamed, Pop smiled, and Mom, a nervous woman, served tea and fussed.

Paul Robeson was a "Negro," which, in the late 1940s, meant that his life was especially hard and unfair. I understood that people who didn't like Jews also didn't like Negroes and used Jim Crow to hurt them and keep them back. This, like all injustice, made me sad and angry. My baseball hero, Jackie Robinson, had defeated Jim Crow and become famous, and so had Paul Robeson, whose great talents as a football player, Broadway actor, and political activist had earned him worldwide admiration.

Although his world-famous voice had resonated throughout my childhood, I was unfamiliar with the scope of his accomplishments and only later learned how he had put his career on the line time and again to further humanitarian causes. On this afternoon at our kitchen table, the mythical being who dined with royalty and hobnobbed with the world's elite gently took my hand in his huge one. I lifted my eyes to his kind face.

"Hello, Alix, I'm delighted to meet you," he said softly, perhaps aware of his power to overwhelm. Smiling, he looked right into my eyes and, suddenly self-conscious, I lowered them. The great voice echoed off our dingy walls as he reached behind me to shake the hand of my neighbor and best friend, Mike. "And how are you this evening, young man?"

"Fine," we answered together.

Paul Robeson had a Columbia law degree, spoke twenty languages, and had made twelve films including *Showboat* in 1936, establishing both his universal reputation and signature tune, "Old Man River." The strapping Phi Beta Kappa Rhodes scholar and all-American football player at Rutgers College who played the lead in *Othello* and other dramatic and musical roles on the major stages of London and Broadway seemed perfectly comfortable sipping tea and chatting with us. I began to relax and would have liked to remain in his exciting presence but had been warned beforehand. "You and Mike can come in and meet him," Mom had instructed, "but that's all!"

From the darkened hall we peeked through the doorway at the grown-ups while my mind raced to absorb the enormity of the moment and maximize it. "Should we ask him to sing?" Mike and I whispered across the doorway, and when Mom emerged from the luminous kitchen we asked her. "No," she shook her head. "It wouldn't be polite." But I knew he wouldn't have minded. Paul Robeson was a very nice man.

"The Toughest Guerilla of All"

I WAS NAMED after my uncle, a handsome, charming, brilliant, drug-addicted, alcoholic, spouse-abusing, revolutionary hero executed by a fascist firing squad in the Spanish Civil War.

A hero of his time, my uncle battled corporate shipping bosses, organized crime, and the NYC police all at once.

In the mid-1930s, when the Albert Anastasia mob ruled the Brooklyn Docks, my uncle was an organizer for the National Maritime Union (NMU).

He challenged thugs like Joe Ryan, front man for the mob, the "phony head," as Pop called him, of the International Longshoremen's Union (ILU) on the docks of the East Coast and Gulf.

"Alex's best friend, Pete Panto, got bumped off by Anastasia," Pop told me in his living room fifty years later, when I recorded his recollections of the family I would be born into. "He was the guy who was really getting someplace in the rank-and-file of the NMU. Well, the Mafia got hold of him and they killed him. Just as simple as that."

"It sounds like *On the Waterfront*."

"It *was On the Waterfront*," replied Pop.

Mom's brother was known as "Cecil" to his comrades, "Alex" to his family, and "trouble" to his foes. "He was one smart cookie," Pop said of his brother-in-law, who taught himself to read French poetry and speak fluent Spanish. Editor of the rank-and-file NMU newspaper, *The Shape-Up*, Cecil Alex carried articles in the band of his hat and often came home battered and bloody. "The cops and the goons beat Cecil up more times than you've got hair on your head!" Pop laughed. "I remember one demonstration Cecil and Pete led for Home Relief, and Mom and I were on a corner with the goddamned cops up on the horses and a horse coming at us. It was scary! The cops took them in an alleyway and they beat the shit out of them. It was horrible, but he took it. He took it all."

In the 1930s, the Roosevelt government was giving working people a New Deal and revolution seemed imminent. A loose coalition of left-wing activists, liberal groups, and labor unions called "The Popular Front" was shifting into high gear, and the "vanguard of the working class" (meaning the Communist Party) would lead the way. Economic and social justice had become a magnet attracting hundreds of thousands of active, politically conscious Americans, and the Revolution was just around the corner. Pop laughed, "We used to say, 'Workers and peasants of Flatbush, seize the railroads!'"

One day in 1934 my uncle asked to have a talk with his new brother-in-law, Pop. "He couldn't understand how anybody could be interested in Art History when the world was being turned over and all kinds of important things were happening," Pop said.

"He told me, 'The world is turning around and here you are, fooling around with pictures!' He needed somebody to take care of the records and talked me, Mom, and Grandma into joining the Party and working for its Waterfront Section." Pop quit his art courses at NYU and the Metropolitan Museum to make politics a way of life.

Uncle Cecil was a womanizer and a thief who stole everything from Grandma's silver to Mom's record albums, pawning it all to buy alcohol and drugs. "He was on drugs way before drugs became popular," Pop continued. "I had a lot of respect for his ability and his intelligence . . . the longshoremen were his brothers, but the rest of the world didn't mean a goddamn thing to him. He was a bum and he treated Martha like dirt. She respected what he did on the Waterfront and in the Party, but she hated his guts for everything else."

Top Party officials were among Grandma's many friends, and for a time she dated an editor of *The Daily Worker*. When she brought her son up on charges for beating the woman he had moved in with, the Party took it seriously and threw him out. He cleaned up his act and went to Spain to defend the popular new Spanish Republican democracy against Franco's fascist treachery. On February 6, 1937, my uncle, in his mid-twenties, sailed on the *SS Paris* with two comrades and signed up with the 14th Army Corps Guerilla unit operating on the southern front, where he earned the rank of major.

I've seen only one photo of my mythical prototype as an adult. Dressed in rugged clothing and dark beret, he stands shoulder to shoulder, between one Spanish and his two American comrades. Among clusters of olive trees they lean easily on their rifles and squint into the sun. Confident and eager for action, in his alert expression I recognize Grandma's strong, sharp features. Mom also inherited Lotte's stalwart air, but with less authority than Cecil, the favorite, the charmer, always sweet-talking himself out of trouble.

In Spain, Alex specialized in planning brazen behind-the-lines sabotage and raids on fascist prisons in which hundreds of prisoners at a time were freed. Another American fighter, Carl Geiser, was close to Alex and admired him a great deal, he wrote in a letter to Pop.

His companions spoke highly of the 'trim, dark-complexioned, 5'10" man with the friendly smile who was totally dedicated to the anti-fascist cause of Republican Spain. . . . He was a leader not because of stripes but because of his ability and concern for his men. In all the time we spent together I never witnessed a single moment that Alex indulged in any drinking or drug abuse. The latter was unthinkable. His conduct in Spain was exemplary and impeccably correct. He was deeply admired by men and officers alike. Everyone in the outfit wanted to go on missions with "the toughest guerilla of all" who "always carefully and completely worked out all details in advance. His last mission was different Alex's section was informed that an entire unit of the 14th Army Corps was captured and wiped out and he was itching to get at the enemy to make up for the losses.

* * *

It was May 1938. They climbed the Sierra Nevada Peak, the highest mountain in Spain, and walked into an ambush in which Alex was wounded in the leg and captured. A fascist soldier who later came over to the Republican side was present at his execution. He reported that Uncle Cecil refused a blindfold, stood against a wall, and with a shout of "Viva La Republic!" raised his fist in the Loyalist salute as he was shot to death.

Grandma clung to the idea that Cecil Alexander was alive and would return home, but two years after word of his death, I was given his name, and Jews do not name their children after the living.

My uncle, I knew, was a hero who had died fighting Franco's fascists in Spain, but beyond that, everyone, Mom especially, refused to elaborate. The war receded into history and his name was mentioned less and less. My self-image was formed in his shadow, but with a twist. "Where did the *i* in my name come from?" I once asked Pop, half expecting, "Why is a cow?"—his response to questions without answers. But this time he replied, "Like Queen Alix of Greece . . . she was in the news around that time."

In the Beginning

WHAT I KNOW about my father's origins begins at the point when his immigrant mother and father first laid eyes on the same New York City waterfront where their son and his family would help organize the dock workers several decades later. In the early 1900s, Russian pogroms had driven Schmuel and Sonia from Katrinislav (Dnepropetrovsk after 1926) near Lithuania halfway around the world to the east side of Manhattan, where Sonia gave birth to Aunt Rose and Aunt Mary. In 1909, Schmuel—now "Samuel"—shifted his family to Alabama Avenue in Brooklyn in time for the arrival of a son who would be called, in succession, "Velvil," "Wolf," "Willie," and, years later, an occasional sharp "William" from my mother to get his attention. But to me, my siblings, and all our friends, he was "Pop."

Pop's father, "The Old Man," moved his family out of Brooklyn to Central Falls, then Pawtucket, Rhode Island. From a horse-drawn wagon, in his wire-rimmed spectacles and small wedge mustache, my stern and sturdy peasant grandfather sold pots, pans, and hardware to farmer's wives in the countryside around Providence. My father was eight years old when Sonia died in a tuberculosis sanitarium and Schmuel moved his children to the Bronx and went into business operating a grocery store on Monterey Avenue with his brother-in-law. There, my grandfather would make the housewives laugh until they protested, "Sam, stop! I've got to get home!" His love of storytelling was passed to Pop who passed it on to me.

"Friday nights after the Sabbath dinner was song time," Pop said, leaning back in the rocker he had put together from a kit. Tape recorder in hand, I settled into the couch, delighted to be sitting with Adrian when she heard these stories about her great-grandfather for the first time. "The old man was an alternate, non-professional cantor who led us in old-world folk songs. Music seemed to bring us together; it was a happy time."

After graduating high school, Pop checked the papers and saw that the University of Michigan had the best football team, so he hitchhiked to Ann Arbor and paid his way through two and a half undergraduate years with tips from waiting tables in fraternity houses and summer resorts, plus the two dollars his sisters sent every week from their own waitresses' tips. Describing himself as "too wild to graduate," my father stumbled upon the history of art, along with a thrilling universe of culture and intellect unsuspected on the Bronx streets—and he went after it. "Art history saved me," he said. "Before that I was a bum!"

The crash of 1929 sent him back to New York City and a dishwashing job in a cafeteria in Greenwich Village. During the Great Depression, Pop supplemented his skimpy salary by renting the key of his Perry Street apartment to friends seeking a venue for, as he put it, "discreet entertaining." To amuse themselves, his crowd of Village intellectuals wrote bogus poetry for their bogus literary magazine, *Fifth Floor Window*, spoofing artistic pretensions with lines like, "*I saw a cello in the window / It was mellow.*"

My mother's name was Martha but for as long as she lived, everyone in the family called her "Mom." She and her mother, Lotte, were living in the Village when my father first came to call. Evicted from one apartment after another for not being able to pay the rent, mother and daughter often went hungry and needed "Home Relief," but "Mom would never go," Pop said, "even when she was starving, she was that proud." Grandma took to Bill immediately, and to ensure his return, she lent him a book. According to Pop, Lotte "was a walking paradox, a contradiction, an amazing mixture of puritanical morals and radical politics, with a foot in each world, a combination of straitlaced and liberal." She recognized his profound goodness and often referred to her son-in-law as "my Bill."

Attracted by her combination of quiet beauty, tough intelligence, and core of steel, my persistent father proposed to Martha three times before breaking through her reserve, and they were married at the City Hall Municipal Building just as 1934 got underway. Pop was taking graduate courses at NYU and needed a better job than dishwashing. He persuaded a pretty friend of his to see a dean who dispensed jobs to NYU students. "Wear a low-cut dress and bend over to light a cigarette," Pop told her, "then say you have a friend who isn't a graduate but goes to school and needs a job." She laughed and agreed. The dean gave her a slip of paper designating a job as a clerk with the Works Projects Administration. She gave it to Pop, who changed "clerk," with a salary of $17.34 a week, to "research worker" at $23.86, which is how Pop got his job at the WPA.

During World War I Pop's father had been a steelworker, and by the time of the City Hall wedding, was back in business as the proprietor of a small grocery store in the Bronx. Pop neglected to mention his marriage but soon afterward at their regular Friday night dinner together, Sam declared, "Willie, I know you're married. Have a good, Jewish wedding and I'll give you twenty-five dollars." It was a good deal, and Pop took it. At the last minute on the day of the wedding, Pop dashed to the waterfront in search of two witnesses and rounded up a couple of sailors, one of whom, comrade "Cockeyed Robinson," was drunk.

The Old Man wasn't impressed with his son's prospects. "When are you going to carry a briefcase?" he'd ask. Samuel died singing in a hospital bed, too soon to see his son carrying an administrator's briefcase and supervise installations of permanent exhibits at the Museum of the City of New York.

Politics and the Party had become my parents' focus because they were good people and it was the right thing to do. "We had some very exciting experiences in the Party," Pop recounted. "I played a minor role, but it was my most shining hour!" The Party called and my father answered without hesitation, prompting a friend to suggest a shrink. "So what should I do, work less hard?" He laughed.

When the Party needed a financial and administrative secretary for the waterfront section, Pop stepped up, and a career in fund-raising was the result. As "Bill Mack," his Party identity, he doled out quarters to NMU organizers every week while Mom kept track of who paid dues. "Once we were up in the Section headquarters," he remembered. "It was nighttime and the cops came . . . they decided to raid the place. A whole bunch of guys were having a meeting, and Martha was collecting dues and making records of who paid dues, who made a contribution, and so forth, and here come the cops. You should've seen her scurry to the toilet, tearing up the records, shredding, scared outta her wits."

Money was so scarce for my parents that they once spent the better part of an afternoon searching in the snow for two dimes my mother had dropped. Mom, who agonized over money her entire life, was inconsolable. Two dimes would have bought a couple of loaves of bread and some coffee. Normally a patient man, my father remembers feeling irritated with her at the time, but less than when she accidentally sat on Duke Ellington's *Black and Tan Fantasy*, his favorite record. "I almost didn't marry her because of that!"

A Hero Once Removed

DURING HIGH SUMMER in the leap year of 1940, Luftwaffe pilots bombed the hell out of London while Berlin rejoiced. Back home, Bugs Bunny first appeared on screen, Woody Guthrie first appeared in New York City, and Republican candidate Wendell L. D. Wilkie resumed his futile presidential campaign against FDR. During this Year of the Dragon, Saturn, after a twenty-year separation, briefly reunited with Jupiter to sprout a crop of idealistic, groundbreaking little Leos like John Lennon, Nancy Pelosi, and me. And on a Friday evening in mid-August, Pop and Grandma celebrated my birth with a pizza at John's, which is still doing business in the Village. A delivery room nurse at New York's Lutheran Hospital dreamed that she saw me singing on stage at the opera. The next day she told Grandma that I would be a great singer, a great star, and that I would perform at the Met. Grandma crowed about that prediction for a long time, never imagining that in twenty-five years, rather than appearing at the Met, I'd appear at Carnegie Hall in a program with Chuck Berry and the legendary guitarist and singer Dave Van Ronk at the peak of the folk boom.

Had Uncle Cecil glanced down from heaven, he might have nodded approval at his tiny namesake being wheeled to the Waterfront in a baby carriage crammed with NMU leaflets. Mom and Pop distributed them while carrying me in their arms so that the longshoremen wouldn't beat them up. "Those hard-boiled guys were sentimental about children and families," explained Pop.

From WPA to WPB

AFTER PEARL HARBOR, wartime priorities overruled political persecution. With the Soviets as allies, fighting the Red Scare took a back seat to winning the war, which aligned perfectly with leftist objectives. Pop's record at the WPA plus his various connections landed him a Federal position and we moved to Washington D.C., "a hotbed of intrigue," he recalled. "They had everybody working in Washington from the ultra-lefts to the center, with the best minds in economics, politics, social work, manufacturing, statistics, any field you could think of."

The War Production Board paid Pop $80 a week as administrative officer for its Statistics Division's *War Progress* magazine; a summary of industrial resources for the Government's all-out war effort. Lacking good writers in Washington, Pop went to his boss and volunteered to bring some back from New York City. "Well, I got permission to go and I went to New York and I got four guys. One of them was a Trotskyite, which was a mistake." Because he could write well, Pop's boss was ecstatic, but the Party bosses disapproved of giving a break to an arch enemy. "I got bawled out for that, but he was a good writer," laughed Pop. "I didn't know he was a Trotskyite."

My first memory is of dust motes sparkling and dancing in the wedge of sunlight from the window above my mother's left shoulder. She was holding a mattress upright to disinfect it because bedbugs had invaded our apartment through the walls we shared with our unfriendly neighbors. Mom said they were anti-Semites, which, she explained, meant they didn't like Jews. Jewish meant that my family was different which meant that for some reason, certain people we didn't know didn't like us. That was pretty much all I knew or thought about what being Jewish meant since we never attended synagogue or observed religious holidays.

Pop could imitate that neighbor leaning out her back doorway singing, "Jaaahhh-neeee . . . Jaaahhh-neeee, come on home or I'll SWITCH ya," like she was calling hogs. Some afternoons, her daughter would come to our kitchen and we'd play with our dolls on the linoleum floor. She said I wasn't allowed inside her apartment, and I wondered if it looked like ours but had no desire to enter a place of nasty bugs and anti-Semites, as they are forever linked in my mind.

On the landing we shared at the top of the back steps I'd wait for this girl, staring at the patch of screen in their door behind which shadowy figures moved about in their kitchen. "You wait there," spoken through the screen, were the only words her mother said to me. This troubled and confused me, but I enjoyed playing with the five-year-old who favored me with her company if no one else was available. She was my only friend in Takoma Park.

One afternoon I was playing in the field behind our apartment when a bunch of kids came over, knocked me to the ground, and jumped on my back. I didn't know what to think except that fighting seemed pointless against so many, so I resigned myself and lay there quietly and thought it over. I shifted my head to watch the orderly line of children calmly awaiting their turn as in a game. They didn't seem to want to hurt me, plus the woolen coat I wore for late autumn protected me from the force of the children's weight, which wasn't much to begin with. In fact, I felt quite comfortable under the gentle pounding of small feet. Relaxing, I gave myself up to wondering why they had ganged up on me and if it was because of being Jewish, and if so, how they knew. They ran off with one of my new sandals, and later Mom and I retraced my steps, searching everywhere because we couldn't afford to lose a new shoe, but we did anyway, and never found it.

Washington wasn't a very friendly place for us and by late 1943 I was ready to head out, and some mornings Mom or Pop would find my crib empty with me sleeping on my tricycle, arms folded beneath my head on the handlebars. So when the WPA transferred Pop back to New York, it was none too soon for me. Or for Mom. We'd both had our fill of Washington. Besides that, we'd be taking the train! The night before we left I dreamt I handed two crude clay suitcases up from the platform through the window of the train to Mom.

Awakening in the still-dark morning, I beheld a shiny white overnight case on the floor by my bed. My heart stopped and I caught my breath. I got up and circled it, hardly believing it was for real. Round like a hatbox, it had a strap-handle and a tiny mirror glued inside the top. I gazed into the glass and a brown-eyed girl with curly hair stared back at me. I was for real too.

Standing in the middle of my room for the last time, ready to travel in my bonnet and dark blue, brass-buttoned woolen jacket, I felt adult and proud. I'd selected my most grown-up books and other toys and packed them carefully. It felt just wonderful to be three and moving back to the city my parents adored. Goodbye and good riddance to Washington, where kids jumped on you and wouldn't let you in their house because you were Jewish.

By the time we settled into our apartment on West Eighty-third Street I was aware of injustice and on the lookout for it. My first Manhattan memory has me sitting beside another little girl on a step of the brownstone next to our building. Newly arrived to the neighborhood, I thought she might be my friend. We were engaged in pleasant conversation when "dirty Jew" caught my ear. She couldn't have known what she was saying, but I did, and if reason and vocabulary were not yet available to me, teeth were. In my memory is first a close-up of her hand, followed by a blank moment, and then the girl's back as she ran shrieking up the street. A rush of pride straightened my own back for taking a stand against bigotry.

Manhattan Music

DUE TO HIS success at the WPB, Pop might have looked forward to a career as a bureaucrat, but the FBI was nosing around his office asking questions, making it too hot for him to continue working there, so he resigned. His top-notch recommendations and top-level contacts came to nothing after FBI visits. Millions of good Americans suffered this kind of pressure and harassment. The Merchant Marines was a stronghold of the NMU and offered political opportunities, so Pop signed up, earned his Able Bodied Seaman's license at Sheepshead Bay, and was elected as an alternate Merchant Marine/NMU delegate to the Party's National Convention.

While Pop was gone, Mom's high school friend, Selma, sent us train tickets to visit her in Chicago. Grandma came along at her own expense. The train ride remains one of my strongest childhood memories: ducking into the smart little bathroom in our private compartment, sipping hot chocolate poured from a silver pot at a table in the elegant dining car, pulling doors open between cars and stepping out into a rush of cold air before the next car, and making repeated trips to the wall with the cone-shaped paper cups to pull down next to a button to push for water. In the darkness of the top bunk in our compartment I watched America roll past and was, for the first time ever, held fast and steady in the soothing heartbeat of a train. *Clickety, clickety clack.* I never wanted to stop traveling, and so far, I haven't.

I loved all of Mom's friends, especially Selma and Margie. High school best friends, the two had provided Mom her only sanctuary from a caustic home life. Selma lived in Chicago, but Margie, an artist, lived only blocks away from us. Margie was deaf, wore a hearing aid, and read lips. She laughed easily and entertained me with her orange puppet, Mollie. Margie encouraged my love of drawing and we drew together for hours, making pictures out of squiggles.

Music was a constant presence in our house. Either the kitchen radio or the phonograph filled our apartment with musical variety from Bach to Meade Lux Lewis. Mom particularly loved complex baroque pieces along with the ragtime piano tunes her whole being longed to play. She would sing along, note for note, with every composition under the sun, or so it seemed to me.

I'd color pictures for Mom to send to Pop in Greenland. One day he was summoned by Naval intelligence and stood in front of an officer behind a desk covered with papers filled with colored markings.

"Dobkin, can you explain this?"

"Lieutenant, are you married?"

"No, I'm not."

"I didn't think so," laughed Pop, explaining that a father would have recognized the drawings of a four-year-old. Chagrined at mistaking childish artwork for subversive code, the lieutenant relaxed and laughed along with my father.

I would sprawl on the floor of our living room and hum along with the mighty Red Army Chorus. Mom told me that I wore out their set of 78 rpm recordings before graduating to *Tubby the Tuba* where I learned the names and sounds of orchestral instruments. Mom and I sang and acted out, "*I dropped my shoe, pick it up, pick it up,*" from Woody Guthrie's *Songs To Grow On* album. Earl Robinson's *Ballad for Americans* featured "The House I Live In," recorded by both Frank Sinatra and Paul Robeson. The voices of Josh White, Leadbelly, and The Almanac Singers with Pete Seeger were often heard in our apartment alternating with the deeply earnest *Six Songs for Democracy* from the International Brigades. This music was shared by a vast community of political and social activists whose record collections, during the 1940s, looked, at least in part, very much like ours.

Music was important to both Mom and Pop and formed a deep, beloved bond for our entire family. Singing all together never failed to lift everyone's spirits and bring us close. I loved singing along with Mom's clear, sure alto, and, when he returned, Pop's sweet baritone. He sounded a little like Burl Ives, but I preferred Pop's voice and often told him, "You sing better than Burl Ives." He'd laugh and wave it off.

Over the years, Dixieland became familiar too: lyrical guitar and violin duets of Eddie Lang and Joe Venuti, Cab Calloway, Duke Ellington, Hoagy Carmichael, and of course Louis Armstrong. Mom admired the piano of Nellie Lutcher. Waving our arms, we'd prance around to "Hurry on Down to My House, Baby (Nobody Home but Me)" and chirp along with Nellie in falsetto. There was no finer entertainment than watching my parents cut the threadbare living room rug executing the intricate steps of the Peabody.

Disharmony

FOR ALL ITS improvement over D.C., life in New York City wasn't easy for my mother. With Pop away, she was living without a buffer against Grandma, whom she loathed, the same mother who years earlier had escaped the state-of-war in her own home by forging a career as a legal secretary.

In Grandma's day, a "sick headache" was a common complaint for women. Mom, who resented Grandma her whole life and usually kept her childhood under wraps, once told me that Grandma often spent four or five days at a time in bed in a darkened room. Grandma was well into her eighties when she told me that my grandfather, named Sam like my other grandfather, had beaten her during their tumultuous marriage. Lotte, I knew, had left Sam and returned again and again before finally divorcing him and scandalizing the New Rochelle Jewish Community, where nothing like that had ever happened. She further shocked the neighborhood by finding work outside the home, compounding her daughter's distress. Threatened with banishment to her father if she didn't behave, young Martha was left to be humiliated by a grandmother, Julia, who begrudged her every morsel, and bullied by an older brother whose brilliance kept her in the shadows.

My mother spent her whole life struggling with the trauma of those years, when music became her ticket out. She was seventeen in 1929 when Grandma lost everything in the Crash and had to sell their belongings, including the piano.

Mom's lessons were cut off and, with them, her lifeline.

Stuck with each other for life, Mom and Grandma's relationship was tense at best and tragic at worst. For as long as I knew her I never heard my mother refer to Grandma as anything other than "Lotte," never "Mom" or "Mother." She avoided or minimized contact, snubbing her and withdrawing in Grandma's company. Childhood ghosts haunted my mother, but when Lotte wasn't around she could be playful company. Then we'd sing or converse in rapid-fire exchanges of improvised languages. She delighted in silly humor and puns, the cornier the better, and would jokingly refer to the "terlet," or declare an odd thing "perculiar."

Other times Mom would seem to drown in a silent, brooding ocean of the past that threatened to submerge us all. I rarely saw her cry but frequently saw her close down, condemning both herself and me to the isolation of a sad childhood. Depressed along with her, abandoned and anxious, fearful of accidentally disappointing or offending her, I also felt responsible for coming to her rescue. Somehow it had become my job, one guaranteed to fail.

A generation later, my daughter, Adrian, asks me, "What's wrong, Mom?"

"Nothing's wrong," I hear myself echo back.

My mother worked long and hard to reduce her suffering before handing it over to me, just as Lotte no doubt sweetened her own bitter legacy from the mean, miserly Julia. Like everyone else in the family, I held my breath through those times when Mom shut us out, trying to take care of her or keeping out of her way. Neither parent stayed angry for long, but I grew up careful to avoid hurting feelings. In my family this was the supreme offense, unspoken, but carrying the severest emotional penalty.

Pop sometimes got angry and scowled, but he wasn't moody and his temperament was steady. He was safer and more predictable than Mom, whose voice might snap coldly and whose piercing glance withered. The first time I saw my father cry was when FDR died, on April 12, 1945. The radio announcer was talking and Pop stood in the middle of the living room in his shirtsleeves, his face turned up, eyes closed, tears running down his cheeks.

Ten months earlier, on the afternoon of June 10, 1944, Pop was released from active duty. I knew that would happen because Merchant Marines didn't fight, so they didn't get killed. This fantasy survived for fifty years until a reading of Marge Piercy's novel, *Gone to Soldiers*, shattered it. Learning that Merchant Marine casualties were proportionately higher than those of the U.S. Army, Navy, or Air Force made me feel faint. Pop taught me the Merchant Marine anthem: "*Heave ho, m'lads, heave ho, it's a long, long way to go....*" Eventually he forgot the words, but I remember them all.

Grandma had signed the lease on a rent-controlled apartment on what I considered the best block of the best street in Manhattan. Stretching five long blocks from the Hudson River to Central Park West, West Eighty-third ran through the heart of our white, middle/upper-middle-income, largely well-educated, liberal, and substantially Jewish neighborhood.

The park entrance, half a block from our building, funneled endless airstream currents off the Hudson River, shooting them up the street to blast us backward on our home-stretch. The "Eighty-third Street Wind" was famous throughout the neighborhood. For another thing, Babe Ruth lived across the street on the corner of Riverside Drive. In all six years we were neighbors I saw him only once, stepping across the sidewalk at the entrance of his building into a cab. Being a Dodger fan, I wasn't that impressed, but can still recall the slope of his back as he squeezed into the backseat. Two years after we moved away he died.

Loew's Eighty-third, the premiere movie house and neighborhood institution, further distinguished our street. Second only to Radio City Music Hall in my estimation, it often featured MGM musical comedies. The plush red drapery and carpet with gold trim inside Loew's Eighty-third gave off that indefinably unique movie house scent infused equally with popcorn and the pure enchantment common to theaters back in Hollywood's glory days. My generation cut our movie teeth on the bewitching, uplifting films my pals and I saw in that theater, when the great studios ruled the film industry with long-term contracts to ensure enduring careers for their shining stars, more lustrous and classy than any before or since.

Brains & Character

ACROSS FROM LOEW'S Eighty-third was Levy Brothers' Toy Store, shining star of the neighborhood. Several times a week I'd go there to Survey and meditate on the latest arrivals. My mother thought it good for my character to be denied longed-for toys, and once refused to let Selma buy me a doll I coveted, which, Selma told me after Mom's death, struck her as ridiculous. Despite Grandma's inclination to indulge me, it was forbidden and she made a point of never going against Mom's wishes. "Your mother says no!" she'd declare, and pleading was fruitless. But my allowance could buy bubble gum packs with the famous paintings trading cards. *Pinky* and *Blue Boy* were the most valuable. He stood squarely in vibrant blue: powerful and grounded while she floated, dainty in gossamer pink and white. Naturally I identified with him, and only afterward pondered the reasons why.

I liked to wonder about things, and was excited to follow a thought and figure a thing out. For example, a friend came to visit and I observed that she folded her toilet paper neatly. Silently I compared it to my own loose wad and determined that her pee would probably run right off the flat surface, whereas mine had many more absorbent hollows and edges. I realized then that I was smart.

However, not all intellectual challenges were so neatly resolved. Profound questions frustrated the impatient pecks and scratches of newly hatching consciousness: philosophical questions that remained unanswered most of my life. I stood on the short step inside Levy Brothers' wondering, *What IS this?* I tried rephrasing the basic philosophical question of all time, but couldn't and was left with repeating, *What am I? What is ME and What is ALL THIS?* There HAD to be an explanation, but verbalizing what I desperately yearned to understand was beyond my powers. Fortunately, there were plenty of stimulating distractions for a budding six-year-old information junkie.

The Wide World

RADIO FIRST CAST its lifelong spell on me in 1947 with *The Lone Ranger*. Staying up until seven thirty represented a milestone of maturity, and I was impatient for more. Eventually I was allowed to stay up for *The Jack Benny Show* with Dennis Day singing the oh-so-slow "Danny Boy," and the predictable closet avalanches on the silly *Fibber McGee and Molly*. Passionately devoted to *Baby Snooks*, I had just gotten used to her time slot when its star, Fanny Brice, died unexpectedly on the air. It was confusing, then heartbreaking, and I felt bereft of a new friend.

Sundays were special because that's when Tallulah Bankhead hosted *The Big Show*. Her Southern accent and jaded sophistication delighted me and I understood most of the jokes, or thought I did. But what did she mean by "ambisextrous?" I'd lower my voice and drawl along with Tallulah's husky "Dah-ling," desolate at the show's end when she led her guests in singing, "May the Good Lord Bless and Keep You (Till We Meet Again)." On one program I heard Bob Hope crack, "Meet me in front of the pawn shop and you can kiss me under the balls." Despite having no clue to the meaning, from the shocked laughter of the audience I knew he had gotten away with something, which pleased me.

Allen's Alley and *George Burns & Gracie Allen* provided great company, but we never listened to *Amos & Andy* because it was racist and made fun of "Negroes," as we were careful to say. My parents would never put up with demeaning a whole people the way that program did and neither would I.

I memorized radio commercials and pictured Bucky Beaver singing, "*Brusha, brusha, brusha, new Ipana toothpaste*," and wondered what "the yellow" was, and where it went, "*when you brush your teeth with Pepsodent*." "Good things for better living through chemistry," was a total mystery. Which "things" and how "better?" And "chemistry?" A can opener was all that came to mind, and for many years I thought that DuPont manufactured can openers.

One weekend my parents borrowed a car and we drove to the country with their friends, Fran and Morris. Fran was beautiful and I loved how she smelled. It was a treat to ride with her in the backseat of the car. We slept at an inn, and after Mom sat with me as she did each bedtime, I lay on a cot in the upstairs screened-in porch and listened to the night birds. The only birds I had known were pigeons and sparrows. Pigeons cooed, but these birds could sing. The next morning, I sat under a tree and composed my first song. It was about sitting under a tree in the country and making up a song. *Songwriting is easy*, I decided. I liked the country quite a lot.

Mom and I were riding the Broadway bus one afternoon. I was cranky and the other passengers were bothered by my crying. I didn't care, and Mom couldn't get me to shut up, so she hauled me off a few stops early. We stepped from the center doors onto the sidewalk and a woman followed us out. On the sidewalk she bent over me and wagged a white-gloved finger in my face. "Little girl, if you don't stop crying we'll have to call the police and have you arrested," she warned, shooting Mom a conspiratorial look.

I will long remember that woman's change of expression as my mother lit into her. "How dare you!" she snapped. "Mind your own business!" I was charmed and forgot to cry. How heroic Mom was in my defense! Her battle lines were drawn with a sharp blade, and her mighty rage at insults and injustice blazes in memory. A patronizing salesman, for example, or a crack about "women drivers" never failed to set her off. We turned and walked on, our conflict neutralized, our bond strengthened. "Imagine telling a little girl that she would be arrested for crying. Some nerve!" It had never occurred to me that crying might be illegal, but I felt relieved when Mom assured me it wasn't.

Grandma loved taking me places, dragging me along on visits to her friends and showing me off. The allure of traveling around the city didn't stop me from resisting these jaunts. My emotional cues came from Mom, and, without knowing why, I resented my enforced excursions with Lotte, but my mother required breaks from me and insisted.

With a son dead and a daughter who cold-shouldered her, Grandma made me her special project, lavishing attention on me that her daughter had done without. Although acquainted with humanity's ugly and cruel aspects, Grandma genuinely believed in the fundamental goodness of people and filled me with a positive philosophy. She trained me to be courteous and friendly to everyone, and taught me not to fear strangers, whom she frequently chatted up.

As if to prove her point, Grandma befriended the FBI agent assigned to her. She was fond of him and attempted to further his political education. In turn, he remembered Grandma's birthday every year with a card, and accepted her annual invitation for an afternoon of tea and conversation. "My agent," Grandma called him, fully convinced that during these sessions she revealed no information and he gathered none, and there was no arguing with her. Pop didn't buy it and would shake his head in resignation on the rare occasion when the odd relationship was mentioned.

During the early 1940s, the New York City Transit Authority ran double-decker buses on Riverside Drive, and riding on the top deck was a given. I don't think I ever saw a child on the lower one. One time Grandma, a male friend of hers, and I, seated on his lap, rode uptown in a crowded bus. A woman stood in the aisle. I popped off the lap with a polite, "You can have my seat." A laugh and approval from an audience of strangers (*did they applaud?*) was my payoff, and Grandma collected another conversation piece.

But as much as I adored buses, the subway was my true love. Accustomed to my disappearances when we walked on Broadway, Mom learned to check the nearest subway entrance and there I'd be, with my face pressed between the bars, hypnotized by the noise, the sight and smell of the Seventh Avenue IRT. My greatest thrill was to ride in the front car of the train and flash through tunnel mazes on the express inside track, barreling by local riders who stood on the outside platform. We had important places to go and couldn't bother to stop for them. The fare, like the price of a comic book or an ice cream cone, was a nickel, and in 1948 it doubled.

The Hudson is the grandest river I've ever known. How lucky to be able to see it from the top of a hill glinting beyond landscaped greenery at the Eighty-third Street entrance to the park. There, a path forked left past the rocks we climbed to the playground with baby swings, big swings, see-saws, and a large sandbox. In a bit of local vernacular, we called the sliding boards "sliding ponds," and made them more slippery by polishing them with waxed paper. A thick sprinkler pipe for hot summer days poked up from the drain at the sloping concrete center, but all that paled in comparison to the jungle gym. While Mom sat reading or chatting with other mothers on a shaded bench, I'd climb and hang, high and reckless. Mom didn't forbid my stunts, and an old family friend remembers being amazed more by her restraint than by my antics, but the risks we both took on that jungle gym paid off for me in agility and self-confidence.

I was six, Mom was pregnant, and I knew it would be a boy. About a week after Mom brought little Carli home, Dr. Finger came to the apartment to check up on him, and asked me about my brother's name. "Does he spell it with a C or a K?" he inquired. "Don't be silly," I answered. "He can't spell." Grandma loved that story too.

Even though it was her idea, I hated leaving Mom and going to school. It felt like punishment. Besides learning to tie a shoelace, my biggest preschool lesson came on my first day. Nothing I said would soften the determined set of Mom's face, and, as my fingers were being pried off the door frame, my most obnoxious resistance did not stand against her will. I hated everything about school, especially naptime. I envied other children who actually slept, and checked their eyelids to see if they were faking, but none ever flickered.

That summer, Mom and Pop wanted time alone with the baby and sent me to an overnight camp for ten days. Feeling rejected, abandoned, scared, and sorry for myself, I boarded the train sniffling, cried upon my arrival, and wallowed in self-pity for the duration. My counselors reported that I was "inconsolable." Finally the dreadful ordeal was over and I was able to return home, which had changed. Fortunately, I had changed too.

Besides a new baby in the apartment, Grandma moved to Florida, and Hattie began cleaning our apartment every other Wednesday. The joy of performing first came home for me when I entertained both her and Mom with "One, two / Buckle my shoe." Puffing up for the grand finale, I swayed side to side, stuck out my belly and growled, "Nine, ten / A big, fat hen!" They laughed and laughed, so I kept it up until they told me to quit. Mom treated Hattie, an African American woman, with great respect. She appreciated her hard work and went out of her way to make those Wednesdays as pleasant as possible. She tried calling Hattie "Mrs. Naylor," who insisted on being called "Hattie" but always addressed Mom as "Miz Dobkin."

My life was too full to leave room for resentment, and if I felt jealous of little Carli I don't remember it. While he was absorbing Mom's attention, my own was turning to Public School 9 and the first grade. A little brother and the universe had forced me, kicking and screaming, out of babyhood. At the same time I found myself increasingly drawn to the more sophisticated pursuits of worldly citizenship. It was time to quit sucking my thumb, I decided one night, and stopped abruptly, the way Mom broke her bad habits.

New Rochelle

IN AN EFFORT to build Mom's confidence, Pop never learned to drive. Plus, he liked being driven around. Once in a while we'd borrow someone's car and go for a ride. At stop lights, Mom taught us to chant the magic "Abracadabra, light (pause) CHANGE," until it did, and when we went through the Lincoln or Holland Tunnel we'd each try to guess the number of burned-out lights. Sometimes we'd drive to New Rochelle to visit my friend Ellen and her family and get a glimpse into the burgeoning world of suburbia.

Ellen and I liked the same movies, music, and books. Our parents had met through political work, and Grandma was friends with Ellen's grandmother who lived in a cottage next door to her family's small but comfortably chaotic house. It had a glassed-in porch and a darling attic where I slept during visits and where, as a teenager, I hung out the small window to smoke. There were lots of beautiful trees, and the air smelled sweet. Ellen had a mind of her own, but as far as I was concerned, being a few months older made me boss. We'd race up and down the stairs in rousing adaptations of movie swashbucklers or sing show tunes like "I'm Just a Girl Who Can't Say No" From *Oklahoma*. I fell in love with the score and memorized it, unaware of the revolution that show and *Showboat* before it had created in American musical theater.

We read the Babar books. My favorite was the story of Zephyr the monkey, whose family lived in a sweet tree house in a perfect jungle village. I imagined living an equally perfect life in just such a place with my family and friends. Grandma had given me the My Book House series and Ellen had her own set. Grandly bound blue volumes offered up poems, myths, and fairy tales from every land with elegant, painstaking illustrations I adored. Advancing through them to Volume Twelve, we tried to keep at least one book ahead of our ages and were quite pleased to move up a number in the series.

The Glass Mountain and other tales of princesses appealed, but whenever romance reared its head, my interest dimmed. I found the heroines' passivity annoying, and in *Sleeping Beauty*, with the most passive heroine of all, my sympathies lay with the witch who had been snubbed. The premise of *Snow White and Rose Red* thrilled me, but the ending was terrible, as usual. What was wrong with those girls and why on earth would loving sisters abandon their precious cottage, devoted mother, and agreeable lives? My heart would sink, and once again I'd brace myself against the inevitable "happy" ending that felt like a betrayal of the sisters, their mother, and girls like me.

A Brownie at PS9

MISS MORRISON'S CLASS 1-1 in room 203 is a place I still try to find during infrequent anxiety dreams. In this and later classrooms I defended my name ("Isn't Alix a boy's name?" "NO, it's MY name!") and was introduced to spunky "Dick," passive "Jane," the adorable "Spot," "Fluffy," and their whimsical bouncing ball. I couldn't identify with anyone in the two-dimensional stories, particularly "Jane," and it seemed to me that Dick, Jane, their pets, pipe-smoking Dad, aproned Mother, and rosy-cheeked grandparents on the farm all added up to cardboard cutouts. But how real were they? New Rochelle had acquainted me with the suburbs, but this strange family lived in a setting I'd only seen through the window of a train. Dull, forgettable stories left me unsatisfied, but the characters wormed their way beneath my consciousness, to model "authentic Americans." Being Jewish and progressive, I was pretty sure that my family wouldn't qualify.

Mom and I joined the Brownies. The girls made connections, I began noticing my peers, and friendships took root. Our Brownie pins were fastened upside down until we did a good deed and we could turn them right side up. On some afternoons we constructed arts and crafts projects, like varicolored potholders woven on the teeth of square metal frames. Mom warned me that during Brownie meetings she would be helping the other girls as much as me, maybe even more, and despite the outrageous unfairness, I grudgingly resigned myself. At the same time, I was proud that the girls liked her and went to her for help. She appeared respectable, like a normal mother. Maybe she wasn't as peculiar as I thought.

Being quick, I loved racing and was proud of my position as the second fastest runner in the troop. Beneath ceilings that seemed low even to me, we'd streak across the floor and around the thick, round pillars stationed throughout PS9's expansive basement which also served as the site for wonderfully exciting PTA bake sales. The entire school gathered there each Friday morning to kick off the school assembly, sing the national anthem, and pledge allegiance to the flag, in the days before children were made to recite, "under God." I wished we could sing "America the Beautiful" instead of "The Star Spangled Banner" because it had a prettier tune and better words.

One afternoon, on a trip to Radio City Music Hall, as our troop gathered in the lobby, someone said, "There's Marlene Dietrich!" I knew she was an important, glamorous star like Tallulah Bankhead. "Where?" I whipped around on tiptoes, looking over the other girls' heads. Mom and Pop didn't like just anyone, but they liked Marlene, whose continental charm reminded me of Tallulah's Southern allure. When my family sang "Lily Marlene," I pictured Dietrich, leaning against the lamppost in a stark circle of light, brave and wistful.

"Over there," someone pointed. Searching frantically, my eyes lit upon shapely calves in a pair of smoky-black, seamed stockings whisking around a corner and out of sight. The sheer romance of that instant struck my heart, leaving me electrified, exhilarated, and wallowing in mysterious yearning.

Our Brownie troop visited Grant's tomb, located about a dozen blocks or so uptown along Riverside Park. My friend Karen and I skated up and down the long concrete paths stretching through lawn and shrubbery known as "the mall." We played hopscotch and jumped rope on those paths, biked from Seventy-ninth well up into the Nineties, wandered around the Soldiers and Sailors Monument facing out over the Hudson, and watched the Italian men fishing for eel. Sometimes we'd stretch out on the grass and just watch the clouds.

Perils & Disillusionment

MY NONRELIGIOUS, anticapitalist parents didn't care for Christmas, which they celebrated one year strictly as a concession to me. One year they even bought a small tree for me to decorate, and I was thrilled to have it in my room next to my bed. On Christmas morning, a teddy bear sat under it, perfect, in a normal American *Dick and Jane* sort of way.

Was Santa Claus real? Undecided, I resolved to find out for myself. On Christmas Eve, in the manner of urban kids, Mom and I taped our stockings to the dining room windowsill. Next to a glass of milk and a plate of cookies for Santa I placed a note reading, "Whoever fills these stockings please sign here," with a line for the signature. It was foolproof. The next morning the cookies and milk were gone, and on the bottom line, "Santa Claus," was signed, but in Mom's handwriting. Doubts confirmed, I put another childish illusion behind me with both satisfaction and regret.

One lunchtime during third grade, I was tearing around the landing between the second and third floors of my building when a man, on his way downstairs asked me to stop. Very politely he inquired if I was a dancer. "No," I said, puzzled and a bit intrigued by the curious question. "Are you sure? You look like a dancer," he persisted, smiling at me in a friendly way. I wasn't afraid, but was unsettled.

"You have the legs of a dancer," he said, reaching out his hand and squeezing my thigh. Up the stairs I flew to tell Mom about the encounter. Her eyes flared and then she was gone, out the door, breathing fire, looking for the man, who had disappeared, luckily for him. On her return I learned that no one had the right to touch me unless I wanted them to, and that I should tell her if any man ever tried that again. I still wasn't sure what it was all about, but I knew Mom would always defend me.

A desperately self-conscious but otherwise uneventful bus ride with Grandma one afternoon taught me the importance of putting underpants on before leaving the house when the realization hit me that I had forgotten to put them on that morning. All afternoon I smoothed my dress along my legs and could think no further than keeping my knees together, my body upright. Girls had to wear dresses and worry about things like the humiliation of exposed underwear or worse.

Where the Boys Were

FOR ME, READING and drawing came second only to playing ball, climbing the rocks in Riverside Park, and running around with my friends. As I had done every afternoon since preschool, I'd come home, rip off my dress, pull on dungarees and a T-shirt, then grab a quick bite before heading out to the ball field. Other days, I'd sprint the block and a half to Levy Brothers' Toy Store to hang out with Trudy, a young woman who worked there and knew my name. I thought she was beautiful and relished her attention.

While examining the window display one afternoon, a vaguely familiar-looking boy approached the entrance with his mother. His right eye was black and blue. *What a shiner!* I thought. He looked my way, burst into tears, and pointed his finger at me. "She did it!" he wailed. "She's the one who hit me." A flash of recognition, and I remembered that I'd fought with him in the park a day earlier and won. I glared at him and stood a little taller. His mother shot me a dirty look and I looked right back at her. A long moment passed before she grabbed her son and pulled him inside.

Small and wiry, I was always active and poised for action. Full of myself, my strengths and abilities, I felt strong and enjoyed fighting with my friends because I was a frequent winner and no one got hurt. Late one afternoon I got into a scrap with Bernard. He'd been getting on my nerves and the fight was unusually fierce. We rolled on the ground for some time before the kids who had circled to watch got bored and pulled us apart. Equally exhausted, bruised, and filthy, we were persuaded to shake hands, declare a draw, and call it a day. I didn't win, but at least I made him cry.

My downstairs neighbor, Mike, was my best friend among the boys. Bernard was next, and although he was a crybaby we had fun together. He was my size, sensitive, and moody, with red hair and freckles. Bernard lived a block uptown on Riverside Drive with his quiet older sister, timid mother, and a stern judge of a father. An enormous table took up most of Bernard's large bedroom, where model locomotives pulled railroad cars around an elaborate track system. Every Christmas day I made sure to visit Bernard and admire his new engine, caboose, or maybe a switching station, and to take my turn at the controls. The best part was organizing the miniature houses, bridges, trees, little buildings, and people, arranging and rearranging small-town America.

Mike and I played sneak-ball with Danny or Liz or any other kid we could find in the lobby of our building. Two played catch with one in the middle trying to intercept the pink spaldeen that one of us was bound to be carrying. Boys from all over the neighborhood congregated in the park to play hardball, and so did Mike and I. Many of us had played in the playground and on the rocks, and we all shared a love of baseball cards.

Mike and I shared a fascination with Hollywood celebrities. Both of us adored movie magazines and would pore over them for hours. One day after lunch I pictured us playing together for the rest of our lives. A profound, moving vision, I couldn't wait to tell Mom, who stood washing the lunch dishes. Stepping up to the bow tied at the back of her apron, I made my announcement: "Mom, I love Mike and I'm going to marry him." The dishwashing continued uninterrupted. "That's good, dear." Speechless with disappointment, I turned away, thinking, *She doesn't CARE about my FUTURE*, and didn't mention it again.

The summer after third grade, our family rented a house on Cape Cod in Wellfleet, Massachusetts, for a month, and the red L-shaped cottage quickly came alive with social activity. It was equipped with white wicker furniture and a dining room picture window overlooking Cape Cod Bay and the beach where I spent most afternoons.

Grandma came to visit, and so did my parents' friends, Sam and Annie, along with their twins, Steve and Eliot, a few months older than I. They lived just outside the city in a two-story house with a fine sliding banister. Steve was a half hour older than Eliot, slightly larger and considerably more reckless. We three forged an alliance and exploded into action, spending most days on the beach scrutinizing the strange-looking horseshoe crabs, older than the dinosaurs and looking more like giant spiders than crabs. Fiddler crabs were everywhere, especially in rock pools. Grasping their middle section beyond the reach of pinching, oversized claws, we'd drop them into buckets and stir with our shovels until Mom reproved us with, "Let the poor crabs go, they are not your playthings!"

On Sunday mornings during visits to their house in Westchester, the boys and I would lounge in the living room and listen to radio programs, reciting along with, "I'm Buster Brown / I live in a shoe / That's my dog, 'Tige' / Look for him in there too!" Provided Mom wasn't in the room, we'd sing along with her least favorite commercial: "Less work for Mother, let's lend her a hand," the sappy tune advertising everyone's favorite, Horn & Hardart Automats. A popular eatery sorely missed by thousands of working class and other budget-minded Philadelphians, Bostonians, Baltimoreans, and New Yorkers, the Automat was not just a cafeteria. For one thing, they were immaculate, and they were the only restaurant at that time that didn't allow smoking. Sandwiches, snacks, and desserts beckoned from marble columns of glass-fronted, brass-trimmed compartment windows. I recall an enormous front window looking onto the street and inside, the grand sense of a lofty hall muted by the absence of pretension.

Had it been up to me we would have eaten every meal there: hamburger, mashed potatoes with gravy, and creamed spinach, accompanied by the finest, richest, darkest hot chocolate on earth with little bubbles of fat floating on the surface. At the center of the room, a woman in a glass booth sold nickels that I'd buy to slip into a coin slot in the marble wall. A small lion's head stuck out by a chrome handle that I'd crank with one hand and, holding my white cup on its white saucer in the other, catch the cocoa pouring from the lion's mouth.

Mom loved Horn & Hardart as much as Pop and I, but she despised their radio jingle, calling it "crap." To her, commercial exploitation was beneath contempt, particularly sentimental appeals to "motherhood," like the H&H ad. She refused to celebrate Mother's Day, condemning it as a phony, cynical holiday whose only purpose was selling candy and flowers. We never dared wish her a "Happy Mother's Day" let alone give her a card or present. When Mom was around, rather than risk her icy glare of disapproval, the twins and I held our tongues during Horn & Hardart radio ads.

Robeson in Peekskill

ONE WEEKEND, LESS THAN two weeks after my ninth birthday, we visited Westchester. Our two families sat in the living room of Steve and Eliot's house and listened to the radio on the afternoon a Paul Robeson concert in Peekskill, New York, was attacked by mobs. Robeson had recently been called before the House Un-American Activities Committee. Long afterward I learned that in their attempt to link anti-racism with "Communist subversion" the Committee had, only four days earlier, questioned Jackie Robinson. Robinson, under enormous pressure, distanced himself from Robeson and repudiated Communists in a statement that, years later, he regretted and apologized for.

A progressive New York theatrical agency, People's Artists, had scheduled a concert for Robeson on August 27, 1949. Although it had become an annual event, *The Peekskill Evening Star* whipped the town into a frenzy. Front-page anti-Communist hysteria incited the Regional Veterans Council, The Veterans of Foreign Wars, The American Legion, and the Catholic High School to disrupt the performance and express their outrage. A dozen people were sent to the hospital while local police looked on and did nothing. All but the left-wing press blamed the violence on "the Communists," and Governor Dewey refused to comment.

The concert had been rescheduled to September 4, and now Robeson was being cursed and his life threatened less than an hour's drive from where we gathered around the radio with our friends in their living room. The reporter's voice crackled with excitement and disbelief as he described that terrible afternoon. Fearing a repeat of violence, the Fur and Leather Workers Union, the United Electrical Workers, and the Longshoremen sent their members to act as bodyguards, so, circling Robeson and the audience, they formed a human shield. When Robeson sang "Old Man River," the song he had made famous on Broadway in *Show Boat*, the great man changed the lyric, "I'm tired of livin' and 'feared of dyin'" to "I must keep fightin' until I'm dyin'."

This time, there was no violence during the show, but following Robeson's performance, the local police and state troopers joined in an ambush and prevented people from reaching their automobiles, numbers of which were vandalized, or their buses, many of which were overturned. American Legionnaires and Catholic high schoolers lined the road from the concert site shouting racist and anti-Semitic slogans and throwing rocks at the cars and buses of concertgoers trying to leave. Slowed by police, they made easy targets.

How could those people do that, especially to such a great American? The adults in the house were grave, their conversation low and serious. In my mind I pictured Paul Robeson sitting in our kitchen and remembered how nice he had been to us. We ourselves might easily have been at that concert, along with our friends and allies, our lives at risk.

In fact, we later learned that our friend Fran was leaving the concert when a rock smashed through a window of the van in which she and her four-year-old daughter were riding. She sat in the backseat and picked slivers of glass from the driver's neck while dropping pieces of chewing gum on the floor in a desperately improvised game to keep little Sally busy and away from the windows. "I could see the troopers lining the road, laughing, doing nothing to stop the violence," she said.

The folk singer Ronnie Gilbert, who would later become my friend, was riding in a bus that New York state troopers prevented from moving out, making it a perfect target for their attackers who stood beside their neat piles of rocks in the incident that sent 150 people to the hospital. Embattled caravans made their way back to the city and to Harlem, a community far less vulnerable to anti-Communist hysteria than white America. People in Harlem considered Paul Robeson a champion and the returning audience heroes, and came out in a massive welcome with food, shelter, and medical care. They recognized racism and most realized that Communists had consistently come through as allies. More often than not, "Nigger-lover'" was paired with "Commie."

The governor of New York, Thomas Dewey, blamed "red totalitarianism" for the riot, and bullied everyone into silence, even the courageous Eleanor Roosevelt, who declined to place responsibility where it belonged. Nevertheless, headlines around the world focused on the violence at Peekskill, and the FBI was forced to look into the blatant breakdown of law and order. In the face of his own agents' reports that the vets had started the riot, J. Edgar Hoover balked at an investigation.

In the 1930s, FDR failed to publicly support anti-lynching bills despite Eleanor Roosevelt's persistent efforts which earned her the fury of racists who hated and ridiculed her. In Harlem she was much admired, as was Robeson, who publicly criticized Truman in 1946 for continuing to buckle under to the vile Dixiecrats who defended the rights of whites to brutalize blacks. The high cost of racist America was old news, and Peekskill clearly located the latest assault in a seemingly endless war upon "Negroes."

We took in every word of the broadcast, fearful of the hostility our politics had unleashed in our fellow Americans, and heartsick about the brutal violence wrought by people living in our own state who, given the chance, would hate and attack us too.

Real Politics

U.S. CITIZENS LIVING in the middle of the last century ran the risk of being jailed for expressing certain ideas interpreted as "subversive," or questioning certain conventions considered "patriotic." People were fired from their jobs based on rumors, like actor Jean Muir, who in 1950 was dropped from the cast of *The Aldrich Family* because of Communist allegations. Americans were too frightened to object and progressive causes were frozen in their tracks until civil rights heated them up in the 1960s.

Most of my parents' friends were liberal. In the 1948 Presidential elections, most of them voted for Truman rather than our cowardly Governor Dewey. My parents campaigned and voted for Henry Wallace, the Progressive Party candidate, FDR's secretary of agriculture and his third vice president. Wallace ran against Truman, who, in collusion with the press, pumped up the anti-Communist hysteria and smeared Wallace "red" in the campaign, further encouraging the atmosphere of fear and hostility against activists like my parents.

A legislative deluge issued from the capital. In 1947 the Taft-Hartley Act required that the labor movement exile its best organizers and most effective members. Truman's 1948 Executive Order banned "Communists, fascists and totalitarians from public life." Regardless of any private reservations, public officials fell all over each other scrambling to get on the bandwagon or out of its way. Wallace did not use anti-Communism to further his political career, but Truman's venal strategy laid a foundation for the Smith Act trials, which began in Foley Square, New York City, in January 1949 and sent eleven Party leaders to jail. The Party was never mentioned within my hearing, and yet its presence was palpable.

"There was a time when the Politboro—a half dozen guys at the top of the [Communist] Political Bureau—used to meet at our house," said Pop. "I could always tell when there had been a meeting because there'd be an ashtray with ashes and a ring from a cigar and I knew that was Browder's brand of cigar. At the time, Browder was the head of the Party."

On certain evenings I would be told, "people will be coming over" and under no circumstance was I to mention it to anyone. On those nights we all left, or tiptoed around and spoke in hushed voices so as not to disturb "them," and Mom would be particularly on edge until "they" finally left. Forbidden to watch these people enter the front door or follow them down the hall as they proceeded to fill our apartment with intrigue, I never once set eyes on them. I knew better than to ask why.

Like all children, I craved safety, and like most Jews and all leftists back in mid-century America, I felt particularly endangered. I understood that "progressive politics," although righteous, was a euphemism for beliefs far from the norm and highly suspect in the eyes of the world. The fact was that there were two worlds and only one was safe for the truth to be spoken or written. In addition to public opinion and news reports about political events like the Wallace campaign, those early secret meetings from which we were banned helped establish in me a perpetual state of alert. Unfairness didn't make sense to me, but it was a fact of life.

While taking pride in the unusual status of my family, and passionately subscribing to my family's radical point of view, my wish was to be like everyone else in a *Dick and Jane* sort of way. Dick and Jane's family didn't have opinions or have to worry about anyone they knew going to jail. I had to worry because I had learned and could see that bad people were in charge and didn't like people who opposed them, like us. The lesson of Peekskill was not lost on me, living proof that in "the home of the brave, land of the free," the most brave were the least free.

Not yet able to comprehend broad events or grasp the finer details of political realities, I knew enough to question authority and mistrust my government. Because of this, public opinion determined that we weren't good Americans, but Grandma said, "I love my country, which is why I want to make it better." Her reasoning made perfect sense to me and made me proud of my family. Good Americans helped make our country better, we were good Americans, and no one, not even Dick and Jane shook my faith in that.

While privately I was proud of my family's politics, in public they embarrassed me and created social tensions. Politically isolated and vulnerable, I tried to avoid discussing the election with my friends, cringing whenever the subject came up in conversation. But sometimes silence was not an option, and my family's support for Wallace became impossible to hide. Having important information to contribute, I felt obliged to educate my friends, wanting them all to be radical, and now that I'm an adult, they are. Only recently I learned that my family's politics made a positive impression on Mike, who remembers our unorthodoxy as admirable rather than odious, as I'd imagined. Karen's parents were sympathetic but her mom was evasive when I brought the election up. As teachers, they were forced to sign "loyalty oaths," and Mom explained that they had to be careful not to lose their jobs by showing their support of Wallace.

Pilgrimage to Brooklyn

IN 1947, BRANCH RICKEY broke Jim Crow's grip on the major leagues and signed Jackie Robinson to the Brooklyn Dodgers. Progressive New Yorkers became Dodger fans and flocked to Ebbets Field to cheer the first "Negro" ballplayer in the majors.

I was born a Dodger fan, and Mike now believes that he should have been one too, but he was pressured into the enemy camp by Bernard, a true Yankee fanatic. It seemed to me that the Yankees were the biggest bores in baseball. Like rich people, they always won. I pictured Yankee limousines lined up at the players' entrance of Yankee Stadium. Rooting for such a dull, stuck-up team with no special personality and only money seemed senseless.

It was, I decided, a class thing, and very likely a boy thing too. Brooklyn would be far more likely than the Yankees to hire the first woman in the major leagues (me). And unlike the predictable Yankees, the Dodgers were endlessly fascinating. They had charisma, drama, took risks, and played cliff-hanger games with pitchers like Rex Barney, who was wild and usually had to be taken out. But on certain days he pitched no-hitters. You never knew.

Pop and I loved the whole lineup and cheered our hearts out for them, but number 42 was special. Pop told me how tough it was for Jackie to break the color barrier and to withstand the insults and taunts he silently endured; plus, we knew that Negro ballplayers had to be much better than whites to play. One day, sick and tired of losing my voice after every visit to Ebbets Field, I vowed to break the pattern and refrain from cheering. So, the next time, during play after thrilling play, I held myself back, remaining perfectly silent. The next day my voice was gone anyway, as usual.

Emerging in Brooklyn from the Prospect Park subway stop and joining the throng on their way to the field made me dizzy with excitement. Every vendor's board awaited my scrutiny. I was allowed one item per game. My first was a badge of Jackie Robinson with a red, white, and blue ribbon at the bottom, meaning integration was truly American and Jim Crow wasn't. I puffed up my chest and fastened it to my shirt. Another sported Jackie over a miniature bat and ball on a chain. Maybe I'd get one of those next time, or a new banner for the wall beside my bed. Pop would buy a souvenir program, and somewhere on the cover would be a caricature of the "Brooklyn Bum," an unshaven slob wearing a ratty topcoat with his shirttail hanging out, which came to be the Dodger logo.

Behind first base, where we always sat, we'd look for the tuba and drums and a few guys dressed in rags and made up as "bums." The "Sym-Phony," our unofficial team band, punctuated the play on the field, encouraging our guys and harassing visitors by putting an exclamation point on their every out and error with musical commentaries and little snatches of current tunes like "Slowpoke," or "Undecided," to serenade a runner caught between bases, and "Three Blind Mice" when an umpire made a call against us. A visiting batter striking out might be accompanied by a funeral dirge played in time to his footsteps all the way to the visitors' dugout where he'd sit down to a dramatic drumbeat and final cymbal crash. The band was not popular with visiting teams, but we loved it.

I remember the fans as being good humored, joking around, yelling fierce encouragement and approval, or shouting their dismay with insults. The vendors, each with his own distinctive singsong pitch, were characters and great loyalists who loved the team as much as we did, and cheered along with us. One or two came to recognize us, sometimes handing me a bag of peanuts before I even had a chance to ask for it. A good part of each game was spent consuming food and passing beers, sodas, hot dogs, pretzels, bags of peanuts, and popcorn across the rows, followed by a reverse flow of bills that reversed again to return change.

Excitement escalated when Jackie came up to bat. Voted "Most Valuable Player in 1949, he usually got on base and the crowd would go crazy waiting for him to steal, which he was famous for and which we saw him do more than once. Smart, fast, and hyper-alert, he rattled opposing pitchers and made fools of their infielders. Once we even saw him steal home, a spectacular baseball feat that to me represented a triumph over racism. My voice was gone the next day for sure.

When I couldn't attend a game, I'd flop on the couch, gaze out the window at the sky above the Christian Science Church across the street and listen to the radio, singing along with the Schaefer beer commercials. Red Barber described the play-by-play in a colorful Southern drawl. No one I knew drank beer or was from the South, but Schaefer was my beer and Red was my announcer. When Bobby Thomson hit that famous triple for the Giants in the 1951 playoffs, I threw some pillows around the living room to express my rage but didn't make too much of a mess because Mom would have to clean it up and it wasn't her fault. Then I stalked out to the park.

Dodger fans were spirited underdogs, and we were good at it. Losing particularly crucial or close games was a cherished Brooklyn tradition. In all my years living in New York we never managed to win a series, but we knew how to comfort ourselves. *"Wait till next year!"* we'd yell, our heads thrown back, while year after year the Yankees continued their tiresome victories. And when they beat us in the final game of the 1947 Series, we were desolate, but in a familiar, satisfying sort of way.

By the time fourth grade rolled around I had made a place for myself within the social circles of the boys and girls who lived in the district of Public School 9 on West End Avenue.

My credentials in the boys' gang had been earned in the street, pitching pennies against the curb and playing stickball. Football never caught on for long, but there was a baseball game going in the park every afternoon throughout baseball season and beyond. Every inch a serious player, with my well-loved, ratty glove, I was good in the infield and preferred playing first base. My hitting rarely made it to the outfield, but my speed could get me around the bases on little hits.

When we weren't playing baseball we were flipping the baseball cards that had replaced the classic paintings trading cards. They too came with a slab of bubble gum no one chewed. Double Bubble was for chewing, or Bazooka. Sometimes we'd flip cards while listening to a ball game. Our fifth grade teacher wrote in the class newsletter, "If some of you knew your schoolwork as well as you know batting averages, the standing of the teams, etc., I would have fewer gray hairs." Endless arguments were peppered with contemptuous sneers. We compared teams, players, stadiums, and sponsors, and put Red Barber up against the Yankees' Mel Allen. Every bar on the street meant a victory for the Yankee fans if we passed a sign for Ballantine Beer, and each Schaefer sign was a victory for me, my neighbor Liz, and the Dodgers. The intense, good-natured rivalry drew us together and sharpened our identities as we learned about belonging to a community and passionately supporting a cause.

Class & Clubs

AT PS9, MATRONLY Lucille D. Collin governed class 4-5 with a vigilant eye. She wore no makeup and seemed comfortable with her middle-aged face and gray hair. A bright, unruly roomful of personalities met their match as unflappable Mrs. Collin transformed us into a coherent community extending well beyond the classroom.

By fourth grade I was straddling the genders, my feet planted firmly in two distinct social worlds. Being the only girl on the ballfield counted as a social advantage, and being best friends with Mike, who was extremely popular with everyone, was another. In addition, I was best friends with Karen, who was also best friends with Michaele, second only to Nancy, who reigned at the top of the class popularity chart. Not a social leader but well positioned, I maintained the status I'd established in Brownies.

For much of my adult life I've tried to recreate those formative patterns set way back at the beginning of my community life. A social model consisting of two best friends, a club, a team and a tribe had its origin there, and for decades I've been favorably predisposed toward anyone named Mike, Karen, Nancy, Arthur, Bernard, Jane, Janet, Alan, and Phyllis. Nancy, in fact, was the name of my first serious love.

I was friends with both of the two Karens in class and wished the other Karen didn't have to take so much time off from school, traveling with her family to places like Europe or Palm Beach. She lived in the fanciest building I'd ever seen. The Apthorp Building on Seventy-ninth and Broadway resembles a palace where imposing wrought-iron gates open onto a huge courtyard with a driveway encircling a fountain.

Karen's father owned the famous Club 21, and when I visited her we'd lounge on her bed and she'd show me her scrapbook, the best I ever saw. Celebrities wrote "To Karen" with real signatures and there were new ones with every visit. Her collection included big stars like ice skater Sonja Henie and Robert Taylor. His name sent a stab of anxiety through my gut. Although I hadn't heard his testimony—"If I had my way [Communists would] all be sent back to Russia or some other unpleasant place"—I knew that he had cooperated and named people before the House Un-American Activities Committee, and that those people he'd named had lost their jobs.

Flipping quickly past his picture I said nothing, and concentrated on the next pretty star hoping it wouldn't be yet another rabid anti-Communist like John Wayne, Ginger Rogers, or Adolphe Menjou, who had betrayed good people so they couldn't get work. That scrap book was a minefield.

Finished with the book, we'd adjourn to the sitting room where a uniformed maid served us milk with sandwiches and cookies as we watched *Howdy Doody*. Karen's TV was the first one I ever watched and it was fabulous, but Howdy and Buffalo Bob seemed oddly creepy and Clarabell scared me.

In spite of her wealth and sophisticated life, Karen was fun and not at all stuck up. Too bad her frequent, prolonged absences from school meant that she also missed the Girls' Club. Most days after school I played ball with the boys, but not on Fridays when the Girls' Club met. Fourth-grade Brownies friendships resulted in weekly gatherings. Attention revolved around the most popular girls who lived in the snazziest apartments and wore the best clothes.

Aside from that, democracy pretty and much reigned, crammed as the group was with strong personalities. Each had her say, but, as I remember it, Nancy's carried slightly more weight. She was pretty, had lots of charisma, a fabulous apartment, and good snacks. We usually met in her feminine, well-appointed bedroom where we gossiped and played canasta.

Until its timely end, the Girl' Club ruled with its own order and loyalties. Membership presented a moral dilemma we managed to overlook. It was not our intention to hurt anyone's feelings, but it was clear that we did, and by the end of the second year Mrs. Collin called us together and told us what we already knew about the hurtfulness of exclusion. Consequently, the club opened to all the girls in class, and soon afterward the Friday meetings faded away.

During Lunch Club on Wednesdays, Bernard, Mike, Karen, and I rotated apartments and our mothers' cooking. All agreed that Mom's hamburgers were the best they ever tasted.

Between class trips, being captain of a winning girls' basketball team, acting in theatrical productions, playing baseball in the park during the week, going to Lunch Club Wednesdays and Girls' Club Fridays, and attending movie matinees Saturdays, I had every activity a kid could ever want.

Topping off the week was Radio Club with Liz and Danny, who lived down the hall, and Mike from downstairs. They would arrive on Friday nights in time for *This Is Your FBI*, a half hour when I tried to forget that the FBI was my enemy and that I hated J. Edgar Hoover more than anyone except Hitler. But politics was not discussed when we sprawled in our pajamas on the floor of my bedroom to play Monopoly, chatting and half listening while we waited for the main event, *Ozzie & Harriet* with David and our favorite, Ricky. Then our ironclad rule, "absolutely *NO* talking except during the commercials," took effect. And we honored it, mutely tossing the dice and pushing our pieces around the board mouthing negotiations and deals. The single exception was when, in one voice, we'd proclaim on cue along with little Ricky, "I don't mess around, boy!"

Nor was talk permitted during *The Life of Riley* with William Bendix as Riley, who always said, "What a revoltin' development dis is!" We chanted, "Whaddya want for St. James Place?" in singsong voices. It became our mantra as, week after week, year after year, we passed "Go" and went in and out of "jail" countless times, rolling on the floor with hoots and gasps, applauding when the richest player landed in jail.

Movies

MY FIRST MOVIE memory is of Pop taking me to see *Pinocchio*, in which the Fox and Cat radiated an evil more menacing than the straightforward brutality of other cartoon scoundrels. They were fools, but these two were sly, and the so-called easy life of no school and unlimited ice cream sodas was a wicked deception that transformed ignorant boys into slaves. No image sends chills through me like that of the fearful duo and their Pleasureland, which was really

Donkeyland inhabited by boys with donkey ears eating ice cream and candy instead of going to school.

My fascination with movies increased each year. Saturday afternoons I could be found sitting in the "children's section" of Loews Eight-third or RKO Eighty-first where white-smocked, gray-haired "matrons" patrolled the aisles, monitoring us with their flashlights and grumpy dispositions. Who were they? Where did they go during the week, and why were they so mean?

I sat with the girls for some movies and with the boys for others, taking in a progression of Hopalong Cassidy, Tom Mix, or Flash Gordon serials, *Movietone News*, coming attractions, and cartoons, followed by the second feature, more cartoons, and the main feature: *Father of the Bride* with Spencer Tracy and Elizabeth Taylor; *Easter Parade* with Fred Astaire, Judy Garland, and Ann Miller; or *The Flame and the Arrow* starring Burt Lancaster. What a relief to know that only grapes and not Tyrone Power's real eyeballs were cruelly squashed in *Prince of Foxes*.

It was immediately clear that I did not belong to the sort of all-American family portrayed in *A Date with Judy*. This 1948 musical comedy featured the Davis family heading the cast of flawless characters too good to believe, much like Dick and Jane. Each Sunday, the family dressed up and went to church. Then, at the dinner table, Mr. Davis carved the turkey or ham while Mother served and smiled contentedly. The FBI was nowhere in evidence.

That carefree American ideal family image was spun by moguls, impoverished Jewish men like Pop's father, who had escaped Russian pogroms and emigrated to New York City at the turn of the last century. Grim poverty of the shtetl inspired a shining fantasy of safe, prosperous American neighborhoods with streets paved of gold. Unlike my grandfather, who only got as far west as Allentown, men like Samuel Goldwyn, Darryl Zanuck, Louis B. Mayer, and Irving Thalberg continued onward to fabricate Hollywood and invent stars like Jane Powell.

Larger and more perfect than life on the big screen in *A Date with Judy*, Jane Powell took my breath away. Anticipating the formula TV family sitcom of the future, the movie co-starred a fetching, adolescent Elizabeth Taylor, but I only had eyes for Jane. Daylight was fading when we exited Loews. I skipped down the slope of Eighty-third ahead of Mom, trying to remember all the words of "It's a Most Unusual Day," the 1948 movie's hit song. The very thought of Jane caused my eight-year-old mind to reel with an unfamiliar headiness, and my heart to be consumed with delicious longing reminiscent of my feelings at glimpsing Dietrich's legs at Radio City.

I wanted to *be* Jane Powell/Judy Davis, and failing that, I wanted to be her best friend. Perky, cute, and, if not particularly bright, spectacularly popular, she was able to charm one and all with a precious giggle, a twinkling eye, and a raised eyebrow. But more important, so prettily did she sing that I dissolved into pure ecstasy at the first note. For many years I remained achingly in love with someone representing those virtues I instantly realized I lacked, and who owned everything I suddenly coveted. In years to come, "Judy" and her family would act as the standard against which to measure my imperfect household in our dark apartment; my inadequate social grace and standing; and my freckles, pigtails, and overbite.

Judy Davis/Jane Powell never had to worry about money, union busting, anti-Communism, or bigotry like I did. She was seasoned, composed, and far too sophisticated to be interested in the childish activities I pursued. I aspired to her calm maturity and self-confident social success, her secure membership in Proper America. And that piercing, sweet voice. Like a live wire to my heart, it thrilled me even more deeply than Paul Robeson's rich, soothing tones or the International Brigade's noble, inspirational ones.

Impatient for new Jane Powell films, I surveyed the coming attraction posters flanking the entrances of the local theaters in hopes of satisfying my hunger for her. Dodger banners on the wall beside my bed gave way to radiant portraits cut from *Photoplay*, *Modern Screen*, or *Silver Screen* magazines and the autographed photo from the MGM publicity department. "Best wishes, Jane Powell," was scripted in the lower right-hand corner of the 8" × 10" head shot sent in response to my fan letter. Of course she hadn't really signed it, but was it a copy of her real signature?

Maturity Strikes

NEVER STRONG ON looks, I developed compensations for a plain face early on. Clothing interested me not at all, and I spent little time worrying about my image, much less trying to improve on it. Mom called me "freckleface," and my family seemed satisfied with my features. As for me, I remained more or less indifferent to the reflection in the hall mirror on my way out the door. Not that I was a slob. Every morning I'd braid my pigtails, leaving irrepressible wild hairs sticking up all over. Of course I'd be prettier with a smaller nose, but my appearance did not yet concern me. Adults frequently commented on my dark brown eyes and long eyelashes. Due to tenacious dark circles beneath my finest feature, they'd sometimes note that I looked tired, even when I wasn't.

After Carl was born and Grandma left to live in Florida, it was up to me to keep him occupied, and later when Julie was born, it was my job to keep both siblings out of Mom's way until she had showered, brushed her hair, and finished her coffee with heavy cream and two thin slices of Pechter's well-baked, seeded rye bread, each lathered with a thick layer of unsalted butter on the wide side of the slice—her butter delivery system—topped off with a Fatima or Pall Mall cigarette. Sufficiently fortified, she could then take over.

Not a morning person myself, I suffered many slow, early-morning hours of baby games and other grim entertainments, my sleepy eye on the clock as I wound the Jack-in-the-box playing "Pop Goes the Weasel," or played favorite records like Groucho Marx singing: "Laugh, laugh, laugh at the gangling giraffe. . . ."

Not many years later, those morning moods suddenly became history. Overnight, Mom no longer spent mornings in a dark room and became approachable, sometimes even pleasant, even before getting out of bed. "I was unfit to live with," she told me long after those dreary mornings had faded from memory. "It just couldn't go on."

Mom was a model of self-improvement, and once she made up her mind there was no stopping her. She'd stick to a commitment like glue and astonish intimates with her iron will. Even before the surgeon general's report, Mom became alarmed by the health risks of smoking, threw her cigarettes away, and quit forever. After a while I forgot that she ever smoked at all.

All I knew about sex was that it was a big deal to adults, who didn't talk about it, and that its mention inspired wily looks and sly guffaws from older boys. I knew that sex was generally located around the pubic area, and had to do with having babies, which was related to women menstruating, but I didn't know what that was either. Nor did I understand its connection to sex, whatever that was. Did the other girls know?

On the corner after lunch one day, we crowded around Karen. School was a block away with only moments before the bell would ring. Karen held instructions she had taken from a Tampax box belonging to her older sister. We jostled each other trying to look at the drawings while she read aloud from the puzzling directions, which precipitated shrieks and whoops. None of us could make sense of the positions pictured in the diagrams, which posed more questions than they answered. We barely made it back to class before the bell.

As our ages entered the double digits, my classmate Bobby and I discovered a common interest in exploring the bright lights of Broadway and the heart of Manhattan. Without telling anyone who might object (our mothers), we'd hop on the Broadway bus after school and ride awhile, decamping on a whim to roam around midtown Manhattan.

Bobby and I felt safe together wandering around the streets sharing a great sense of adventure, careening in and out of fine hotel lobbies, dashing up escalators and riding elevators to the top of office buildings. Back on the street we ogled the gags displayed in novelty shop windows around Times Square, then leaned on the rail at Rockefeller Center to watch skaters circle the ice on the rink below. From time to time my parents had taken me there and to the Wollman Rink in Central Park. I'd try to balance on collapsing ankles and duck oncoming skaters, grateful when it was time to return the rented skates so we could dash to a nearby genteel Schraft's tea room and sip hot chocolate.

Thesbian

SOMETIMES ON PASSOVER, my family traveled to Flushing, Queens, where Pop's sisters lived side-by-side in little brick houses. I loved them and my cousins and the great, warm, hubbub of the big, crowded family gathering. I loved that the way that in their Conservative Jewish household Pop led the Passover Seder and got away with occasional political asides, likening HUAC to the Egyptian oppressors, or "accidentally" starting to say "Nixon" for "Pharaoh."

In later years we celebrated Passover with Liz and her younger brother, Danny, who lived down the hall with their parents and maiden aunt. A year or so older than I, Liz was quite well read and my sole Dodger ally, while Danny played ball in the park and was the only New York Giants fan I've ever known. Every year Liz would write a Pesach play. She'd be Pharaoh and would rehearse Danny and me for weeks. "Work, you dogs!" she'd snarl at us Jewish slaves as the silhouette of a whip snapped over our small backs bent behind a backlit sheet tacked up in the doorway. The adults smiled and applauded, then we read from the Haggadah and drank Mogen David wine, a wonderful sweet treat.

Mike's mother gave him a record of *The Emperor's New Clothes* on Young People's Records. Mom liked the music, written by Douglas Moore and Raymond Abrashkin, and bought it for me. When Danny and Liz got a copy, we decided to put it into production, made props, and began rehearsals. Mike was the Emperor, and Johnny would be the Prime Minister. Liz narrated, and Danny and I played the deceitful tailors, obsequious and cunning with our song: "We are two tailors who hail from the north / We have invented a wonderful cloth. . . ."

My parents let us use the apartment for the performance. Our stage was the dining room, and families and friends sat in the living room. The big sliding doors between them served as curtains for one performance to benefit the March of Dimes against polio, a scourge that killed and crippled many children. We hotly debated whether to charge a nickel or a dime admission and finally compromised on seven cents, which we collected from each adult on the big day when friends and family flocked to our living room.

The show was a great success, although Johnny missed his cue in the last act, forcing Mike to walk two extra large circles in his underwear. For months, the proceeds, about a dollar and a half, remained in my top bureau drawer under my socks. After struggling with temptation, I finally sent it off with a sigh of relief. I was honest after all.

My parents had bought me a set of records: Englebert Humperdink's *Hansel and Gretel* with Jane Powell as Gretel. "Brother, come and dance with me," she sang brightly on side one. Naturally, I was delighted by Jane, but it was the witch voice of Basil Rathbone that enthralled me. His demonic cackling falsetto scared me so much that I generally went from side three directly to side six, but its dramatic power acted as a magnet, and eventually I made it mine. When Mrs. Collin settled upon *Hansel and Gretel* as our fifth-grade production, I was ready. As always, the part of the witch was the best female role and I had no competition. None of the other girls was nearly as eager for it as I.

More important, no one else had heard Basil Rathbone, let alone huddled on the floor stiff with terror at his chilling performance. No other girl's mother had endured the racket of her daughter making herself hoarse trying to duplicate his timing, his delivery, his ghastly shrieks on their descent-into-evil chuckles.

"On the morning of December 21st, there was a rush of changing into costumes," began Nancy's review on page five of the June 1951 issue of *Out of 5-5's Inkwell*. "There was great excitement as our class started up to the assembly to present the operetta *Hansel and Gretel*." Nancy noted, "The play was very well received and was a big hit. . . . Everyone was afraid of the big, bad witch, Alix Dobkin." It was my first review in print.

Our performances included a dress rehearsal for visiting Girl Scouts, and was repeated for the children in the second and third year, whose fear-filled faces warmed my heart. I thrilled to the applause and wished the run had been longer.

On my next report card Mrs. Collin wrote, "Thank you for portraying the

'Witch' in *Hansel and Gretel*. You did a good job there and helped a great deal in making the play such a success." Recalling the thrill of applause, her praise further strengthened the resolve of a budding performer. The experience also drove home the value of good material, and thirty years later, when my daughter announced that her fifth-grade class would present *The Wizard of Oz*, I urged her to try out for the Wicked Witch of the West. In an echo of class 5-5, the futility of competition became immediately clear to her classmates as it had to mine. Well coached in "the laugh," my daughter was a chip off the old block. Small children screamed and cowered in the front row of the Woodstock Town Hall, courtesy of Basil Rathbone, via her proud mom.

Music Lessons

LONG AFTER MY mother's death I began to wonder how she felt about the Steinway upright, a gift from Grandma on my eighth birthday. It sat in the dining room facing the wall across from the front windows, and not once did I ever see Mom sit at it. As for me, I loved pounding the keyboard, an experimental sound grating on all ears but mine, and Mom started investigating music schools. She believed music to be the highest form of art and Bach to be the finest of all music, while composers such as Liszt and Rachmaninoff she dismissed as lightweights.

My mother didn't take to many people, but she admired serious musicians and liked Mrs. Kravitt, a teacher at the Metropolitan School of Music, and in the fall of 1947 they teamed up to see to my musical education. The school was located between Central Park West and Broadway. I'd turn east at Seventy-second, where the Beacon Theater is still in business. My only memory of theory class is sitting on a small chair in a room filled with kids banging on percussion instruments. I was given a triangle. Smacking it produced a sharp but fragile tinkle, puny and of no consequence. It bored me, and so did theory class. And so did practicing, which proved a frustrating challenge and no fun. However, I wanted to play and if I was to learn to read music it must be endured for an hour, "*Every* day," Mom emphasized, "even if it isn't a whole hour."

"She was a stickler," as Pop put it. Honest mistakes didn't bother her, but carelessness did. Alert to the first sign of distraction in the dining room she'd chide from the kitchen, "Alix, pay attention!" or caution me to "slow down!" as I galloped through an exercise in an effort to steamroller mistakes and get it over with.

"Keeping correct time is more important than playing fast," she'd remind me.

But mostly, "Stop looking at your hands!" because she always knew when my eyes strayed from the music, which was most of the time. This explains how, despite three years of piano and theory classes, I successfully avoided musical literacy.

My lackluster effort must have disappointed Mom, who accepted that neither of us would become the pianist of her dreams. Each week I'd resolve to do better, but practicing scales and exercises just wasn't that much fun. Today I can barely follow a line of music, yet thanks to Mom, I did learn to pay attention more as well as to value practicing every day. Her advice proves true in life as well as music, and eventually some of it did manage to sink in. "Find the weakest section of the piece," she'd say, pointing to a consistent trouble spot. "Work on it until it's the strongest and everything else will fall into place." Or, "Repeating a mistake will set you back and will also be harder to correct later on."

My mother's vigilance, my teacher's indulgence, and my ability to quickly memorize musical phrases allowed me to squeak by with "fair" in "preparation" enhanced by "very good" for performing Schubert's "March Militaire" at the school recital. Performance was clearly my strong suit, rating "especially good" from Mrs. Kravitt on her June report. "Excellent work for a beginner," she wrote, but I knew it wasn't as good as I could have done.

Fine Arts & *Lady*

POP LOVED MUSIC but leaned toward visual art and the art history that had saved him from being a bum. Free to choose between the two, I wanted to oblige both Mom and Pop with some of each. My formal art training began across town at the Ninety-second Street YMHA (Young Men's Hebrew Association), and one day a week after school I climbed onto the Eighty-sixth Street cross-town bus winding across the Central Park transverse.

Not even nature abhors a vacuum more than I, filling my walls with pictures and my songs with words. Girlhood advanced, and with it, specters of Dick and Jane's mother as well as the glamour-pusses in evening gowns at the top of staircases over captions saying, "Modess, because. . . ." The advertisement was as mysterious as womanhood itself and a treacherous shadow from the future. Beneath my eagerness to learn what femaleness had in store for me lay a sense of dread about how I'd ever look, act, and think compared to the ways a real woman was supposed to.

During this time of growing into adolescence, I was confounded by the conflict between my eagerness to learn what femaleness had in store for me and my dread of it. Perhaps as a way of trying to resolve this conflict, much of my artwork outside of class was focused on sketching profiles and hairdos of women.

The result was *Lady* magazine, an illustrated monthly outlet for my sketches and skepticism. I could draw to my heart's content, and explore what being a "Lady" meant. Satire would, I hoped, help me sort out truth from advertising, which tried to trick people into buying stuff they didn't need. Mom was a whiz at that and "women's" magazines, which she considered beneath contempt, were never seen in our apartment. Naturally I shared her opinion and devised a way to ridicule them and, hopefully, entertain Mom too.

Lady was produced entirely in pencil in case of mistakes. An issue was four or five stapled 3" × 5" cards, the kind Pop always carried in his shirt pocket in case a note was called for. A front cover of blue, yellow, or salmon might display an exaggerated feminine profile with the most outrageous outfit and hairdo I could devise. At least I hoped they were outrageous, since *Lady* was a parody. In this odd mix of convention and satire, a gossip column reported on the doings of fanciful celebrities with silly names, a recipe copied from Mom's card file passed for a "food column," and since my friends resembled the Hardy Boys more than I resembled Nancy Drew, a mystery series featured detectives named Mike and Red. This feature was discontinued after three issues for lack of a plot. The murder remains unsolved to this day.

Grandma, who returned from Florida to stay with us each summer, was my biggest promoter. She loved the little monthly, created exclusively for my own and my family's amusement, and proceeded to crank up business by soliciting subscriptions from her friends. She'd hand me a dollar and all of a sudden I was locked into publishing yet another issue every month for someone I didn't even know. As Grandma strong-armed more and more of her friends into subscribing, I began to dread the approach of each issue and was running out of ideas. What had begun as a labor of love and entertainment ended as a belabored chore, and *Lady* folded after six issues.

Insomnia

EVEN THE BIRTH of Julie when I was almost nine didn't keep Mom from sitting with me at bedtime to read our favorite books, like *Winnie the Pooh*, when we laughed so hard at Piglet's hysterical, "Holl, Holl, a Hoffable Hellerump! . . ." that we'd have to stop and compose ourselves before continuing.

Starting on my ninth birthday, Mom took out a yearly subscription to *Little*

Lulu comics in my name and we would both eagerly await each issue. After the nightly reading aloud, we'd review the day's events. During this special time I could enjoy Mom's focused attention and connect with her, ask questions, and get assistance in solving life's puzzles. For example, I did not understand the big deal about the kissing I was seeing on the screen at Loews Eighty-third every week. One night I asked Mom why people kissed for so long in movies. She thought a minute and replied, "When people love each other they like to kiss," an evasive, unsatisfying answer. I never wanted to kiss my friends that way, certainly not the boys. Did that mean I didn't love them? I loved Mike, but didn't want to kiss him. In the half light of my room, determined to discover the secret appeal of this bizarre adult practice, I could think of only one way. Surely, I loved Mom more than anyone. Her familiar features were almost entirely covered in shadow, softening the curve of the moon-shaped scar on her chin, the one she had gotten in a mysterious car wreck as a teenager. ("Tell me about your scar," I'd ask her. "It's too long a story," she'd say, "forget it!")

"Let's kiss the way they do in the movies," I suggested. "Okay," she agreed, still amused and a little self-conscious. Although loving and quick to show affection, this experiment is the only time I remember Mom letting me kiss her on the mouth. In the darkness I looked up. Did the corners of her mouth twitch? Was this "romantic?" I pressed my lips to hers and, instead of the usual quick smack, I stayed put, and so did she. This definitely didn't feel like a movie, not even a funny one, like *The Paleface*, where, having just gunned down three men, Jane Russell kisses Bob Hope then conks him on the head with the butt of a pistol, explaining, "Sorry, son, but I've got work to do." But that was a comedy, and movie kissing was usually serious.

We remained mouth-to-mouth for several seconds. I could feel grinding hardness of teeth behind both sets of lips and there was nothing even remotely pleasant about it. I had thought that pressing hard had to be the exciting part of kissing, but more pressure would be more painful and I was uncomfortable enough. If pressing wasn't the answer, what was? Regardless, it wasn't worth continuing. Waiting a few more seconds to be entirely sure, I finally gave up, more baffled than ever. I can't imagine what Mom made of it.

The failed kiss experiment was part genuine curiosity and part delaying tactic, for if this precious time with my mother was a favorite part of my day, her departure was the worst. "Good night, sleep tight, don't let the bedbugs bite," signaled the dread farewell. Each night I begged her to stay longer, to postpone the bleak landscape of boredom poised to spring into the void her withdrawal created. Insomnia dogged me in my own bed as surely as it had at naptime on a preschool cot. Many years later, Mom confessed that of all her mistakes raising me, my greatest childhood torment was also her biggest regret. "I should have let you read in bed," she told me and I could hardly believe my ears. Insomnia tormented me until the moment of my daughter's birth, when suddenly I could fall asleep anytime, anywhere.

Night after boring, sleepless night, I would turn to fantasies of a private island, part primitive village and part highly civilized secret compound with a select population of friends, our pool and underground facilities complete with bowling alley, although I'd never bowled. Sometimes I'd begin imagining myself a pro ballplayer, but that fantasy was too complicated because first I'd have to explain women playing in the majors, which was exhausting and depressing. I often imagined oratorical confrontation and debate with a succession of enemies from Hitler to J. Edgar Hoover. My passionate speeches, supremely logical and witty, would be overheard by reporters and troops milling outside, who, upon finally hearing truth spoken aloud, would see that justice was done.

Boy-Girl

SOMEWHERE IN FIFTH grade, "maturity" began to close in, its vague, ominous shadows seeping into my social life. The kids started playing spin-the-bottle at parties, where one unlikely couple after another adjourned to "neck" in the closet. The best parties were at my friend Warren's apartment, where his famous dad, the columnist Leonard Lyons, loved watching us square dance.

At one of these parties, a boy I didn't know sat beside me on the floor of Warren's hall closet. Square dancing was more fun than sitting there pretending to make out. I had learned all I wanted to know about kissing and was not interested. Fortunately, neither was he. If not square dancing, then I wished I was in the living room, watching the flat, thin TV screen that folded down into a cabinet. After a calculated time of not talking or touching, my partner and I stepped out, oozing all the casual mystery we could summon.

Social dancing class began in fifth grade, and an unfamiliar sharp edge sliced through our formerly easy equilibrium. I was happy to play, or to even dance, as an equal with boys. I didn't mind choosing teams either, mainly because I was usually either among the first chosen or the team captain. Boys were no better than girls, but the boys got to choose just because they were boys. Without anyone saying anything, they had suddenly been transformed from comrades into bosses, and even though it wasn't their fault, I resented them for it.

Of all the boys, Arthur was the best dancer, and although he wasn't particularly athletic and didn't play ball with us, we were pretty good pals. I hoped he'd ask me to dance. Or Mike. When Bernard asked me to dance twice in a row, I decided that I didn't like being taken for granted, especially by Bernard, because he was too wimpy.

"Uh oh, here comes Bernard . . . I don't want to get stuck with him," I whispered to Karen, turning away from him with a bored look on my face. He sailed past me and over to another girl. Now I had no partner at all, like the unpopular "Cheese" from "Farmer in the Dell," forever standing alone. Wimp or not, Bernard still had the power to rescue me. I thought about what great friends we were and hoped he hadn't heard my whisper, that I hadn't hurt his feelings with my snotty attitude, now extinguished.

But Bernard never asked me to dance again, and the implications of the enforced boy-girl coupling felt none too clear or comfortable. Power and injustice were clearly involved, meaning politics, yet no name in my political vocabulary conferred reality upon it. Already off the beaten track due to my family's politics with which I completely agreed, I couldn't bring myself to think about the hopelessness of women ever being hired to play professional baseball, let alone the hopelessness awaiting womanhood in general.

Near-perfect life on West Eighty-third Street as I knew it would end shortly, when the twins' father opened an office for Israel Bonds in Philadelphia and offered Pop a job working for him at a higher salary than he'd ever made. The arrival of little Julie made the apartment crowded, and Mom fretted terribly about having enough money to pay our bills. Pop would say, "They all go in a hat and the ones that get picked get paid this month. The rest will wait." As long as his steady paycheck came in, we'd be okay, he told us, and we were.

But the new job would take some financial pressure off the family, so, despite my fervid objections, I would be living in Philadelphia before my twelfth birthday. Everyone signed my autograph book, and Karen's father wrote, "To the best baseball player on Eighty-third Street."

PART TWO

1952–1954

Philly

The fight against Communism diminished us. It dulled our love of dissent and our sense of life's adventure.

—JOHN LE CARRÉ

ONLY NINETY MILES from West Eighty-third Street, the City of Brotherly Love felt as distant as the moon and as removed from childhood as I suddenly found myself. Feeling utterly alone in my culture shock, without a friend or anywhere to go by myself, I was suddenly a stranger in a strange house on a quiet, tree-lined road in Ardmore, Pennsylvania, where we were staying with friends of my parents' until our own place on the other side of Philadelphia was ready.

Summertime in New York had never seemed so hot, nor so dull. Relief from the sweltering monotony could be found only at the movies. Peter, the family's older boy, took me to the local theater to see the first of the modern horror films, Howard Hawk's *The Thing: The Story of Modern Science that Challenges the Imagination*. Dimitri Tiomkin's eerie score had me crouching under the seat before the opening credits had finished, but Peter hissed "Chicken!" at my hunched back, forcing me up to my seat and fixing my attention back on the screen.

Realistically documented in black and white, this creature of "modern science" disturbed me far more than the Technicolor Fox and Cat in *Pinocchio*. The "Thing" might be REAL, a mysterious, frozen vegetable monster so terrifying that even the camera's eye couldn't bear to focus on it for more than a second. *Such a movie couldn't be for kids*, I thought, desperate for a good look while also dreading it. Images of the thawed-out monster's severed hand creeping along the floor haunted me for days. At nights, the throbbing midsummer darkness resounded with a new sound of crickets' staccato song. Sleepless, I lay in bed wondering if I should worry about "The Thing from Hell." Adult privilege came with a world of adult worries I'd never imagined: a realization that weighed heavily on me. Yet there was, I knew, no turning back.

Life in Ardmore seemed to go on forever, but ended in August, when our three-bedroom apartment just north of City Line Avenue in Elkins Park became ready for occupancy.

Acres of woods and fields had been laid waste to make way for a sprawling brick maze of one- and two-story apartment units comprising Lynnewood Gardens. It would age gracefully into landscaped walks and shaded lawns, but during the summer of 1951 when we settled into the inner corner of a *U*-shaped courtyard at 1941 Mather Way, many streets were still incomplete, and naked-looking buildings sat on stretches of raw mud and clay.

A few hundred feet from our backyard was a minimal playground where I'd keep an eye on my brother and push my toddler sister on the swings, scowling disapprovingly at them. The anger at my parents, especially my mother, had cooled, but residual resentment for my shattered life shortened my fuse with everyone, especially my unlucky young siblings. Peevish and restless, I surveyed the unfinished vista. Everything here fell short of Riverside Park, but beyond the small playground was a field, and beyond that some promising woods not yet leveled by development.

Luckily Steve and Eliot soon moved into an apartment half a block up the street. While our fathers set up their office downtown and our mothers settled into our apartments, we roamed the woods armed with slingshots whittled with pocket knives, and shot at trees and telephone poles. As freckled, lean, and as scrappy as I, the twins were also as restive. Steve generally took the lead in "boy" activities. He was the best shot throwing rocks at telephone poles. In games of mumbledy peg he could throw his jack knife closest to his foot, on the dirt of the front courtyard where we also scratched circles for shooting marbles. My parents bought me a second-hand bicycle, a clunky yellow Schwinn I named Charlie. The boys and I rode everywhere, exploring Lynnewood Gardens and beyond.

Inventive and mechanically minded, Steve devised high-tech pranks like pulling a black wool cap over an electric train engine, which muffled the small headlight, making it glow eerily in the dark of night. Operating the remote from behind parked cars, we'd confound drivers who'd slow to a crawl and gape at the fuzzy beam gliding back and forth across their path. Some cars circled the block and returned again and again to puzzle over the ghostly signal.

Eventually, young families filled the remaining apartments and livened up the neighborhood. A toddler moved in next door, and when Mom was at home I was able to earn fifteen cents an hour babysitting. I applied for my own card at the Glenside Community Library. Like the newly planted trees outside my window, I was finding my center and sinking roots.

Red Scare: Home Front

THE POLITICS OF fear surged through the early 1950s and, for people like us, discretion and keeping a low profile had become rules of survival. Outside of trusted friends and family, appearing indistinguishable from everyone else offered the only safety, and the last thing I wanted to be was noticed. In school, along with the Pledge of Allegiance—we had to recite The Lord's Prayer. The phrases were alien and somewhat menacing, but being able to drone along with everyone else provided a curtain of safety. Strangely, words I couldn't remember memorizing slid off my tongue. *But MY father was at the Bonds office, NOT in heaven*, I thought defiantly to myself. Those kinds of thoughts I kept to myself because no one who went to this school would understand.

Paul Robeson had been attacked by high school kids in Peekskill and the whole country hated "Godless" Communists. So, thankful that no one could read my mind or know that I had personally shaken hands with Robeson, I bowed my head and mumbled, *"Our Father who art in Heaven . . . ,"* along with everyone else.

"Communism," said Lyndon Johnson of the 1950s, "was the great beast to be feared," but for thousands of Americans like us, the hysteria of anti-Communism was even scarier than *The Thing*. Besides defining American foreign policy, it kept America small-minded and fearful, removed unconventional points of view from the public discourse, and made equality and justice suspect.

With the 1919 Palmer Raids two years after the Soviet Revolution, the U.S. Government initiated the first big Red Scare. Young J. Edgar Hoover initiated his career in public service by overseeing the arrest of six thousand "Communists." Two hundred forty-nine aliens were deported to the fledgling Soviet Union. The hysteria gathered momentum in a frenzy of investigations, court rulings, purges, and legislation leading up to the 1939 Hatch Act, which initiated government loyalty oaths. For citizens with a social conscience, the anti-Communist tide was chilling. But for certain politicians it was a golden opportunity to bathe in publicity that only the 1941 attack on Pearl Harbor and a world war could temporarily divert.

The government's single-minded attention to the war had no doubt been a source of frustration for power brokers and aspiring political leaders eager to exploit anti-Communism. However, Martin Dies, chairman of the House Special Committee on Un-American Activities, continued undaunted. Refusing to be distracted, the fanciful Texas Democrat published, in 1944, a six-volume report listing twenty-two thousand "fellow travelers," and even questioned Shirley Temple's patriotism. Dies's inquisitorial methods and attention-getting hyperbole were not lost on young Joseph McCarthy, who, a decade later, adopted them to advance his own political ambitions.

Fear increasingly divided friends, severed family ties and discouraged community action. A succession of laws made every American think even harder about speaking out, signing a petition, attending a meeting, a rally, or even a picnic, or supporting any cause not approved by the American Legion and *Reader's Digest*. The intention of these laws was to expand a growing list of political hostages. Blood may not have been running in the streets, but fear was in the air and my family was at risk.

No one had to explain the cruelty and stupidity of anti-Communism in the days when examples were everywhere. The Cincinnati "Reds" changed their name to the "Redlegs," and FBI informer and Screen Actors Guild President Ronald Reagan regularly updated J. Edgar Hoover on "disloyal actors," earning himself the approval of political kingmakers, steady B-movie parts, and a TV career promoting General Electric for a larger salary than President Truman's.

Family conversations were now joined by a newly anxious edge to my parents' voices. I sensed their distraction and how secretive they had become about their activities, how careful with their language. Sometimes a certain young blond couple came by for what was clearly not a social occasion. Mom suddenly turned brisk and businesslike and everyone would be shooed from the dining room so she could sit with them, their heads together over the table, their voices low and serious. They seemed pleasant enough, but never stayed to chat or have dinner. Was Mom helping them hide from the FBI? As curious as I was I knew not to ask about this mystery couple. Even in our own kitchen, anti-Communism divided our family, drawing a line between me and them.

Although still unmentioned, the Party asserted its presence as a cloud in our midst, darkening when sharp tension arose from my parents' concern with news reports of multiplying laws, investigations, and arrests. The wrinkles in Mom's forehead deepened along with her piercing look of determination. Gravely, she'd sit, eyes fixed, a Pall Mall cigarette between her elegant, bony fingers, the smoke curling gracefully upward. Pop would sit quietly on the couch, reading the paper, his eyes hard, his attention turned inward in what seemed like a private trance. I observed them both carefully, frightened along with them, but permitting myself to be comforted by their thoughtfulness and resolve. I don't remember discussing it, but knowing that we were all in it together and seeing that life kept on as usual helped.

The only direct reference to our vulnerability I recall was Mom instructing, "If the FBI comes to the door, don't open it. Tell them, 'I have nothing to say to you.' That's all you say, no matter what." The opportunity never came.

The year 1950 had produced the Internal Security Act compelling registration of Communist or Communist "front" groups. In 1951, the Supreme Court upheld the convictions of Communist leaders under the 1940 Smith Act for "conspiring to teach and advocate the forcible overthrow of the government of the United States." "Subversives" could legally be deported under the McCarren-Walter Act of 1952.

In order to ensure continuity in the event of mass arrests, the Party sent its second level of leadership—approximately two thousand women and men—into hiding. For the first time in American history, thousands of responsible citizens suddenly disappeared and went underground. Although membership itself was not illegal, the Party leadership was either in jail, on their way to jail, or in hiding. I personally didn't know anyone in prison, but my parents must have. Nothing was ever said in my presence but I thought if the secretive young couple weren't in jail, they were probably fugitives.

One day during recess, some of the girls in my grade formed a circle as I walked by them in the schoolyard. "Your father's a jailbird, your father's in jail," they chanted in singsong. My heart clutched. I barely knew them. Were they singing to me? What was paranoia and what was real? I fixed my gaze forward, and, without appearing to run, left the yard as fast as I could. Once home, I asked Mom, "Are you or Pop going to jail?"

"I don't think so," she said, fixing her brown eyes on me for a long moment before shifting them to the darkness of the window. I trusted her, but anxiety remained a knife hanging over our heads. I longed for an end to the atmosphere of gloom, doom, and dread, the sudden fear poised to slice through any relaxed moment, triggered by anything from a glimpsed headline to a casual remark. I was scared because my parents were, and once or twice I imagined them being taken away but couldn't bear that for more than a second. Mostly I trusted that we'd be all right and that truth and justice would win out. Then I'd put it from my mind.

Spies & The Politics of Fear

SPIES WERE EVERYWHERE. There were FBI spies in the Party and "Russian spies" all over the press. The anti-Communist zealot, Wisconsin Junior Senator Joseph McCarthy, and HUAC dominated the media and reverberated within our walls. My bedroom window faced the courtyard and sometimes I'd peer out and try to spot agents who might be lurking about. I'd examine our neighbors' front doors and wonder who among them were informers.

On July 17, 1950, Julius and Ethel Rosenberg were arrested, along with their friend, Morton Sobell, and accused of betraying nuclear secrets to the Soviet Union. The case attracted global attention, massive support, and pleas for clemency. It had to be a frame-up like so many the government had engineered, used by anti-Communist politicians to stir up more hatred and hysteria. Everyone knew the Rosenbergs were innocent. Pablo Picasso, Albert Einstein, and Jean-Paul Sartre—the world's foremost artist, scientist, and philosopher—signed a petition for their release. In August 1951, the left-wing *National Guardian* ran a seven-story series documenting the trial, and, soon after, the National Committee to Secure Justice in the Rosenberg Case was formed.

Our dining room table was constantly piled with brochures and mimeographed updates. There were pamphlets to distribute, meetings to attend, protest demonstrations to organize, door-to-door petitions to fill, and letter-writing campaigns to conduct. Before long it seemed as if we had always been working to rescue this doomed couple—so like Mom and Pop—from an obvious government frame-up. Surely they would be saved. They had to be!

Through discussions at home, I learned that although no documentary proof of their guilt was ever offered, in August 1951, Judge Irving R. Kaufman condemned the Rosenbergs to death and sentenced Morton Sobell to serve thirty years in prison. The Supreme Court refused to review the case, and Judge Kaufman refused to modify the death sentences unless the Rosenbergs confessed and named others. However, the couple continued to declare their innocence,

Truman didn't respond to an appeal, and, after his 1952 election, Eisenhower denied the appeal.

The media was part of the problem. Except for radical newspapers like *The Daily Worker, I.F. Stone's Weekly, The National Guardian*, and *The Daily Compass*, the entire press hated us.

And I hated *My Weekly Reader*, distributed in class at the week's end and filled with lies. I hated being talked down to and found the reactionary distortions infuriating. It was perfectly obvious what answers were expected on the little back-page quiz. As my eyes forced themselves across the page, flinching at each "totalitarian," "Communist menace," or "Iron Curtain," new wrinkles engraved themselves in the space between my eyebrows. Was I the only sixth grader who knew anything? Did anyone else even have a clue?

Speaking up at school about "current events" was risky. Nor was it safe to talk candidly to neighbors, some of whom were bigots, some of whom might be FBI. The only kids who understood anything were Steve and Eliot, but they didn't go to my school.

Our Hit Parade

ELIOT DISCOVERED "BUSYBODY," a spectacularly clever song recorded by Jerry Lewis in his characteristic frenzy. It consisted of three long verses in rapid-fire rhyme, sung in three long breaths, which, at age twelve, I could just barely do. Beginning with "I'm a little busybody . . ." it exposed the secrets of "Mrs. Jones," "Mr. Klunk," "Mrs. Dunn," "Mabel," "Joan," "Mortimer," and "Mr. Shore" with a cunning string of insults. Now I wonder if, in a world filled with spies where political dissent had to be coded, Jerry Lewis was mocking tattle-tales and informers.

We listened to Frankie Laine's spooky "Ghost Riders in the Sky," and "The Wild Goose," and mimicked Johnnie Ray's heart-wrenching million-seller, "Cry," with "The Little White Cloud That Cried" on the flip side. Phil Harris sang about the unnamed "thing" found floating in a box in the bay and we sang along at the top of our lungs. But what was it? We'd never know.

All three of us had been raised with the Weavers, Josh White, Leadbelly, Woody Guthrie, Pete Seeger, and the Almanac Singers, who recorded an album of union songs. Our favorite was Seeger's "Talking Union." *"He's a bastid!"* we chanted along with Pete who described "the boss." *"That BAAS—tid!"*

"Busybody," however, remained number one on our hit parade. Monitoring each other against extra breaths, we rattled it off to each other while hitching rides on unauthorized sightseeing excursions through the nearby Pennsylvania countryside, or flying model airplanes in the parking lot of the new Big B supermarket on City Line Avenue, the first supermarket any of us had ever seen.

Our imitations of Jerry Lewis's scratchy voice peppered the air while we perfected yo-yo tricks like "Rock the Cradle," "Over the Falls," and "Dog-bite," at which Steve excelled. He eventually tired of "Busybody," but Eliot and I stayed with it, intently monitoring each other for any sign of sneak-breathing. Both of us could usually manage to cram the deluge of words into three side-splitting breaths. We also sped flawlessly through the chant: *"One smart fellow, he felt smart / Two smart fellows, they both felt smart / Three smart fellows, they all felt smart."*

Recreation

EXPLORATIONS HAD DRAWN the twins and me to a modest clearing in the woods beyond the back field. We dragged some logs in from the thickets and arranged them around a circle of rocks arranged for fires. The main attraction was a tree at the site's eastern edge, its wide limbs ideal for climbing and lounging. About a dozen feet up was the perfect spot for a platform, which we built. Laboring after school and on weekends, we added a roof, walls with two windows, a doorway, a small bench, and a table. It was perfect for smoking, reading comic books, and telling dirty jokes.

Comfortable with boys, I was used to being treated as an equal and took my peer status for granted. Being the female exception was nothing new, but unlike my gang on West Eighty-third Street, the new boys who came around were strangers, and I didn't trust them. Although cordial to others, my true hand of friendship extended no further than Steve and Eliot.

It was summer. Seventh grade and junior high loomed, I had just turned twelve and was sitting around the fire pit with some kids. A boy flashed a pack of Camel cigarettes. He lit one, took a drag, and passed it on. I watched, intrigued, as the butt made its way around the circle, each kid taking a puff in turn and trying not to gag. It was passed to me and I held it between my fingers like Mom. It felt natural and looked good.

"Inhale," I was instructed. "Take a big drag and breathe it all the way in." I sucked up a big puff and choked. Hacking and gagging, I couldn't imagine why anyone would want to do this. The butt made its way around the circle a second time.

"Are you gonna try it again?" Everyone was looking at me. This time the smoke went down smoothly and produced a rush. I felt dizzy and my head swam. I slipped gently down off the log onto my back. Treetops circled over me against the sky. Wow! I could hardly wait for the second cigarette to come around.

From that day on, an overflowing ashtray sat on our tree house table. We smoked while reading comics and between renditions of "Roll Me Over, Lay Me Down and Do It Again" or "Casey Got Hit with a Bucket of Shit and the Band Played On" and "They Are Shifting Father's Grave to Build a Sewer," with exaggerated Cockney accents.

We told dirty stories: "Did you hear the one about Johnny Fuckerfaster?" we'd ask each other knowingly in between puffs. "Wanna hear a dirty joke? A boy fell in the mud. Wanna hear a clean one? He washed his face."

At the beginning of the 1950s, Bill Gaines took over his father's E.C. Comics and, with Al Feldstein, published the first *MAD*, which was a comic book before it became a magazine. Within a month of publication, the twins and I had it, as well as *Panic*, an even more outrageous E.C. product. The arrival of either, especially *Panic*, resembled a religious occasion. Each issue was passed around with care and every other activity was preempted for painstaking readings. I still loved *Little Lulu* and was glad Mom continued subscribing for me, but in those drab fifties, the lunacy of Harvey Kurtzman and his staff blazed like fire. We began introducing smugly subversive E.C. references and terms like "fershlug-iner" into our conversation.

Eventually Mom relented and we got a second-hand table-model TV, but television watching was limited at home, so on babysitting nights I'd be glued to it. Sometimes our set was in the dining room, and sometimes hidden in my parents' bedroom because "It's so ugly!" Mom would say. Mom believed that almost all TV was trash designed to highlight the mediocre and sell unnecessary products, whereas I'd sit through the flag waving along with the national anthem at midnight when the broadcast day ended and the screen filled with snow. I wanted to watch everything, from John Cameron Swayze assuring us that a freshly brutalized Timex watch "just keeps on ticking" to Dinah Shore throwing a kiss from Chevrolet ". . . America's the greatest land of all!" I could even tolerate Kate Smith singing "God Bless America." Mom, of course, couldn't stand it, but to me, it was all entertainment, like a movie theater in your own home.

My favorite, *The Ernie Kovacs Show*, was not to be missed. Milton Berle occupied the same Tuesday night time slot at eight, and, like all TV hosts of the time, always wore a fancy smoking jacket between skits, whereas Ernie would appear in front of the curtain, a ratty, threadbare bathrobe hanging on him and the inevitable cigar poking out from the corner of his mouth. As long as Ernie wasn't canceled and *MAD* and *Panic* comics kept coming, there was still hope for nonconformists like me.

Starting late in the spring after sixth grade, the twins and I would hitchhike to a city swimming pool in a suburb across the city. Alone sometimes, I'd catch a bus and trolley car to whisk me there, fanned by a breeze through open windows as we glided through leafy green corridors sprouting branches close enough to touch.

In the ladies' locker room, changing into my bathing suit, I looked down at my stomach. It used to be flat, but now there was a bulge, and I noticed the beginnings of breasts. When did that happen? Was I getting fat? I sucked it in and walked outside to find a place to spread my towel and put my book. There were lots of kids but no one I knew. A group of boys roughhoused by the diving board. "Hey, ugly!" they yelled, laughing. *Me?* My head snapped around in alarm.

"She looked, she must be ugly!" They laughed harder, pointing at me.

Face flushed, I turned away, walked to the grass on the other side of the pool, spread my towel, sat, and stared at my book. Burning with humiliation for having been tricked by their game, I hoped everyone would forget the insult. Who was gawking now to affirm my ugliness? I didn't want to know. Was I really ugly? Big nose and dark circles. I was. They wouldn't have yelled at Jane Powell and she wouldn't have turned around. Or, she would have laughed with them about how untrue it was. I missed Steve and Eliot.

Girl to Woman

THREE EVENTS WOULD, I believed, signify my official passage into the realm of adult women. These consisted of the appearance of armpit or pubic hair, wearing a bra, and getting my period. Womanhood brought on the sweaty moment when I rounded the top of the stairs and noticed an unpleasant, acrid odor. Sniffing my armpit, I was shocked to discover that it was me. The next day at the drugstore, Mom and I bought a squat white jar of Mums cream deodorant, neat and round, with a red cap.

My lifelong wish to drink coffee at breakfast was granted when I turned twelve. For the first few weeks, Mom diluted this undeniable symbol of adulthood with an equal part of cream, which I poured in my cup before the coffee the way she did, because "You don't cool the coffee, you warm the cream." We both preferred a teaspoon of sugar.

The time had come to shed the eternal undershirt, familiar as my skin, and although I've never actually needed a bra, I whined and wheedled until Mom gave in. She took me to a lingerie store and bought me a size AAA32 "brassiere," as Mom called it in her embarrassing, old-fashioned way.

When the long-awaited blood of womanhood finally appeared on my underpants, Mom set me up with sanitary napkins and the awkward belt to secure them in place. Did I want to talk about this? she asked. Not with her, I didn't, sincerely assuring her that a talk wouldn't be necessary. She directed me to rub out bloodstains quickly in cold water before they set. Cold water was absorbent, Mom said, adding that cold running water absorbed smoke.

Sex Ed

I WAS PROUD of "menstruating" but detested hearing the word spoken, especially by Mom, as well as "vagina" or "brassiere." The blessedly few sex talks she forced on me made us both squirm. We sat on her bed and she tried to explain the mechanics of sex and reproduction while I repeatedly interrupted, saying that I already knew it, partly out of my own discomfort and partly because I actually did. I certainly knew enough to distance Mom (and Pop) from anything even remotely sexual. The very idea made me shudder.

Despite blocking out Mom's dutiful, "when two people love each other, lovemaking and sex is beautiful," her words came to mind unbidden one afternoon as I fought off a boy who was pawing me on the floor of an empty garage. Mom's reverence certainly didn't apply in that case, just as her kissing explanation hadn't applied almost half a lifetime ago. Fine with me, because Mom and sex did not belong in the same thought.

Boring diagrams and romantic euphemisms aside, my entire being had started to tingle with speculations about sex, which might explain how I came to be in the garage with a boy I didn't like or even know. After a short and unpleasant few moments, I escaped, convinced that this was not what Mom had in mind and certainly not what I was looking for.

Nor was it the half dozen strange boys I came upon unexpectedly one afternoon in the tree house. Where had they come from? We introduced ourselves. A sharp edge unsettled the space that had always felt like mine and I suddenly felt unsafe.

"Wanna play cards? Let's play strip poker," one of the boys suggested while the others fidgeted and leered. In a flash I was down the tree, through the woods, and across the field, heart pounding.

By age twelve, my sex education had moved briskly along, independent of adult input. Sex was increasingly the major subject of smirking discussions with the twins. Together we bought Mickey Spillane's *I the Jury*—published in 1947 amid great controversy—and other Mike Hammer books, only to find few, if any, scenes of the promised sex. We studied Irving Shulman's controversial 1948 novel, *Amboy Dukes* (not as sexy as we'd hoped), and on futile quests while I babysat we searched the drawers and bookshelves of our parents' friends, who had entrusted me with their children.

We found nothing, but at least we could smoke and listen to records of *Porgy and Bess* and *Carousel*, singing along with, "What is the curse that makes the universe so all bewilderin'? / Necessity!" and "When you walk through a storm keep your head held high. . . ." By now, fully resigned to the inevitability of sex-role stereotyping, I could appreciate the wit of "Soliloquy" with minimum resentment.

I babysat as much to smoke as to earn money. Also to examine the kitchen cabinets of each new customer in the hopes of finding instant cocoa mix and chocolate sprinkles, favoring those clients who stocked the agreeable tins and slender jars. Over months I consumed moderate amounts, keeping track of the levels. Mom stocked neither of these delicacies. Besides, she'd miss even a sliver from the giant chocolate bar by her bedside.

Great Explorations

OF THE TWINS, Eliot was the less aggressive and more musical. He was also more lecherous, a special recommendation for partnership in sexual inquiry. All three of us were attracted to dirty jokes and songs, but Eliot and I were driven. Sex was exciting, especially to thrill seekers like us. We shared a certain creative impulse that first produced repulsively exaggerated, age-appropriate drawings, and that eventually led to the silent explorations of Eliot's hand between my thighs as we lolled on my bed and pretended to read comics. Many agreeable hours were enjoyed at both ends of those probing fingertips without a word or regret about it.

Mom might have suspected something, because every so often she'd open my door without knocking and look at us sharply. There would be Eliot, sprawled across the foot of the bed, and me, propped up against the pillow at the head, my eyebrows raised in innocence, surrounded by comic books strewn everywhere and covering everything including the open fly of my dungarees. "It's so quiet, I wanted to make sure you were here," she'd explain, and leave the door open.

Strangely, my sexual curiosity did not extend to masturbation, although the subject was frequently mentioned in jokes, as was virginity. I was almost certainly a virgin, but how could I be sure? Unable to fall asleep one night, the perpetual showdown with boredom sent my hand investigating. My period was underway and my sanitary napkin had to be moved aside to permit the poking around that would, I hoped, provide the answer to the status of my "cherry." No pain, but a sudden gush saturated the pad and sent me to the bathroom to replace it with a fresh one. It was impossible to distinguish the types of blood, and the first blood-less penetration eight years later confirmed that I had indeed deflowered myself.

I made friends with a darkly beautiful girl named Jean. After school while her mom was at work, we'd brush out our long hair and experiment with makeup in her Penrose Street apartment. When she danced to her native Hawaiian music, I could have watched for hours. She taught me to dance the hula to "The Little Grass Shack," explaining the legend and translating the hand signs. Her interest in boys piqued my curiosity enough to follow her conversational lead. Although we became best friends and gossiped constantly, I didn't confide to her my silent episodes with Eliot. Like every other girl I knew, she was interested in Eric, an older boy in the neighborhood and the only one worth noticing. He was tall, dark, handsome, and muscular, much admired from a distance.

One night I was babysitting at home with Eliot keeping me company. We were watching wrestling on TV in the dining room, when there was a knock on the back door. Exchanging looks of horror, we quickly stamped out our ciga-rettes and hid the ashtray. While Eliot fanned the air frantically with a magazine, I walked slowly through the darkened kitchen to the back door. "Who is it?"

"It's Eric. I want to talk to you."

I opened the door, relieved that it wasn't Mom and Pop returning unexpect-edly, and thrilled that it was Eric. How, I wondered, had he known I'd be home without my parents?

"Where are your parents?"

"Out."

"Don't turn the light on." He was inside, standing close in the middle of the room. "Is anyone here?"

"I'm babysitting. Eliot's here." Eric gripped my arm and, with a decisive, "Don't come in!" to Eliot, leaned on the swinging door into the dining room to head off Eliot who, dying of curiosity, was on his way into the kitchen. But Eric was too big to argue with. *This was really exciting*, I thought, backing away. He stepped forward until we were standing toe-to-toe in the dark. "I've been noticing you," he said quietly. I thought, *Oh wow! Maybe I'm not so ugly.*

"I can see that you're maturing. Starting junior high in the fall?" Yes, I told him. "Junior high isn't anything like elementary school, and you're gonna need to know what it'll be like. It's time to start learning about boys." He moved behind me and cupped my breasts with his hands. Thank goodness I was wearing a bra! I felt him unhook it, reach underneath and squeeze my flesh as I was hoping he would.

"This is what big boys like," he whispered in my ear, "so you'd better get used to it." *How fabulous*, I thought, weak with delight.

"Make a muscle in your right breast," he instructed, and I did. He approved. "Now flex the other one." I was doing very well, clearly proving myself mature enough for seventh grade. If Eric spoke the truth — and I hoped he did — I was more than ready for junior high.

"Let's go in the living room," Eric suggested.

"But Eliot . . ."

"Don't worry, just go into the living room. I'll take care of him," he reassured me.

My only response to Eliot's sky-high eyebrows was a helpless glance as I slunk past him into the blackness of the living room beyond. It was like entering a movie and I was like a woman in a trance, being drawn by an irresistible interior force galvanized by my handsome neighbor. Back in the dining room the boys conversed privately for a moment and then Eric was back in the living room with me. We groped our way to the couch and lay down. The exquisite lesson resumed, but in a different direction.

"Are you going to tell your mother?"

"No . . . I don't think so."

"Have you ever seen a penis?"

"Maybe my brother's, I don't remember."

"Ever touched one?"

Had I? Did I ever brush Carl's by mistake, and did that count? Eric took my hand and, guiding it down his leg, deposited a warm, firm piece of himself into it. "Think of it like a bird," he murmured. "Hold it tight enough so it doesn't get away, but gentle enough not to crush it. Now move the skin around it up and down." I concentrated, wanting to get it right. He complimented my grasping and rubbing. This was weird, and not nearly as sexy as in the kitchen, but still interesting. His hand reached between my legs. "How about if I put my penis in here?" he whispered gently.

I froze. Absolutely not!

The phone rang. Rather than face Eliot on the way to the kitchen phone, I ran upstairs for the extension. It was for Mom and I took a message. When the conversation ended, I hung up the phone, which immediately rang again with Eric's voice on the line. "Come back down," he crooned in my ear. "I'll put my penis in your vagina."

"Then I definitely WILL tell my mother!" Eric knew when to quit and didn't press it. I went downstairs and we walked companionably back through the dining room and kitchen. He fondly wished me good luck in junior high, said goodbye, and vanished out the back door into the night, leaving my head spinning, my heart pumping, and my skin vibrating.

My lips were sealed to Eliot, who pleaded for a report in vain, but I couldn't wait to brag to Jean. It was so romantic, and she would be so jealous. After school the next day, I gave her the full story and she asked for the details, which I was happy to relate, and she *was* jealous. Demystified, Eric became more distant than ever, and the shared adventure drew Jean and me even closer.

On a gray day in June 1953, the *Philadelphia Inquirer* front page declared the awful headline across our dining room table. I couldn't imagine Julius and Ethel Rosenberg actually being dead, but they were. We had no defense for them, and all of our work, our protests, the worldwide outcry had proved fruitless. Worst of all, our certainty that right would triumph over wrong and good over evil had been destroyed. There was no telling who would be next, and everyone I loved went deeply into shock.

Camp Heaven

SIXTH GRADE ENDED, and Mom and Pop announced that for the last two weeks in July I'd be going to a camp. The time had come for me to start connecting with my cultural heritage, and Kinderland was a "progressive," meaning leftist, Jewish camp. "And," they reminded me, "you hated staying home last summer. You were so bored."

I was stunned. What I'd hated was overnight camp the summer after Carl was born, and I didn't want to go. I didn't know anyone there, and besides, this summer would be different, I protested, thinking about biking to Taflin and Schwartz and hitching around the farm country with Steve and Eliot. And where would I smoke? My parents were disrupting my life once more. Fuming to myself, I vowed that no child of mine would ever suffer this way.

"Well, I'm not bored *now* and I want to stay *here*," I persisted, but Mom fixed her course, held it steady, and sailed through my sullen resistance in much the same way as she had weathered my preschool tantrum. Steve and Eliot were also sent to camp that year, and like it or not, I was in for a life-changing summer adventure.

Situated those days in Hopewell Junction, near Peekskill, New York, Camp Kinderland immediately felt like home. Older women with strong personalities and distinct styles were in charge. Elsie, the warm-hearted, no-nonsense director, had a daughter, Dina, in my group. Edith Segal, a well-known poet in left-wing Yiddish culture and a camp institution, directed the dance program. The staff was friendly and didn't talk down to us. Suddenly my values were the norm, my politics were taken for granted, and my music was part of the standard repertoire. Most campers and staff lived in the Bronx with Socialist, even Communist, parents. We compared stories from Henry Wallace's presidential campaign and I could brag about knowing Paul Robeson. Everybody was militantly antiracist, pro-union, and pro-peace and supported every one of my family's causes.

We shared Sylvan Lake with other camps, notably our distant cousin and arch-rival, Camp Kindering, run by Workmen's Circle on the opposite shore. The socialist, anti-Communist branch of the Yiddish-speaking left-wing secular family was part of a community of feuding factions about which I knew nothing.

Adjacent to the children's camp, Lakeland, the adult resort, occupied separate and adjoining waterfront, lawns, and dining room, but both kids and adults used the large recreation hall called the Casino and purchased treats at the canteen, which sold *The Daily Worker*, *The Freiheit*, and *Jewish Daily Forward*. Generations of relatives, friends, and comrades rented cabins and relaxed in massive redwood lawn chairs to discuss the terrible fear that had our nation in its grip.

The poetry of Ethel and Julius Rosenberg circulated among the vacationers, along with poems, essays, and tributes. They knew Pete Seeger, Josh White, Leadbelly, and Woody Guthrie. The canteen sold egg creams, and everyone was a Dodger fan. The nightly "sing" in the Casino was conducted by Mattie, who organized a chorus and led us in the familiar union and Spanish Civil War songs. There were wonderful new ones like "Follow the Drinking Gourd" from the Underground Railway and "Dark as a Dungeon" from the Appalachian coal mines. "Joe Hill," a plodding tune, seemed to last forever. "Miner's Lifeguard" warned, "Keep your hand upon the dollar, and your eye upon the scale." When we sang "And the banks are made of marble / With a guard at every door . . . ," I pictured the steep, winding bank of a river, with uniformed chauffeurs standing by. The repetitive "Everybody Loves Saturday Night" taught us verses in every language I could imagine. "Ren-ren see waaah-lee pai-luuuuu . . . ," we sang, and "Yedderay-nah-hut leeeb Shabbos bi naaaaacht."

We sang our history, Jewish and otherwise: "I saw Jesus on the cross on the hill called Galilee / Do you hate mankind for what they did to you? / He said, 'Talk of love not hate, things to do, it's gettin' late / I've so little time and I'm just passing through.'" At camp, even Jesus was on our side. The poem by Jewish writer Emma Lazarus inscribed on the Statue of Liberty was set to music and we sang it. "Give me your tired, your poor. . . ."

We rehearsed plays about the German immigrant John Peter Zenger, the first American who went to jail in 1737 to defend the freedom of the press, and Crispus Attucks, a Negro who had been the first American to die in the Revolutionary War. Our skits incorporated Yiddish stories and tunes and folk dances originating in old Europe. The Yiddish tunes I sing in my concerts I learned there, along with the history of Jewish immigrants on the Lower East Side, where young Jewish women and their Italian sisters worked in sweatshops and organized the International Ladies Garment Workers Union. Our skits incorporated Yiddish stories, tunes, and folk dances originating in old Europe and adapted to the new land. In an audience spanning multiple generations, staff, campers, families, and Lakeland guests crowded the casino for our Sunday performances and the folk dancing that followed. The adults, especially the Holocaust survivors, cheered vigorously and extra long for the songs of resistance.

World peace came alive during the annual camp Olympics, when everyone divided into teams representing the countries on the Security Council of the UN: the United States, France, England, the People's Republic of China, and the Soviet Union. Together, we would surely be able to compete in friendship and help bring peace to the world. Mattie taught and rehearsed us for campwide performances of traditional songs from our country and Edith instructed us in the dances, while an enthusiastic athletic and art staff helped us prepare our national exhibits and trained us for the competition.

Teams sat together at the large tables during Olympics, amplifying even further the usual racket in the dining hall, typically resonant with sounds of bunk or table cheers, loud groans and tunes vilifying the cold "bug soup" (with prunes) or the "bug (fruit) juice." After lunch on Olympic Sunday, the entire camp congregated outside behind our national flags to sing the UN anthem with Paul Robeson on the PA system: "United Nations on the march with flags unfurled / Together fight for lasting peace / A free, new world."

It seemed to me that Annette and Judy from the Bronx were the cute girls while Barry and Aaron from Philly were the cute boys. The girls in my bunk were a community. We shared clothing, and my best friend, Bernice, was from Mt. Airy in Philadelphia, not too far from me. Toby's sense of humor was enhanced by a wonderful Bronx accent. Our counselors were a contrast in styles. In a letter home I described Silvia as ". . . the motherly type, and Toby is great to pal around with. They are both terrific! Today was general cleanup and the place was moped [sic], scrubbed, dusted, and the linen changed. (I mopped!) Right now the girls are writing to an ex-bunkmate and they are in histerics [sic] . . . Sometimes we have bunk nights, and we invite a boys bunk over and play post office. Last night the boys next door had a bull seccion [sic] and we heard it all the way in here. It was very funny!"

For Kinderland campers, Lakeland was forbidden territory, but I found a spot to smoke unseen behind a distant cabin. Scrambling through the brush and woods left me with a row of blisters emerging across my forehead days before my departure. The nurse painted them with "gentian violet," camp cure-all for every skin problem, including poison ivy. From a distance, the short, jagged strokes of dark purple beneath my tight hairline resembled bangs. It looked good to me and prompted my first change of hairstyle in six years.

Once home, the dread poison ivy rashes erupted all over my arms, legs, torso, and even between my fingers. Worst of all, my face ballooned, my eyes swelled shut, and my lips bulged with juicy blisters. Day after dreadful day I lay with blinds drawn, a pathetic, bloated, coated blob, unmoving on my bed in the dark, calamine-drenched air. Once or twice a day, a hideous monster worse than the Thing forced its eyes open to little black slits. Gory pink bulges stared in fascinated horror and glinted at me from my mirror.

To break up the time, Mom drew cool baking soda baths for me and brought ice water with a straw for my inflamed mouth. She'd sit quietly on the bed to stretch a cool washcloth across my forehead and reapply calamine lotion that felt good at first but then dried out to feel more uncomfortable than before emanating a smell that has sickened me ever since. In due course, the blisters dried up and the rashes faded, leaving me a pale frail survivor with eyes now like black coals stuck onto a gaunt white mask. They beheld the bright world as I stepped, blinking, onto the school bus and back into life, weak and grateful for my deliverance.

TW Junior High

THE SCHOOL HANDBOOK of the Thomas Williams Junior High in Wyncote, Pennsylvania, advised that the penalty for smoking was immediate dismissal. Assemblies ended with the whole school singing together, accompanied on piano by Mr. Long, the music teacher. Lyrics were projected onto the big screen, and a bouncing ball lead us through "Finiculi, Finicula," "I'm Always Chasing Rainbows," "(I Love Those) Dear Hearts and Gentle People," and other corny pop standards that everyone knew. Every so often, the ball would bounce an irritating fraction of a beat behind the change of syllable. Singing had never been so boring.

A select group of cheerleaders from the eighth and ninth grades practiced on the lawn every day after school. They were the role models with a touch of show business, moving together and kicking high like the Rockettes at Radio City Music Hall. Within a week I'd learned the steps and arm motions and could cheer along with a few routines, but I had no personal cheerleading ambitions myself. It wasn't me. Neither pretty nor popular enough to make the squad—the closest girls could get to serious sports—I found myself seriously wanting to get close to a cheerleader, which was about as close as I would come to being pretty and popular.

Eric's prediction notwithstanding, I was being drawn to older girls in general and one cheerleader in particular, with a preoccupation throbbing more around my heart than between my thighs. This round-faced, dark-haired ninth-grade beauty wore the white pleated cheerleader skirt with the orange and black "TW" on the front of a heavy white sweater. "Frav-lee-oh Eeeeee, Frav-lee-oh aaaahhh . . . ," we chanted. She too lived in Lynnewood Gardens, and because we rode the same school bus, I was able to strike up a conversation and cajole my way up to a friendship.

Now after school, instead of bike rides and hours searching out prurient material with Steve and Eliot, I sat at the foot of my cheerleader's bed while she modeled her new felt skirts, cashmere pullovers with short puffy sleeves, and small silk scarves of orange or turquoise, casually tied around the neck to the side, above the "fertility" circle pin, popular with all the girls but me. It was a female thing but I had no interest in fertility. Nothing even vaguely political passed between my cheerleader and me, but that didn't matter.

Her father made lots of money selling seat covers for cars. She and her mother shopped exclusively at Bonwit Teller and Lord & Taylor. "I wouldn't be caught dead buying clothes anywhere else," she confided, undeniably shallow and spoiled. But I refused to let it bother me.

For her part, she must have enjoyed my adoring, younger company, a foil for her glamour and sounding board for her gripes and gossip. We read magazines and discussed her outfits, her makeup, and the other girls, like Irene, who was "fast" and dyed her hair green on St. Patrick's Day. Besides clothing, we talked about older boys in general and her boyfriend in particular. The light of my life and the spark in my school day spoke of guys in the heady, romantic way I thought of her and it stung to hear it. What did she see in these dull boys? Nevertheless, I celebrated the successes and sympathized with the setbacks in her dating melodramas as if they meant something to me. To comfort her in times of despair was a privilege and a pleasure, but her attraction to the on-again-off-again steady remained a mystery and a heartache.

Although the social advantages of dating were plain to see, it wasn't the least bit tempting. On the other hand, intimacy with my perky, popular heartthrob was almost like being close to Jane Powell, and for a while I longed for each of them alternately. But as the year slipped by, my heart turned more and more toward Kinderland and my thoughts focused more and more on my new crowd. Thrilled with this new gang, I had fallen in love with a whole company of girls my age. I had best friends who championed unions, justice, equality, and freedom. They too hated war, wanted peace, and shared the same low opinion of *My Weekly Reader*.

The Bronx Co-ops & The Philly Shul

MY REAL BEST friends were from camp and none of them lived in Lynnewood Gardens or went to Thomas Williams, but my progressive Yiddish education and its social life would soon overshadow junior high, while interest in my cheerleader would wither and fade.

Two camps, Kinderland and Lakeland, were run by the JPFO (Jewish People's Fraternal Order), which also ran a network of secular Jewish Mittleshuls, attended by kids my age in New York and Philadelphia. My shul was located in Strawberry Mansion, an ancient Jewish working-class neighborhood. The homes of many camp friends were located only blocks away from the school in cramped row houses on the narrow cobblestone streets still used in that section of town. Getting there required catching a streetcar and a bus, then an electric bus like a trolley car minus tracks and powered by antennae wired to an overhead line.

The largest percentage of Kinderland campers and staff lived in the Bronx. As kids assembled from all over the east at the beginning and end of each summer, cries of jubilant reunions or anguished farewells filled the air. The camp bus stopped on Allerton Avenue across from "The Co-ops," the project of an unsung New York City cooperative movement.

The Co-ops had been designed and built in the 1920s by Communists and Jewish garment workers. Built to facilitate community and political action, the complex, although considerably past its heyday, wowed me. In a deliberate departure from tenement housing, two thousand rooms housed three thousand people in seven hundred fifty units, each with a high ceiling, at least one sunlit room, and a view onto a common courtyard. At ground level, a community room and auditorium were surrounded by a maze of small offices and rooms in which to meet, read, study, play a game, take a class, dance, sing, or socialize. How amazing it would have been to grow up in a place like this, with my own values embedded in the very concrete.

But Yiddish was not spoken at home and although Pop was somewhat fluent, he and Mom had not participated in the culture or the heritage of radical activism surrounding the language that was sometimes known as " Jewish." If it hadn't been for camp, I never would have known about the Co-ops or Yiddish-American history. I would not have been able to imagine peace in the world.

In a telling letter I wrote to my parents at age thirteen, "I have always felt a little inferior to everyone else that I knew and tried to make it up by being smart and clever and saying fresh things. If you saw me with the shul kids, you'd come to realize that I don't act this way around them. I don't try to make anything up by being wise because I feel so much like part of them. They are my whole life. . . ."

Yiddish class began at nine on Saturday, but I preferred sleeping late. Then, two buses and a trolley delivered me to shul in time for lunch with my friends. In the afternoon we danced the Russian Troika and Israeli My-im and, sweating, panting, and singing along in ecstasy, I let the music take charge. An indifferent scholar with a booming social life, the only Yiddish I remember learning besides songs, was, "Sammie ess fis una cup," meaning "Sammie eats fish without a head."

About a dozen girls from various sections of Philadelphia made up the bulk of my shul crowd. Lorraine and Micki were my favorites, along with Bernice, who we called "Nicey," and Sandy, the smartest of the group. The boys were okay, camp-approved fellows, and I liked them well enough, but being with the girls was far more exciting and fun.

It would be twilight as I headed up the long blocks on Penrose Avenue, where one afternoon, an unappealing boy from my class had offered me a quarter if I'd pull down my pants and let him pull my hairs. Yes, a few hairs had appeared and, although dimly suggestive of sex—always worth noting—his proposition was stupid, might hurt, and was definitely not worth a quarter. "No!" I said and looked past him, thinking, *That bastid*, like Pete said it. The spelling, when I learned it later, seemed all wrong because "Bastard" sounded inane. So did "prick," although "dick" didn't, maybe because I was used to hearing it.

The width of Lynnewood Gardens lay before me, long blocks before I would turn away from the campus of the Stella Elkins Tyler School of Fine Arts. The school grounds bordered those of an equally well-tended convent, neighboring mansions bequeathed to art and religion by widows of tycoons. How inviting the orderly gardens appeared, glimpsed through graceful wrought-iron gate-ways and neat hedgerows. Despite their proximity, these estates had escaped our rambles, protected by a dignity too intimidating to breach.

Lots of girls carried photos of boys, but I was never without the closeup of Micki and Lorraine from camp, their eyes closed, their nearly smiling lips puckered and barely touching in a chaste yet heart-stopping kiss. I dared show this precious summer souvenir to a few select schoolmates. "That's disgusting," they scoffed, bunching up their noses at the queer image in my hand. "I think it's funny," I countered, with the only defense I could think of. Without under-standing my powerful response to the image, and with my lifetime of training to hide unconventional thoughts in public, I automatically suppressed those feel-ings I knew were forbidden, and didn't let on when they surfaced.

"Once I had a secret love that lived within the heart of me. . . ." The tune, riddled with delicious hidden knowledge, cycled in my head and tugged at my heart. But what did it yearn for? Even Doris Day was forced to sing in code, promising to "shout it from the highest hill . . ." whatever "it" was. The mean-ing of her big hit, "Secret Love," remained a secret, perhaps even from Doris herself.

At least I didn't have to hide my politics from camp and shul friends. We came from similar political backgrounds, spoke the same language using the same references and assuming the same givens, like that workers should be paid fairly and our government was usually in the wrong. It was one thing to be free to be politically honest with the kids, but feelings were another thing entirely. Some songs brought these feelings on in a rush like a punch to the heart. But how could I describe the deep longing that erupted with the sound of Jane Powell's voice or the image of my girlfriends' lips? Like witnessing the twinkling night sky and apartment windows lit by Christmas lights on the way home from a Brownie trip one December evening, and thrilling to the flash of Marlene's legs disappearing around a corner at Rockefeller Center.

The same stars glittered and the familiar ache churned inside my chest as I trudged up Penrose. Another week to endure before I'd see the girls again.

My pockets were loaded down with the penny candy found nowhere in our neighborhood. Each Saturday before leaving Strawberry Mansion, I stocked up a week's supply for the twins and me, neat rows of pastel-colored sugar dots stuck on strips of white paper, black wax mustaches, red wax lips, and sets of white upper teeth, excellent for long lasting chews.

High Holidays

OUR HIGH HOLIDAY season began on Thanksgiving weekend at the bus station between Arch and Race. It was the first reunion of the year and we were hopping with excitement in the tiny waiting room. Then the bus pulled in, releasing our Bronx and Brooklyn friends into our open arms. The long weekend flew by, ending at the bus station where it began with choruses of "See you next month!"

Converging again on the first day of Christmas vacation, our $5.50 round trip tickets in hand, the Philly kids boarded the bus for Manhattan's Port Authority where our former guests gathered us up and whisked us off on the A train to the Bronx, or the D train to Brooklyn. Their old-world term for suitcase was "valise," and they said "train" for subway. I stayed with Toby whose Yiddish wit was enhanced by her Bronx delivery. Yiddish was spoken in many of my friends' homes, unintelligible but comfortably familiar. When he met my friend Mona's mother, Pop called her "the salt of the earth," which was good because I wanted our parents to like each other.

The annual Hootenanny at Town Hall attracted a community of political lefties and mavericks and starred the cream of American Folk Music. Kinderland kids were among the crowds cheering Pete Seeger and Ronnie Gilbert with the Weavers, Martha Schlamme, Leon Bibb, Cisco Houston, Earl Robinson,

Sonny Terry and Brownie McGhee, and other legends who dazzled the packed house and sent us roaring to our feet. Unable to sit still for our grand reunion, campers lined up against the back wall and joined the streams flowing in and out of the lobby, minding the music with one ear and taking in the news with the other.

Then, Ronnie Gilbert's vibrato was soaring throughout the hall riding the rich Weavers' harmonies, "We wish you a merry Christmas / And a happy New Year." My hands were sore from clapping and my heart vibrated in my chest sending joy out to every cell in my body. With my dearest friends at this very concert and a round of parties coming up, it had to be the best night of my entire life! Too soon after the final party to welcome 1954, dozens of us again converged on Port Authority. Our tearful farewell dramas seemed all the more heart-wrenching for the six-month lapse before camp united us all again.

The rest of the school year couldn't move quickly enough for me, but at least I had shul every week, and mail to look forward to, especially letters from Gun Hill Road. My heart nearly sprang out of my chest on the afternoon I received Toby's unexpected eight pages of fat script in exotic green ink on baby blue stationery. As instructed, I proudly shared the letter, but not my crush, "with all the girls."

Crushes

The House of Wax was playing downtown and we met at the theater where, along with our tickets, we were handed 3D cardboard glasses, which put us in the screen with Vincent Price. Mostly we went to musicals like *Three Sailors and a Girl*, in which Jane Powell sang duets with Gordon MacRae and tap-danced with Gene Nelson. On a damp, slushy evening, we gathered in Center City to see *Kiss Me Kate* with Howard Keel, Kathryn Grayson, and other favorites Ann Miller and Keenan Wynn. The combination of great songs, great stars, and the company of my girlfriends set me on fire.

And Cole Porter's score knocked my bobby-sox off, topping even *Annie Get Your Gun*. The Irving Berlin tunes were still clever and wonderful, yet less sophisticated than I now was. Each *Kiss Me Kate* tune was a songwriting lesson in itself. One favorite, "Where Is the Life that Late I Led?" rhymes "puberty" with "Schubert-y," plays with interior rhymes like "stinking pink palazzo," and strings out "itty, bitty, pretty Pitti Palace." Lyrics didn't get much smarter.

Despite Jane Powell's absence, *Kiss Me Kate* was the best movie I had ever seen with some of the most brilliant songs I'd ever heard. True, Kathryn's distracted air and fuzzy edge felt a bit unsettling, yet until her surrender, Kate's passion riveted and enthralled me. Her sharply raised eyebrow and fiery stare made me wonder how the far more grounded Jane Powell, who could raise her eyebrow with the best of them, would have belted out a rousing "I Hate Men."

At home I listened to original cast recordings nonstop. Mom liked them all right, but not as much as Bach or ragtime. *Oklahoma, The King and I, South Pacific,* and *Annie Get Your Gun* had been memorized long ago, and I had since added the spectacular *Guys and Dolls,* and much of *Show Boat, Carousel,* and *Porgy and Bess.* The *Finian's Rainbow* score was outstanding, especially "When the Idle Poor Become the Idle Rich" and "When I'm Not Near the Girl I Love (I Love the Girl I'm Near)." Margie had taken me to see Ray Bolger in *Charley's Aunt* on Broadway, from which I learned "Once in Love with Amy." On a quiz show with a Broadway show tunes category I would have won the grand prize.

Broadway was exalting America's musical standards and Tin Pan Alley was flattening them. After my journey to Strawberry Mansion on Saturday afternoons I'd sip lemon Cokes or egg creams at the luncheonette, gossip with my friends, and slide nickels into the jukebox for songs like Rosemary Clooney's "Botch-a-Me," or perhaps, "You, You, You," by the Ames Brothers. With inward groans I endured each interminable note of "I Believe," Frankie Laine's sentimental hit and the biggest song of 1953, according to *Your Hit Parade.*

On the weekly collection of dramatized top ten songs on TV, *Your Hit Parade,* the robotlike smiles of the regular vocalists Snooky Lanson, Dorothy Collins, and Giselle MacKenzie headed each week's brisk march behind the Lucky Strike Victorian picture frame. On better weeks, Rosemary Clooney's cheery face injected life into the stupefied visage of official pop music. Little scenes on the show attempted to dramatize top tunes in the blandest of scenarios. For every week that a song remained popular a new drama had to be produced, and the narrow possibilities of some songs really pushed the limits. The passive "Harbor Lights," with no action whatsoever, was a particular challenge for each of the twenty-nine weeks it stayed popular. Worse, "How Much Is that Doggie in the Window?" sold over a million and hung in the Top Ten for months and months.

The Weavers' recordings of "Irene Goodnight," "Tzena, Tzena," and "Kisses Sweeter than Wine" were huge hits, but the 1952 blacklist quickly shut them down. The group had been investigated and refused to cooperate, but when Pete Seeger, who had brought his banjo to the hearing, offered to sing the very songs

HUAC considered subversive, the Committee turned him down. Among the popular songs then current, two haunting show tunes alone, "My Secret Love" by Doris Day and Tony Bennett's "Stranger in Paradise," seemed noteworthy.

Unrivaled for gut-wrenching or heart-stirring, the tune "Ebb Tide" had been popularized by Al Hibler and Roy Hamilton, but I bought Vic Damone's version to add to my expanding collection of 45 rpm singles. The sweet Italian crooner could sing circles around the far more popular Eddie Fisher, beloved of Debbie Reynolds, Elizabeth Taylor, and virtually every one of my girlfriends. While they all pined for him and gushed over "Oh My Papa," I remained indifferent.

All the songs were about boys with girls. It was perfectly clear that I was supposed to like boys and not girls, and if I didn't, no one was ever going to know. Putting up Vic's photo was one of several tactics in a campaign of disinformation. Another was hiding the depth of feeling that Jane still evoked in me.

No one had to tell me that I was expected to love boys and to display male images on my wall, and Vic's pretty face could reasonably be swooned over. His equally pretty voice pleased the ear but in fact I was lukewarm to his singing. Nevertheless, a couple of Vic's photos went up over my bed to provide respectable, boyish company for Jane. From the little square record player on my shelf, Vic's wistful voice crooned "The Breeze and I," always ". . . ending in a strange, mournful tune." I could identify with his torment. It seared my heart as my eyes floated above him to rest on my greatest love, still reigning unchallenged from the wall.

"This is me and my boyfriend," I bragged to my school friends, just in case they suspected my disinterest in boys. "He lives in the Bronx." Proof was a photo of me in baggy jeans and a striped, sleeveless shirt, my head resting upon Davy's handsome collar bone, my face radiating smug satisfaction. His arm draped around my shoulder, shirtless with muscles bulging, he was wearing baggy khaki army pants, dark glasses, and a crooked grin. Not really a boyfriend but a good-looking pal from Allerton Avenue, he and his best friend, Gitchik, drove down from the Bronx. I told my schoolmates about how the three of us cruised through Fairmount Park and I sat between them listening to Nat King Cole croon the haunting "Nature Boy" over the radio.

It had taken two years in Lynnewood Gardens for my life to finally work for me. Then one afternoon, Mom called me over to the sink to tell me that when eighth grade ended we would be moving to Kansas City. My sister, Julie, then four, now remembers me stomping my foot and shrieking, "No, NO, I'm NOT GOING! I WON'T GO! I WON'T GO!!"

No one in my family really wanted to go to Kansas City, but we needed to make more money and there weren't any manager's jobs on the east coast. Pop could get a raise only by opening a Bond office in the small but growing Midwest Jewish Community. It was a good job, and we could come back after a couple of years.

Seven of Mom's friends signed an elegant card; a lino cut of a rose, made by "the children of Holland for the World Friendship Committee of the Women's International League for Peace and Freedom." The note inside said, "with all our love, and with sorrow that you are leaving." Mom was sorry too, but not as sorry as I, fiercely guarding that distinction, bitter spoils of my defeat.

Politics seemed to occupy Mom and Pop less and less; there were no more mysterious visitors or warnings about the FBI at the door, and the Party's presence seemed diminished. The thought crossed my mind that Kansas City offered a break from the FBI and maybe even the Party, but it didn't matter. I just knew I didn't want to leave my new friends.

Nicey and the girls found a recording studio and made a 45 rpm record for me. Their individual voices and messages of love, cheer, and hope were threads to sustain life in alien lands.

Flat Kansas

We are forever mixing ourselves with unknown quantities. What is to come, I know not.

—VIRGINIA WOOLF, The Waves

IT WASN'T UNTIL we reached the airline counter in the Philadelphia airport on the afternoon of July 23, 1954, that Mom remembered she had left our tickets in the top drawer of the dresser, which was by then heading west in a moving van. A bit of a fuss, and Grandma, Carl, and I boarded an airplane taking us to Kansas City. A cab then whisked us thirty-five miles away to Excelsior Springs and a three-room cabin, booked for ten days of sweating and languishing. Meanwhile, my parents and three-year-old Julie motored through the sweltering Midwest in my parents' grand old maroon beauty of a 1946 Packard Clipper, with no air-conditioning.

We arrived in time for Kansas City's hottest summer since 1936. A swarming plague of black locusts arrived with us. They stripped vegetation, blackened the sides of buildings, and blanketed the pavement with a twitching carpet that popped and crunched with each footstep. I couldn't remember experiencing anything stranger or more disgusting.

The temperature hit 110 degrees and stayed there for two weeks. "That is hot enough to affect your eyeballs," Pop commented. Dogged, Midwest humidity slowed movement and thought, while daily, the brutal sunlight flattened already flat fields and turned low buildings into cardboard facades on a barren landscape. They looked no better after sundown. As Pop noted, "The best that can be said about Kansas City is that no matter how hot it gets in the daytime— there's nothing to do at night."

Pop wrote to friends that we had "a nice time" at Excelsior Springs, and that "Alix is flourishing . . . more of a lady every day." *Flourishing? Lady?* Hardly. I was thirteen, hot, bored, and displaced once again. I read and re-read movie magazines and searched for shade, trekking back and forth between the cramped kitchen and a spot on the scrubby lawn separating the cabin from the road. There was no TV or radio, and no stores within walking distance, which made smoking problematic.

One afternoon shortly after we arrived, a boy about my age approached on his bike and hopped off to chat. After a time, he said he had to leave and extended his hand. When I reached out to shake it, he jerked away, saying, "Left hand for niggers," and rode off, laughing.

Kansas City was hell itself.

Brand-new ranch-style houses lined each side of our brand new dead-end street named Sagamore. The unfinished Johnson County suburb echoed Lynnewood Gardens three years earlier in the same raw piles of gravel and clay. A lonely sapling drooped on the front lawn, reflecting my despair. I'd felt exactly that way three years ago when first confronted by Philadelphia, the city for which I now pined and against which Kansas City paled.

In our new middle-class development, every third ranch-style house was identical with a picture window overlooking its regulation lawn. Grasshoppers and daddy long-legs patrolled interchangeable backyards wondering where the wheat fields had gone. In the blazing sunlight I saw my first praying mantis, green and luminous. In the bleak, bleached landscape I soon located a vacant strip across the main road where I could smoke unobserved. Slipping a Pall Mall or Fatima from Mom's pack, I'd tell her I was taking a walk, and beneath sheltering weeds and thorny brambles, I'd unearth a tin-can ashtray from the scattered litter, light up, and breathe in a lungful of smoke to occupy, if only momentarily, the barren space around my lonely heart.

Magnificent Obsessions

Magnificent Obsession was playing downtown, and Mom dropped me off while she did errands. The theater was crowded and I found a seat midway in a center row. A man holding a newspaper to his chest slid into the seat on my right. The movie had barely begun when I felt fingers touching my arm. Before I knew it, they had made their way to my right breast and were squeezing it. From the corner of my eye, I could see his left hand holding the newspaper, concealing his straining right arm as it crossed his chest to reach me. No movement was visible from beneath the paper.

I sat perfectly still, eyes fixed forward as his hand loosened my white peasant blouse from my waistband, and creeping, clutching fingers kneaded my bare skin. We both stared straight ahead at Rock Hudson, blurring before my eyes. I couldn't focus on the story for the tingling spreading through my midsection. My body throbbed with excitement while my mind raced with anxiety. No one had noticed us, but the prospect felt dangerous, quickening the thrill.

After a while, the man released his grip on my breast and moved to my thigh. His unobtrusive moves and outward immobility were impressive, but how did he plan to reach into my panties without attracting attention? Suddenly he gripped my hand and pulled it down to his lap beneath the newspaper, a shift immediately escalating my trotting anxiety into a wild gallop. Wriggling my hand free, I quietly tucked the blouse back under my wide, elastic cinch belt. *Now what?* I wondered, and when again he shifted toward me and reached for my hand, a warning clanged in my head. Time to leave! Clutching my purse, I got to my feet and excused myself across the row to the aisle. In the lobby I considered my options. Mom wasn't picking me up until the movie ended, and there was no point in leaving the air-conditioned theater on a wickedly hot afternoon. Although I had no idea what the story was, I decided to find another seat and finish watching the film. I bought a Peppermint Patty and found a seat on the other side of the theater.

But my mind stayed fixed on the memory of the man sitting next to my now-empty seat, and my body longed for his hand groping my breast. Still unable to concentrate on the movie, I finished the candy and got up, my hunger unsatisfied. He was still there, a balding, bony man, sitting motionless in the center of the row. I made my way back to him, on fire for more fondling, but before I had reached the empty seat he sprang up and disappeared, probably thinking that I'd set him up for arrest. Disappointed, I sat down and began imagining what might have happened had I stayed in my seat. But what about the armrest between us? How did he expect to . . . what? I couldn't imagine. The music swelled, "The End" came up on the screen, and I shuffled outside to meet Mom, frustration giving way to gratitude for the lack of complications.

Never having turned my head to see what the man looked like, his face blurred in my mind, and my first sex fantasies began with a silent, lanky, middle-aged white man, a model for anonymous, unadulterated sex, free from respon-sibility or consequence. However, the vacuum of my adolescence wasn't totally satisfied, so I concocted a fantasy that played like a double feature, alternating raw, lustful episodes with romantic reveries: impersonal male hands and body parts or a nebulous and intoxicating sense of fusing, usually with female crushes like Jane Powell. More conversational than tactile, my Jane Powell fantasies evolved into rich, erotic bonding consisting of mostly me talking and her listen-ing rapturously. The barely touching lips of Micki and Lorraine in the photo had unlocked explosive passion and made me wish that one of those mouths was mine. Frustrated, longing for the romantic adventure of the page, screen, and airwaves, I couldn't imagine who in this endless prairie would ever want to love me. And whose faceless lips could I almost feel brushing my cheek each night, what voice murmured unintelligible endearments in my ear? Beneath consciousness lurked the hope that they would belong to a boy who would make me a normal girl.

Movies and cigarettes alone made life worth living. Although always raised, my high expectations were rarely met by films that stayed with me about as long as the chill of the theater in the Kansas heat. But some films surpassed my expectations.

It was beyond imagination that the stuff of family legend would be lionized on the big screen, and although Communists were not mentioned, let alone credited, in *On the Waterfront*, the film depicted honest, courageous, union or-ganizers. Marlon Brando could have been uncle Cecil in the last scene when he stood up to the mob. During the weeks the film played in the neighborhood, I returned time and again to watch Brando mumbling to Eva Marie Saint, playing with the glove she accidentally drops and he picks up, or tearfully confronting his brother who'd sold him out to mob leaders like my uncle's enemy, Joe Ryan. The thin stream of Vic Damone's charm had long since run dry, and more than ready for a new male heartthrob, I fell for Marlon as hard as I possibly could.

In 1954 I saw *On the Waterfront* and *Kiss Me Kate* six times each, topped only by Jane Powell's *Seven Brides for Seven Brothers*, which I saw seven times. In this movie the girls all got to live together, which was good, but married their kidnappers, which was bad, and truly loved them, which was Hollywood. Suspension of disbelief and the cost of a ticket was a cheap enough price to pay for the athletic dance sequences, high points in an air-conditioned hour and forty-two minutes with Jane.

Across the street from the theater, a record store with a row of "listening booths" enabled potential customers to browse the latest hits as well as Broadway and movie scores. The songs from *Kiss Me Kate* sharpened memories of the Philadelphia girls, while *Pardon My Bloopers* provided some laughs. "The fog was as thick as sea poop," declared an announcer who cracked up on the air at his own mistake. I'd sit in a booth with my stack until a clerk tapped on the glass of the door.

After weeks of nagging, Pop finally brought home a *Kiss Me Kate* album, but instead of Katherine Grayson and Howard Keel from the film version, he mistakenly purchased the Broadway cast album. Disappointed but resigned, I played it often enough to permanently engrave every syllable on my brain. In the process, I couldn't help noticing a number of differences between the film and show. For example, in "I Hate Men," Patricia Morison sang, "mother *had* to marry father," but Katherine Grayson sang, "mother *deigned* to marry father." Similarly, "the business that he *gives* his secretary," became, "the business with his *pretty* secretary," all of which meant sex.

It was hard to find people we liked in Kansas City. "There are so many of them and so few like us," Pop lamented. My parents had made a few friends, but they weren't nearly as interesting as the ones in Philadelphia, and Mom and Pop must have been lonely too. I saw no evidence of political activity and the Party seemed to have vanished. Pop went to work and Mom sewed curtains into the wee hours of the morning until Pop joked that it wasn't safe to leave a rag around for fear it would wind up on somebody's window. Julie was enrolled in kindergarten, freeing my mother to register at the University of Kansas City as a part-time freshman majoring in music.

Commitment to school changed Mom's life entirely, a challenge demanding every ounce of determination and focus my mother could summon. Her day was figured down to the minute. If we were going to interrupt her, it'd better be for a good reason, and we'd better not make any extra work for her either. That year, frozen TV dinners may have flooded America but despite her tight schedule they never made it onto my mother's table. Even with her tight schedule, compromise was unthinkable when it came to precooked dinners, which she rated about as high as TV.

Ruth McKenney's story, "My Sister Eileen," first appeared in *The New Yorker* and was published in a collection of stories in 1938. A smash 1940 Broadway hit, *Wonderful Town* followed with music by Leonard Bernstein and lyrics by Betty Comden and Adolph Green. It starred the incomparable Rosalind Russell as the narrator, Ruth, who flees Ohio with her pretty younger sister and winds up in a Greenwich Village basement flat surrounded by artists, writers, intellectuals, "Freethinkers," and other oddballs like my parents.

In his autobiography, *Really the Blues*, horn player Mezz Mezzrow chronicled a freewheeling 1930s and '40s jazz scene with a look at hot spots like the Village where creativity reigned and races mingled without fuss. The description was riveting. Nothing could have been further from my monochromatic present than the Village of Ruth McKenny and Mezz Mezzrow. I devoured both books and projected my adulthood as a sparkling social whirl centered on a "neat" Greenwich Village basement apartment. "Such interesting people live on Christopher Street!" Green and Comden wrote, and I knew that's where I belonged.

Shawnee-Mission

ONLY THE UNMARRIED female PTA members saw their first names listed in the 1954 Shawnee-Mission High School handbook. Everybody else was "Mrs. G.V." this, or "Mrs. Everett" that. Parent instruction sessions were scheduled in a section, "KNOW YOUR CHILD AND HIS SCHOOL . . . Meet His Teachers . . . Attend His Classes (October 18) . . . Understand Him Emotionally . . . Understand His Problems . . ." and "Examine His Work." Page two set out a list of objectives and ended with a "Parent-Teacher Prayer." I can hear Mom's teeth grating now.

The Philly kids would, I knew, be mystified by the importance of "Pep Clubs" to Midwestern student life. Neither I nor anyone I knew had ever heard of them, but in Kansas, there was one in every school and students were actively encouraged to sign up. Membership required a small fee and the purchase of a pricey red corduroy jacket. It had black collar, black trim, and a felt chest pocket shaped like the profile of an "Indian chief" in full headdress. Pep Club members were expected to show up and cheer for our "Indians" teams at every game. Something about having an Indian for a mascot felt wrong, but it wasn't anything I could name, so I recast the image as a tribute. Pep Club offered camouflage and on Fridays I was indistinguishable from 90 percent of the student body. The idea of a uniform appealed to me, and given a choice, I would have worn the same outfit every day, which, as an adult, I often do.

In anticipation of the Friday game, Pep Club members were expected to wear the jacket to school along with a white top and black skirt for girls (black pants for boys). The halls swarmed with black, white, and red and the few non-Pep Club members stood out. After classes, the grandstands in the gym over flowed with energetic, uniformed teenagers who crowded in for the semi-required, pre-game pep rally. Synchronized group choreography had thousands of us chanting, cheering and mirroring the cheerleaders' hand motions. I found it oddly stirring.

The prettiest, most popular junior and senior girls wore letter sweaters like the varsity and junior varsity athletes, and led cheers far more elaborate than "Fravlio Eeeeeee" from my junior high school crush. Would my heartthrob measure up? If so, she'd be the only Jew on the squad.

Halfway through the year I met the three other Jews in Shawnee-Mission's twenty-five hundred students, but they struck me as geeky and boring. The religious atmosphere in the only Johnson County synagogue I visited once. It felt safer and somewhat easier to take than a church, and although the unfamiliar Hebrew was spoken instead of Yiddish, at least I didn't feel like a total alien. They were pleasant enough and if I made an effort to be geeky and boring, I imagined I could fit in.

With state-of-the-art science labs and first-rate academic programs, Shawnee Mission High was bigger and more well appointed than any school in my experience, and took boys' sports more seriously than I thought possible. Attempting to pass as normal, I tried to care about the teams, but the novelty of rallies and games quickly flagged. Nothing could persuade my mother's daughter to join the Hi-Y's, Y-Teens, 4H, or FHA (Future Homemakers of America). As far as I knew, like women's clubs, they all added up to a lot of nothing.

"What's school like?" Pop asked me. I visualized the expansive parking lot filled with the late-model cars of confident, nattily dressed students. "A country club." They had everything except culture. For example, did anyone at Shawnee-Mission besides me know who Pete Seeger was? Or Leadbelly? Had anyone heard Tom Lehrer's wickedly clever songs spoofing sacred American cultural stereotypes and institutions from Christmas to the Boy Scouts?

Academically, Shawnee-Mission demanded far more than any school I'd attended. Working hard became survival for an East Coast urban Jew during a lonely freshman year in the bosom of suburbanized former farmland. I was proud to achieve a B in every subject and an A in Phys Ed, where my gym teachers, Miss Ness and Miss Brawn, inspired mixed feelings in me. Their love for sports compounded by a lack of interest in makeup impressed me. However, they favored a clique of girls, and I was neither Anglo-Saxon nor Protestant enough for inclusion. Fortunately, athletic ease and confidence saved me from becoming a target for the little meannesses the inner circle inflicted on the less able girls, but despite my athletic ability, I grew to dislike gym class.

Being an outsider everywhere in Anglo-Saxon farm country soon became tedious. Sophistication was my refuge, sarcasm my defense. Eve Arden delivered the driest wit of all at the expense of Messrs. Boynton and Conklin at Madison High School on CBS TV each Friday night. Too bad *Our Miss Brooks* didn't teach gym at Shawnee-Mission instead of Ness and Brawn, who were not amused by my sly humor. On my next report card, they wrote, "Attitude needs improvement," and reduced my lone A to a B.

Comfort with visual images, not to mention a crush on my geometry teacher, helped me through tenth grade plane geometry. Tall, slim Miss Kahn, a sturdy, broad-boned young woman with a dark bob haircut, prominent cheekbones, and fun-loving eyes, stood with authority and moved comfortably around the room. I adored her sense of humor, sprinkled with irony and sophistication. In my fantasies she appreciated my deep insights and sophisticated wit as our friendship became closer and closer. Thinking about seeing Miss Kahn was how I got myself out of bed in the morning.

Toward the end of the term, Mrs. Gibson, my kind and motherly Spanish teacher, spent a short time in the hospital and I missed her. Before paying a visit to her hospital bedside, I stopped at a drugstore to find a stuffed bear, which was what I'd have wanted if I was in the hospital. "Heartbreak Hotel" was playing through the store's sound system. All of a sudden, Elvis was getting lots of play. Boys liked him and girls loved him, but like Elvis himself, I failed to see what all the fuss was about.

On the other hand, he certainly was shaking things up, which I appreciated. I wanted everyone to question authority like I did, and if that wasn't possible, I wanted to be like everyone else. At least I wanted to *appear* like everyone else, and the older I got, the trickier that became. Fitting in now, given my attraction to girls and indifference to boys required greater vigilance than in my younger, simpler days when I had only my parents' Communism to hide.

One unexpected advantage of living in farm country was the restricted driver's license available to fourteen-year-olds because farm kids drove tractors. Mom, foreseeing a battle of wills, refused to teach me, so in return for twenty-five dollars' worth of babysitting, a neighbor across the street agreed to do it. Everyone was all for the deal: the neighbor and his wife got Saturday nights out and, besides driving lessons, I got to smoke, watch a big 14" TV, and pilfer instant cocoa mix. Plus, I had an excuse for not going on dates, not that anyone was asking. It was win-win.

I practiced braking with my right foot, steering with my left hand, and keeping my elbow off the window ledge, even though it looked neat. This was before cars had directional signals and drivers had to use hand signals: up for right turns, straight out for left, and down for stop. Mom was happy to take me to the county building for my license and I drove her home in our 1952 Chevy Bel Air hardtop coupe, top seller in America during the early days of planned obsolescence. The Packard Clipper had been wrecked during a routine servicing by a mechanic who drained the oil and forgot to replace it, wiping out Pop's pay raise with one stroke.

During the previous decades, polio, or infantile paralysis, had been the greatest of all parents' nightmares. It killed or paralyzed children who, to breathe, needed to lie helpless inside mechanical cocoon-like contraptions. Terrifying specters of iron lungs hovered everywhere above us on billboards, and, on a summer afternoon during my fourteenth year, a mobile exhibition rolled down our street and kids lined up to view the display inside. It was like a freak show. The head of a mannequin stuck out of a giant glass and metal cylinder, its plastic body visible within. Deep rhythmic gasps from the respirator heightened a torture-chamber atmosphere. Later that year, Jonas Salk came up with a vaccine against FDR's dread crippler, and the iron lung seemed to vanish overnight. Parents could relax and send their children back to public swimming pools, where the polio scare had shriveled attendance.

Anti-Communist frenzy seemed to have peaked with the Rosenberg executions and Korean War cease-fire. The FBI probably visited us in Kansas but I wasn't aware of it and remember nothing of political activity on my parents' part during that time. Of course we were heartened to see much of the press, including the *New York Times* and the *Chicago Tribune*, join American newscaster icon Edward R. Murrow in breaking the silence of fear engendered by Joseph McCarthy. The Senate took heart and censured their colleague to further brake his momentum, and new ground began emerging for slightly less demented hysteria. I still didn't know if my parents were in the Party, and still didn't want to. With Pop's attention turned to establishing the Kansas City Bonds office, and Mom completely focused on schoolwork, the weight of politics lightened around the house.

In 1954, the United States Supreme Court officially numbered the days of Jim Crow when it ruled that "separate but equal" education was not equal and could no longer be racially separate. Beneath the tight control and bland surface of Eisenhower's tenure, other long overdue remedial forces rumbled and gathered to shake up the rule of mediocrity and, unobserved, rock 'n' roll prepared to shatter the sound and structure of popular culture worldwide. Decades after an early rhythm & blues recording in which the Boswell Sisters first put a name to rock 'n' roll, white musicians were busy adding their touch of blue-eyed soul before delivering it to America.

Music, Music, Music

"TIN PAN ALLEY" referred to Forty-eighth Street between Broadway and Sixth, the center of the music business in Manhattan, which kept coming up with losers like the depressing "Let Me Go Lover" or the equally sappy movie theme, "Three Coins in the Fountain." "The Happy Wanderer" and "The Yellow Rose of Texas," both aggressive male choral pieces, contained lyrics inane enough for the bouncing ball at a Thomas Williams assembly.

White popular music on the radio was, as a rule, boring at best and pathetic at worst. Besides Broadway shows I listened to what my parents listened to: classical, blues, jazz, and folk. Personally, I found that faking a taste for most of it only intensified my feeling of alienation, especially from myself.

Patti Page's hopelessly square, million-selling "Cross Over the Bridge" tried too hard. More successful, her "Steam Heat," from the new Broadway hit, *Pajama Game*, swung as much as any white music I'd ever heard on the charts, yet even that lacked the ring of authenticity. Having been raised with a love of music played and sung by real people for real people about real experiences, it wasn't hard for me to appreciate the difference between songs manufactured to sell and the product of genuine individual creativity. A few cute ones, like the peppy "Mister Sandman" by the Chordettes, or the Gaylords' "Little Shoemaker" told a story like a folk song, but they paled beside the music I happened upon while flipping the radio dial one Saturday night.

After driving lessons were paid off, I could earn thirty-five cents an hour watching TV, eating powdered hot chocolate mix, smoking my head off, and tuning in at midnight to an outsider culture that spoke and sang my language. Dame Fortune, who had tossed "Busybody," *MAD*, and Ernie Kovacs my way, now guided me to a radio station playing one hour of rhythm & blues on Saturday night. Like *The Lone Ranger, The Big Show*, and *Ozzie and Harriet* before them, this R&B program instantly soared to highlight of the week.

Due to cheap, accessible record players and affordable 45 rpm records, rock 'n' roll was able to break Tin Pan Alley's grip on popular music. At the same time, the magnetism of R&B reeled in my generation of white kids with money burning holes in our dungaree pockets. Dissatisfied with the stale succession of lifeless tunes and anemic lyrics of mainstream culture, we were hooked by the energy and directness of rock 'n' roll and cracked the code in no time, realizing that words as commonplace as "work," "dance," and certainly "rock 'n' roll" itself, meant sex, the way "to die" meant sex in the Middle Ages and "gives the business" or "had to marry" meant sex in the Broadway version of "I Hate Men."

Spinning on the margins of the mainstream at seventy-eight revolutions per minute, "race music" had existed for twenty years before 1949 when *Billboard* magazine dubbed it R&B and assigned it a separate chart. As Little Richard remarked, "It took people like Elvis to open the door for this kind of music, and I thank God for Elvis Presley!"

Black Network Radio formed in 1954. Their programs, like my Saturday Night Special, steered me to black record stores in search of labels like Savoy, Checker, Chess, VeeJay, and Atlantic so I could add to my mushrooming collection of 45 rpm singles. White producers hired white artists to water down great R&B hits, then sold them to white audiences either too timid, insulated, or racist to appreciate the originals. To the educated ear, Lavern Baker belting out "Tweedlee Dee" sounded nothing like the chipper, genteel Georgia Gibbs cover, and I made sure to track down the Penguins' "Earth Angel" rather than buy the Chords' version.

My Saturday night radio show played Hank Ballard and the Midnighters' obvious sexual challenge, "Work with Me Annie." Etta James answered with the equally brash "Roll with Me Henry." No song on *Your Hit Parade* even came close, not even Mercury's 1955 hybrid cover "Dance with Me Henry," in which Johnny Otis, Hank Ballard, and Etta James collapsed their witty original into junk for Georgia Gibbs to record. I listened, outraged, but had to admit that pathetic as white covers were, they did manage to perk up radio airwaves.

In an exception proving the rule of mindless pop music, Tennessee Ernie Ford sang, "I owe my soul to the company store" as "Sixteen Tons" flew to the top of the charts. For a moment, it seemed as if the hits would finally start educating people. I envisioned pop music becoming real and transforming lives, but no further class consciousness was heard. Only scattered voices of color, like Bo Diddley, Fats Domino, and later Chuck Berry, singing their own songs made their way onto the airwaves.

Bill Haley and The Comets cleaned up Joe Turner's original "Shake, Rattle and Roll" by moving the lyric from the bedroom into the kitchen and up the charts. But rock 'n' roll wasn't all positive: the message for women in many of these originals was unambiguous and made me nervous, although at the time I couldn't have said why. Beneath consciousness, rock 'n' roll troubled me, and now I know it was a hyper-male coziness with violence, and an absence of the strong female voices I'd grown used to hearing in the blues tradition. With rock 'n' roll effectively disappeared Ma Rainey, Ida Cox, and Bessie Smith. Also gone were Sippie Wallace, Dinah Washington, Pearl Bailey, and other independent blues women who, at least some of the time, stood tall and refused to be victims.

Three years before Elvis's two-million seller, Big Mama (Willie Mae) Thornton recorded "Hound Dog" for fifty dollars, but where was she? Prior to rock 'n' roll's takeover, pop vocalists like Doris Day, Rosemary Clooney, Georgia Gibbs, Kay Starr, Gale Storm, Teresa Brewer, and Patti Page lent a female presence to pop music, but, like their sisters of color, they were knocked clean out of the spotlight by rock 'n' roll, some for years, others for good.

Big changes continued through 1955. In Oceanside, New York, Betty Robbins became the first woman cantor accepted in a synagogue and Marian Anderson became the first African American singer to appear at the Metropolitan Opera. Out in Southern California, Disneyland opened its doors. Mickey Mouse Club ears and Davy Crockett "coonskin caps" appeared on little heads throughout the land.

The TV networks, whose profits were just beginning to exceed those of radio, had also started running two thirty-second ads in place of the customary single sixty-second spot. "Now they're going to squeeze in more and more commercials, just wait and see," Grandma *tsk'd*. She was staying with us through summer and into the fall, as she did every year, trying to be helpful and tiptoeing around Mom.

For my twelfth birthday, Grandma had taken me to a Johnnie Ray concert at the Steel Pier on the Atlantic City Boardwalk. After the show we went backstage for Johnnie's autograph. He had sung with great feeling, falling to his knees on stage, but more thrilling was standing close enough to touch his undershirt as he sat at a table by the door of his dressing room. He looked tired, but patiently wrote my name on the program I offered him before signing his own.

The Steel Pier was big-time showbiz, but I preferred the intimacy of the smaller Kansas City theater where, for my fifteenth birthday, Pop treated me to a road company production of *Bus Stop* starring Albert Salmi. I thought my heart would explode with delight, my usual reaction to show business that began with the magical glimpse of Marlene Dietrich's leg at Radio City Music Hall, and Toby Tyler joining the circus in my fourth-grade book report. *Kiss Me Kate* was tops in my book because of the score, but mainly because it was a play in a play about show business.

Had it been up to me, *Bus Stop* would have lasted all night and the rest of my life as well. The exhilaration of the theater so eclipsed my boring existence that having to leave wrenched my heart, so Pop indulged me and we trooped backstage for autographs. Actors received their fans in a seedy dressing room smaller than Johnnie Ray's. The scruffy floor and chipped paint revealed the reality behind the facade. I found it thoroughly transporting.

Green, Yellow, Pink & Black

GREEN AND YELLOW, the colors of our Chevrolet, were not to be worn on Thursdays because that's what "queers" wore then. All I knew about "queers" was that they were "homos" and "perverts." Homos were mostly men, but also "masculine" women, and both were more hated than Communists. Junior Senator Joseph McCarthy had waved list after list of unsupported accusations against "Communists and homosexuals" before the press and government committees. Like Communists, queers could lose their jobs and go to jail, but they were ridiculed as well. Apparently "queer" applied to Liberace, and even his tremendous popularity with women did not protect him from ridicule. I looked up "homosexual" in the school library's big dictionary but found no help there.

My chief political passions, justice and equality, had always landed me outside conventional circles, but the older I got, the clearer it became that some of my private inclinations were even more abnormal. In a lively discussion at Kinderland, my bunk mates and I had concluded that "ab" meant "above" and bragged to each other about how "ABnormal" we were. At camp it meant special and smart, but in Kansas it meant isolated and lonely.

During this time I checked out a book from the school library that described a future society of strong women who eliminate males through science. The idea of a life lived exclusively with females seemed farfetched and perilous. There were no men and no "homosexuals," who must have been too dangerous to name. The story's doleful ending confirmed the impossibility of life lived with women.

The right clothes and appearance could help someone blend in and be accepted. In 1955 pink and gray dominated teen fashion. Cashmere pullovers and button-down blouses were worn over pleated or poodle-decaled felt skirts, held aloft by stiff crinolines flaring over half-slips. Girls wore saddle shoes, while boys wore neat white "bucks," or "buckskins." Girls curled their hair and some of the boys' all-American crew cuts were being grown out and slicked back into duck tails or "DA's," like bad boys: Elvis, James Dean, and the "jaydees" (juvenile delinquents) from *Blackboard Jungle*, the movie that introduced American teens to rock 'n' roll.

Pop used to say, "If we had ham, we could have ham and eggs if we had eggs." If I was pretty, I'd be popular if I was "normal." A permanent wave might be the miracle to help me look more like Jane Powell. During my high school career, the number of beauty parlors rose 38 percent, but two dismal beauty parlor experiences only reinforced my poor self-image. I knew better, but still, on each occasion I entered the shop only to have my faint hopes extravagantly encouraged by gushing yet indifferent hairdressers. Shampooed, rinsed, and toweled off, my resemblance to a pale, drowned rat in the giant mirror confirmed a lost cause.

Harsh salon lights exaggerated my worst features. Dark circles had never looked darker, a washed-out complexion never more blotchy or sickly looking. A rabbit-like overbite pushed my upper lip out in the middle of a too narrow face in which my nose ballooned larger than life itself. No beauty parlor on earth could make me look like the pictures on the walls or in the magazines stacked beside dryers awaiting heads to bake. Nevertheless, cotton wads were stuck behind my ears, my hair was rolled in little curlers and dabbed with evil-smelling goo so toxic that rubber gloves were required to apply it. I'd have preferred large rollers and large, graceful waves, but I deferred to the breezy stylist because what did I know? Beauty was *her* business.

Eventually, she freed me from the giant helmet, sat me down in the glare of the mirror, unrolled and combed out my crackling hair, and, shielding my eyes with her hand, sprayed a healthy layer of varnish over her work. "That's *much* better . . . so pretty," she crooned.

I paid and left in total despair, my pretty new hideous hairdo glistening in tight little rows around the exact same face I had walked in with.

Sports, especially football, was a very big deal, and halftime shows on the field with the school marching band and cheerleaders were first-rate. Like the microscopes in biology lab, these spectacles affirmed the importance of my education and made me feel valued as a student. I cheered along with schoolmates and tried to feel as if I belonged, as if I cared about football and wanted to be there, but it didn't work.

Despite my ardent wish to fit in with the school crowd, Homecoming left me cold, and I longed to be home watching Eve Arden on TV. It was easier to relate to my smart-mouthed role model than to the pretty homecoming queen driving around the field with her less pretty runner-up attendants. They set the standards, dated varsity captains, lived in a popular whirl, and had the most fun. If Jane Powell went to Shawnee-Mission she'd be sitting on the back of the black Cadillac Eldorado convertible costing five thousand dollars, more than half of Pop's yearly salary. She'd fit right in, but not me. Not in five thousand years.

The worst time was Friday night after the game, when, eager to proceed with their carefree social agendas, the crowd broke into couples and bid each other hasty farewells. Stadium lights dazzled from on high, throwing black shadows over mysteries hidden just beyond my grasp. The parking lot emptied out, leaving groups of hyped-up boys to linger near their hot rods and eye the girls passing by. Their whistles and comments cut through the chilled air and accented my solitude as I made my way to the bus.

Friends, Near & Far

NORMALLY, MY SARCASM met with little or no response from classmates. But at the beginning of tenth grade one of my mumbled comments about crinolines was not lost on the skinny girl with long, straight black hair standing in front of me in the cafeteria line. Dee had a fine olive complexion; big, bright, dark eyes; and a turned-up nose. She laughed and told me that she too changed into pants immediately after school, which surprised me because of her delicate looks. Feeling equally displaced in our upscale surroundings, we recognized the outsider in each other and I quickly bonded with this gentle yet spirited girl.

One afternoon, Dee told a story about someone who, she said, "tried to Jew me down." The phrase was new to me yet I knew it couldn't be good, and when I asked, she explained that it only meant being able to bargain like Jews, a compliment. "I wish I knew how to handle money too," I said, hoping she'd get the point. Nothing more was said and the friendship, essential to us both, continued undisturbed. She spent evenings with her boyfriend, Paul, in his souped-up white Ford, barreling down the straight Midwest roads, skimming over hills, trying to break ninety miles an hour.

I wasn't jealous of them, but I envied their access to crucial slices of teenage life that coupledom afforded. Apparently, dating consisted of hanging around the drive-in, driving around, and "parking." "Parking," the reputed site of "petting," held neither mystery nor the slightest appeal for me. I could get along well enough with boys as pals, but if I didn't "love" them when I got older, would I have to pretend I did for the rest of my life? It was too hard to think about, so I didn't.

However, I had to give it a try and once or twice, Paul arranged dead-end, beer-and-awkward-backseat-groping blind dates for me. Somehow I acquired a steady named Lee for a few months, an awkward, gangly farm boy with a crew cut and little to say. I had nothing to say either. We double-dated with Paul and Dee for a dance at school, in an unlovely, self-conscious evening. Trying to appear happy and graceful, I sat on his lap, balancing on his bony thigh, my hand gripping his shoulder, unable to think of small talk. Was this kind of discomfort normal? Everyone acted as if dating was fun, but it wasn't. It was boring. Equally insecure and passive, Lee and I were doomed by mutual disinterest, and when he eventually stopped calling I understood why and was grateful.

Earning money on Saturday nights with my solitary, self-indulgent routine felt like redemption. Plus, I needed money more than ever. By saving my allowance and babysitting fees, I would be able to accumulate eighty-five dollars for a round-trip coach ticket on the train to New York for Christmas vacation with the kids in Philly and the Bronx. Saving for it would be a lesson in responsibility, said Mom and Pop, and if I organized this trip myself, they'd give me an extra fifty dollars.

Once again worth living, my life became wholly dedicated to preparation for the early December morning when the seven A.M. *Colorado Eagle* on the Missouri/Pennsylvania Railroad line carried me to St. Louis, where I would board the *Knickerbocker* headed for Grand Central Station. I stowed my suitcase in the overhead rack and settled into my window seat, dizzy with joy and anticipation. Then the first glorious Lucky from a fresh pack. Soldiers and families swarmed through the car. I inhaled deeply, focusing on the landscape flowing beyond the window.

The sun went down and so did activity in the car. Lights dimmed and went out leaving a sprinkling of insomniacs to dot the darkness with solo spots that clicked off one by one. I snapped off my own narrow beam, closed my book and leaned back into the coach seat. The darkened countryside flickered by and the wheels swept an unfamiliar symphony through my mind. I closed my eyes and listened until it slipped out of range. I was on my way to big gatherings, small get-togethers, and slumber parties. I'd show off my new baby-doll pajamas and we'd all brush and roll our hair. We'd go to movies, the annual Hootenanny at Town Hall, and a New Year's Eve party. I would eat bagels, drink chocolate egg creams, and see absolutely everybody. We would folk dance, sing folk songs, talk politics, and have a better time than anyone in Kansas City could ever imagine in their wildest dreams. At Grand Central I stepped outside and saw tiny black flecks of something I realized must be pollution floating in the air. I wondered if I'd get used to it, and sure enough, as I was drawn into the whirl of the great metropolis, it disappeared, and I never saw it again.

The visit lived up to my every expectation, and as the end neared I was presented with an opportunity to go with Sandy and some other kids who were driving from Philadelphia to Chicago for a Labor Youth League conference. I got permission to change my return ticket and stayed on an extra weekend. Five of us shared one night and two days driving to Chicago with little sleep but much socializing and politics: manna from heaven. What I remember is the feeling of fellowship with hundreds of activists, all committed to social and political justice. They milled about the big bare hall, hundreds of "youth" of all ages debating revolution, tactics and strategies, flexing their class analysis, and wowing rookies like me.

The "ALIX CECIL DOBKIN aka 'LEXIE' [sic] DOBKIN DOSSIER

The Labor Youth League, or LYL, was run largely by middle-aged Party "youth workers" who swarmed the conference along with the usual informers and agent/agitators. Secret power struggles and hidden agendas provided intrigue; whispered huddles and privately delivered urgent bulletins prompted sudden, unexplained departures. Gatherings of like-minded progressives always charged me up, and I needed a big dose to withstand the cultural wasteland, which is how I viewed the Midwest. At my assigned housing, a small child in the family whose couch I was making up for the night asked, "Are you a girl or a woman?" Having never thought about it before, I had to wonder too.

"On February 11, 1956, photographs of persons entering the Ben Mittleman Center, Chicago, Illinois, were taken by Special Agent [redacted]."

In 1956, the FBI started my very own adult dossier. Of course, Mom, Pop, and Grandma had dossiers which I never saw but, thanks to the Freedom of Information Act, I now own a two-inch-thick pile of paper, all about me. Many pages are entirely black or "withheld" ("No duplication fee for this page"). Most pages are somewhat redacted, like the beginning, containing the legible remains of two paragraphs. Under the title, "BACKGROUND," is a short biography followed by *"AFFILIATIONS WITH COMMUNIST PARTY FRONT GROUPS. On June 1, 1956* [redacted] *subject had prepared an autobiography dated October 21, 1954, which set forth information that subject attended Camp Kinderland during the summers of 1952 and 1953. While there she met and became friendly with* [redacted]."

On the second page: *"the Sunday edition of the 'Daily Worker,' an east coast Communist newspaper, of April 29, 1956, contains information to the effect that Camp Lakeland and Camp Kinderland are managed by DAVID GREENE, a 'notorious Communist Party member'."*

A small, slick magazine, *New Challenge (for Youth)*, was launched at the conference, and I returned to Kansas City a correspondent. Luckily, my dossier fills in the blanks: "[redacted] . . . *advised that ALIX DOBKIN had telephoned his office and had identified herself as a reporter for a magazine called 'New Challenge'. Subsequently on this same date ALIX DOBKIN, accompanied by a teenage girl giving her name* [redacted] *These girls advised* [redacted] *were required to write for the magazine, BOB ROLFE, manager and editor of 'New Challenge,' 673 Broadway, New York City. They stated they were not being paid and they were to do this to gain experience and to develop their knowledge concerning young people's problems in the Kansas City area.* [redacted] *said he reviewed a copy of 'New Challenge' and noted the magazine identified itself as a young people's magazine believing in the principles of Marxism and believing that Marxism presented the best opportunity for the youth of America.*

"Subject: [redacted] *advised* [redacted] *they were interested in the progress and problems with regard to desegregation in the Kansas City area, particularly as it affects the youth. ALIX DOBKIN indicated her main interest was in attempting to call together in Kansas City a youth group interested in these common problems so they could be freely discussed."* The report has me interviewing a few other informants on

behalf of *New Challenge*, but I don't recall writing an article or who was with me at those interviews. What I do remember is that nothing was happening with the youth of Kansas City.

Moving to the Midwest had been an experiment; it was an opportunity for Pop to earn a higher salary, pay some bills, and stabilize the family finances. It also served to distance my parents from the Party, which no longer seemed present in our lives. Had we settled in and gotten comfortable after two years, we might have stayed longer. But, in addition to feeling politically, culturally, and socially deprived, we deeply missed Philadelphia and our beloved friends back east. A vibrant Kansas City Bonds office had been established, so Pop happily accepted the cut in salary and demotion to assistant manager working for Sam, the twins' father in Philly. He hired his replacement and, at the end of the 1956 school year, my family headed back to where we belonged.

PART FOUR

1956–1962

Driving My Red Blood

We will be enormously strengthened if we can show that we are willing to fight to the very last ditch for what we believe in.

—ELEANOR ROOSEVELT

OTHER FAMILY MEMBERS may have been happy to close our Kansas chapter, but I was in ecstasy! Moving west had put more than a geographic distance between us and the source of a certain kind of fear and tension in the family. My parents had never discussed joining the Party, but I knew that they'd quit and blamed it for deceiving them and wasting twenty years of their lives. The absence of tension and a new lightness about my parents was a welcome change in the atmosphere at home. Their commitment to justice and equality continued, but with fewer grave political discussions and less of a fearful edge to their voices.

Faking an interest in the Shawnee-Mission Pep Club and the high school boys, their sports and cars had made me feel like a phony. The desperate loneliness and frustration of exile was ended forever, my future was finally looking good, and in a matter of weeks I'd be back at camp. We rented a cottage for a week on the New Jersey shore and my pathetic facade was left behind in the wheat fields of Johnson County.

The air in Kansas had never felt so invigorating, the sky had never looked so blue. Almost sixteen and feeling light as a bubble, I straddled my bike, soaked up the sunshine, and savored snatches of passing conversations seasoned with delicious Philadelphia accents. Months earlier in a conversation at Shawnee-Mission, a classmate had remarked that I sounded like a New Yorker, but she was wrong. My accent was a mix of Philadelphia and Manhattan. "I think *you* have an accent," I told her. "No," she insisted, "ah don't hay-ev uh ay-ex-say-ant." After two years of broad Midwestern dialect, giveaway Philly vowels, like "awn" for "on," sounded like music to my ears.

A white wicker couch in the living room of our cottage proved an excellent site to begin work toward my goal of reading every great writer and every great book. To top it off, I could buy cigarettes and smoke anywhere but in front of my parents. *It doesn't get much better than this*, I thought. But it did.

As final compensation for two years of misery, my parents agreed to pay more than they could afford for three weeks at Camp Kinderland. At least I didn't have to make excuses to my friends, because in that crowd, lack of money was neither uncommon nor embarrassing. Compared to other camps, Kinder-land was not expensive. Even so, few families could afford an entire season.

Each of a handful of modest bunkhouses on a hillside housed about fifteen senior girls who expressed themselves in the high-decibel range. We rotated jobs and cleaned the bunk together, planning projects and plotting standard pranks, like short-sheeting a cot and balancing a bucket of water above a door. We played complicated circle games, notably, "Who Stole the Cookie from the Cookie Jar?" It was a tough challenge to keep time clapping hands alternately with your neighbor's hands. On top of that you had to think fast, remember your number, instantly call it out, and then call out the number of someone still left in the circle, all at the right places in the verse.

As before, to the regular sports, arts and crafts, dancing, singing, acting, and nature programs was added Olympic week, dedicated to world peace. As the second-fastest runner in the PS9 Brownie troop, I dieted ("No sweets or fats!") and trained under the strict supervision of Paul the Zealous ("Keep going, one more lap . . . you can do it!"). The darkly intense, handsome counselor with an attractive overbite took competition seriously. I soaked up the attention, ran my hardest, and finished third in the fifty-yard dash. There were swifter runners in the camp just as there were more accomplished artists, but it didn't matter because I belonged to a team and my contribution was valued, like everyone else's.

The boys' bunks played baseball games and the losers wore their clothes inside out. Some girls had crushes on CITs (Counselors in Training) or boys in our group, but intense speculation was centered on our sophisticated counselors, veteran former campers who knew their way around. After lights out, the appearance of an exasperated counselor—very often the subject under discussion—quieted us only until her departure. We loved our Flo and most of the other counselors, but, as I recall, none more than Ethel Goldstein (later Ethel Raim) a frequent focus of after-hours discussion. In spite of being adored by a coterie, "Ettie," as she was called, wasn't at all stuck up, and although she wasn't my counselor, I wished she was. She was smart and graceful with a gentle manner, twinkling eyes, and a rich voice that unloosed sparkling energy and never once uttered a mean word within my hearing. She played guitar, knew more songs than I did, and rendered them in a velvet soprano more sweetly resonant than Jane Powell's. Luckily, I was able to love her without feeling disloyal to Jane. A perpetual swarm of girls buzzed around Ettie, particularly before mealtimes when we hoped to be the one to hold her hand and walk with her to the dining hall.

Walter, Ettie's boyfriend, played guitar and sang folk songs too. With Joyce and Ronnie, another counselor couple from the Bronx, he and Ettie formed "The Harvesters" and sang the most exciting arrangements since the Weavers, achieving richness and depth through dissonant chords and unconventional harmonic lines. I loved and admired them all, except for Walter, who was surly and abrupt with us, always competing for Ettie's attention and whisking her away from the constant press of teenage girls.

We saw films like *Salt of the Earth*, which documented how ordinary working people prevailed despite intimidation and violence used by mine owners against the Mexican-American miners and their wives striking for decent conditions. Those film makers were blacklisted McCarthy casualties, and Rosaura Revueltas, the lead actress and one of the few professionals in the cast, was jailed by the Mexican Government for her activism and this film. We left the dim hall and stepped out into the afternoon, fired up for revolution.

When Mom visited on my sixteenth birthday, I greeted her in front of the dining hall, cigarette in hand. She glanced at it, then eyed me for a long moment. "Happy Birthday, Lexy," she sighed. Our deal was that from this day on I would have, if not her approval, her permission to smoke. The advent of my birthday meant recognition as an adult from my mother and from the State of Pennsylvania, in which I could now legally drive.

"Coplas"

WHEN WE LIVED in Lynnewood Gardens, my father had purchased a guitar at an auction, his favorite place to shop. The gigantic, blond "Buckaroo" boasted f-holes and high action that meant trying to hold a string to the fret board killed your fingers. Pop was a fine singer and I thought it would be great for him to learn to accompany himself, but he gave it up after a few frustrated attempts. Doing my homework one evening, I overheard him practicing the two chords of "Down in the Valley" in the next room. Between phrases I caught a mumbled "Fuckin' fatty fingers!" and I was shocked to hear that word spoken in our house by anyone besides me. The guitar went back into its case and didn't come out until we returned to Philadelphia two years later.

Eliot had started taking guitar lessons and was soon playing chords and songs. Singing sounded a lot better with accompaniment, and when he placed the needle on "Coplas," a racy Mexican duet from his new record, *A Young Man and a Maid* by Cynthia Gooding and Theodore Bikel, I knew I had to rescue Pop's old Buckaroo from retirement.

My music partner figured out the strum and showed me how to tap and brush the strings in a sharp pattern suggesting flamenco. The barred F with the left hand made already tough fingering even tougher and was compounded by the wicked Buckaroo action. The fingers on my right hand had to hold the strings tight enough not to buzz. But like Mom with Bach, I was driven. For two weeks I felt as if broken glass had been ground into the tips of my left fingers, but daily I picked up my guitar and practiced. In a matter of weeks, blisters became tough calluses and finger picks stayed in place for the strum. After that, the standard chord progressions of most songs were easy. Like learning to dance with lead shoes. "Coplas" taught me to play guitar, In a few months I taught myself to both play and sing at the same time, which made me a folk singer like Cynthia, Theo, Pete, and Eliot.

Playing and singing nonstop," Eliot and I soon had the arrangement down for two guitars, complete with suggestive mugging. "Coplas," meaning "couplets," was full of sexy metaphors and double meanings. The tune initiated my international performing repertoire, and from that song, Eliot pursued his taste for raunch with blues and rags like "Take Your Fingers off It," and "Hesitation Blues."

Before the days when folk singers wrote their own songs, our mostly traditional material was supplied by Cynthia Gooding, Theodore Bikel, Leadbelly,

The Weavers, Woody Guthrie, Pete Seeger, and Josh White, not to mention Camp Kinderland. The challenge was coming up with our own arrangement to everything from the hearty "When I First Came to This Land," to the melancholy "Delia's Gone," or "Bring Me Little Water, Sylvie." Our repertoire blossomed and still there were plenty of good old folk songs we had yet to learn. Eliot's robust tenor combined with my firm alto for songs with uncommon harmonies and important social messages, like "Which Side Are You On?," "Times A-Gettin' Hard," and "Dark as a Dungeon." We began carrying our guitars to parties for sing-alongs and spontaneous performances. "Cigareets and whiskey and wild, wild women," we sang, "they'll drive you crazy, they'll drive you insane. . . ." The song was short on verses, with only one about cigarettes, so we wrote one each. Eliot's was, "Liquor ain't nothin' but Satan's own tool / A man who drinks whiskey, he don't go to shul . . . ," and mine, the first lyric I ever wrote, warned of the dangers women presented to men: "Now come all you young men untainted and pure / So finely ennobled, in virtue secure / From sensuous women, your honor defend / They'll ruin your life and they'll hasten your end."

Party Hard

"I'M THINKING OF joining the Party."

I'd intercepted my parents on the stairs, knowing full well their resentments against and distrust of the CPUSA, the irresistible force meeting the immovable objects. Pop and I made eye contact and we all took a deep breath. His look was fierce, and my heart pounded in my throat. "Your mother and I forbid you to join."

Like any good church, the Party had for thirty years provided its constituency with a moral center, a philosophical structure, and an energetic, like-minded community. Communist Party strength and purpose kindled progressive, world-changing work to far greater effect than its membership numbers would suggest. A stable force in the lives of tens of thousands from every walk of life, the CPUSA had found itself ravaged by internal crisis. The Party's Marxist discipline and activism had been a given for my parents and many others, but power struggles, plots, intrigues, and FBI infiltrators split the Party from top to bottom and from coast to coast.

In private conversation, comrades were expressing second thoughts and starting to openly question certain sacred cows. For speaking out, loyal members were accused of crimes against the Party, put on trial, expelled and shunned. Others, like my parents, quit, disgusted and frustrated by FBI harassment on one hand, and bureaucratic decisions handed down from the "ninth floor" of the National Office, on the other. Some caved and named names, signing on to the army of FBI infiltrators and informers. The informant system had at last reached the point of diminishing returns and informants were duplicating one another's reports. "More than half the Party membership was FBI," said Pop. "Their dues kept the Party alive for years."

We stood in the charged silence as cool autumn sunlight spilled through a window onto the piano. Mom glared down at her feet, her body shaking, her eyes too angry to meet mine. "I'll think about it," I said. But I had already joined, and the only thinking I had to do was about how long to wait to tell them.

The decision to join was not meant to rebel against my folks but to remain close to study group members who were smart and whose politics I admired. I respected Mom and Pop and regretted hurting them, but I craved political action. More important, after belonging nowhere and doing nothing for two years, an invitation into an elite club was not just flattering, it was a dream realized.

A militant radical outlook had carried me through the two dreadful, lonely years in Kansas City. My contempt helped keep the isolation at bay, my political analysis had made a virtue of not fitting in, and my moral righteousness had conferred the power to reject: essential survival tactics and good reasons to love politics. Most important, the lure of membership in an exclusive group meant a full social life unimaginable to Shawnee-Mission "Indians," so I stood my ground.

My parents didn't understand, but they would just have to get used to it. Grim-faced, they continued upstairs and never said another thing about it. "From that I learned not to forbid you to do something," Pop told me long afterward, "because you would just do it anyway," and from that I learned not to forbid my own daughter, Adrian, to do anything.

Years later I learned that Pop's first doubts about the Party had emerged at sea on his way home from Greenland in 1944 when he had spent his free hours reading "fancy theory" by Earl Browder, Communist party chief at the time. Browder changed the rules of Marxist-Leninist theory and made some capitalism okay, distinguishing "good cartels" from "bad cartels." "I'd lie in my bunk and read it over and over and it never made any sense," Pop laughed, shaking his head at the theoretical jargon I grew up hearing. But by the time I was old enough to understand what it meant, the familiar words and phrases had disappeared from my parents' vocabulary. Over the years, their faith gave way to doubts and disaffection, and they drifted from the Party.

The last straw came early in 1956, the same year I joined the Party, when, at the Soviet 20th Congress, Khrushchev revealed Stalin's brutal crimes and abuses. Along with an estimated thirty thousand similarly disaffected comrades, my parents and Grandma walked away from the CPUSA.

As far back as I could remember, Marxist publications like *Political Affairs* and *Mainstream* had been familiar sights around the living room, along with the progressive *I.F. Stone Weekly* and *The National Guardian*. They represented connections with the Communist left, but, like the lingo, they began to vanish and were gone before I learned to appreciate them. Now, considering myself an adult, I kept my copies out of sight in my room next to *The Worker* and the literary *Monthly Review*. In less than a year my parents and I had accomplished a complete role reversal, and now it was them not asking and me not telling. I was the "card-carrying" Communist without the card, which, sadly, the Party no longer issued. Had Mom and Pop ever carried cards? I knew Pop's Party name had been "Mack," and I longed for more information about their activist past, but asking would only call the rage back into Mom's eyes and fix Pop's mouth into a hard line.

Mom's stalwart loyalty to women led her to Women's Strike for Peace and the Women's International League for Peace and Freedom, and both she and Pop joined Singing City, Philadelphia's groundbreaking interracial chorus led by Elaine Brown. *Not good enough*, I thought but didn't say. They seemed to have devolved into liberals, and a wisecrack I thought was clever, "Scratch a liberal and you find a fascist," angered Pop, who called it irresponsible.

The children of Party, ex-Party, and progressive parents, we had been vigorously courted and recruited by Manny, a Party organizer with the brilliant mind, patience, and thoroughness of a good teacher. His reserved demeanor, glasses, blond crew cut, and stony expression gave him the look of a bureaucrat or a square.

A quick survey of his literature on our dining room table during his first visit was all Mom needed to ban him forever. It had been all I could do to persuade her to let us hold a study group meeting at the house. "No, Mom, we DO listen to other points of view," I protested afterward, but she knew better and turned her face away. Manny never set foot in our house again. Nor did his wife, Polly, second in command, with a generous, easy smile, who was no slouch in the theory department. In their late twenties or early thirties, they were considered "youth" by the Party and gave us lots of attention, guided our political education via "educationals" (advanced study groups), and helped us assume our political responsibilities.

Having been raised in progressive Jewish families, schooled in social justice, and readied for political action in an activist culture, we ate it up. For me and my friends, nothing was more exciting than a good political discussion or theoretical debate, unless it was united action against injustice or for peace. So overjoyed was I to be with my dear progressive friends that I have no memory of the day, let alone the exact moment I signed up. It just seemed as if suddenly the seamless process, its mission successfully completed, had delivered us to the Party and I was a proud member. I belonged!

Week after week, Manny laid out the convincing logic of Marxism, reasoning with us through resistance and doubts. Yes, he explained, there had been lapses in the past. The Party hadn't known how bad Stalin really was. At fault was the "cult of personality," a condition, he assured us, never to be repeated. No single person would ever have so much concentrated power again. In my parents' day, questioning USSR policies had been unthinkable, but not now. Didn't *The Worker* condemn the Soviet invasion of Hungary? The Party had learned from its mistakes and had corrected them.

Mom and Pop believed that Party leadership was incapable of change, but we knew better. Eager to forgive and with nothing to forget, we trusted that past failures were best put behind us. A newly inspired and revived Party could withstand free discussion within the "monolithic unity" of its "Democratic Centralism" which, I learned later, really meant that we could discuss as much as we liked, but Party word was law.

On "... *June 3, 1956,* [redacted] *advised that* [I] *was absent from school on Monday, February 12, 1956. An excuse signed by her mother, MARTHA DOBKIN, dated February 14, 1956, states, 'Alix was away for the week end and did not get home until last night and so was not able to come to school yesterday'."*

To be fair, the weekend in question had been spent at one of a series of "intensives" in rustic Brown's Mills, where Manny and Polly had access to a family cabin where we camped and studied. About a dozen of us shared food and housekeeping, and explored "Dialectical Materialism," "Structure and Superstructure," "The Theory of Knowledge," "The Dictatorship of the Proletariat," and the like. I brought my guitar along for evenings when we raised our voices in working class hymns invoking peace, equality, and justice in the world and celebrating the "brotherhood of man": "Our fathers bled at Valley Forge / The snow was red with blood. . . ."

We read theory and history, courtesy of International Publishers, from the great Negro social thinker and writer W.E.B. DuBois and Marxist theoretician William Z. Foster. We asked each other, "Are you a Materialist or an Idealist?" —a phony question since only one answer was correct. My favorite was the "form vs. content" debate. Which is more important, the chicken or the egg?

Change is the sole, universal, constant, explained *The Dialectics of Change*. We learned that each system contains the seeds of its own destruction, even socialism, but especially capitalism. Change happened "quantitative to qualitative," like water slowly accumulating heat until the instant it becomes steam.

I heard the term "male chauvinism" for the first time when Manny applied it to himself in the new practice of "Criticism and Self-Criticism" developed by Chinese comrades to reveal and correct personal faults. At first I believed that Manny was being extra hard on himself to make a point, but I listened and learned about male supremacy. I also learned that honest confrontation could be loving and constructive political work. This discussion excited and stimulated me, as did the camaraderie of my smart new gang.

Older female comrades in their early modeled how to be a young woman in the world and I took my cues from them, observing how they carried themselves and interacted with people. I noted one's self-assured grace and another's worldly sarcasm. Like Mom, they used their brains, cracked jokes, and stuck up for themselves, but they were more relaxed and less wary than Mom. These women intimidated, held their own space without apology, and didn't stuff their emotions down inside the way Mom did.

In the group were two brothers who were comrades and sweet guys; Aaron tended to blush and stammer while Lionel cracked jokes. I'd try to grab a seat next to Lionel at meetings so we could mutter back and forth, avoiding eye contact, trying to break each other up. I'd peek sideways at his dark head bowed, his fingers spread over craggy features, his broad shoulders hunched and shaking with laughter.

Germantown High

COMPARED TO MY rigorous Shawnee-Mission schooling, Germantown High was a cinch and classes bored me. However, my interest in school perked up on the first day of English class with Mrs. Pollack's snapping dark eyes. She was slim in a voluptuous sort of way, and this was her first year teaching. Besides plenty of makeup, Mrs. Pollack wore her black hair in a big, stiff bouffant and spoke in a nasal Philadelphia whine. A thinker who took my opinions seriously, she got my attention right away. More important, my bright, young, Jewish, working-class English teacher responded well to adoration and succumbed to my campaign to win her over with my literacy and sophistication.

My fantasies started to evolve from the earlier Jane Powell scenarios. In cozy, sensual reading sessions, my brilliant discourse kept her rapt attention. I adored being her pet and it took only a few months to wear down the teacher-student barrier and wangle invitations to her apartment on Roosevelt ("Roo-zeh-velt") Boulevard while she prepared dinner for a husband whose arrival signaled my departure. Though a romantic failure, our friendship was a raving intellectual and literary success. I wasn't a pervert, I just wanted beautiful, successful women to adore and admire me. What transpired after that I could not imagine.

During the first two years of high school in Kansas I'd had no one but Dee and my fake self for company. Now at Germantown with my comrades Sandy and Sheila as allies, I sailed through my junior and senior years in a bubble of deliverance. Sheila met Maidy in an English class, and it wasn't long before her D'Artagnan joined our Three Musketeers.

The three girls accepted me as I was and believed what I believed. We didn't share classes, but we were in the same building, sitting in the auditorium at school assemblies and holding a place for each other at lunchtime. The posh diner by Maidy's house near Temple Stadium became another site for coffee, serious political analysis, gossip, and griping. We moaned about our awful history classes, how after World War I colonialism and imperialism magically disappeared from the textbooks, and the only thing mentioned about unions was the respectable AFL and Samuel Gompers who presented no threat to capitalism.

I complained about my history teacher, whose "better dead than red" brand of patriotism grated on my every nerve. Mrs. Duffy adored Teddy Roosevelt above all, loved capitalism, and sang its praises all year. "Competition," "The Law of Supply and Demand," and the "free enterprise" system were superior to "totalitarianism," which meant Communism, which she kept confusing with socialism. Mrs. Duffy rejected every point I made, no matter how much I watered it down, chiding me with, "You can attract more flies with honey than with vinegar." Bent on making my point and educating my classmates, I'd close my eyes so she wouldn't see them roll, and, released from class, I'd rage through the halls.

Knowing more than the teacher and having to keep phrases like "the alienation of labor from the means of production" to myself when they were crucial to what we were studying frustrated me no end. As Mrs. Duffy rambled on, the tension of holding myself back escalated, and I waited for the opportunity to strike.

My chance came in the form of an extra-credit report we could write about one of the "captains of industry who made this country great," like Rockefeller, Ford, or Carnegie. Instead of concentrating on their philanthropies as Mrs. Duffy urged, I tracked down every piece of dirt I could dig up on the banker J. P. Morgan. The result was a well-documented, muckraking chronology of a fortune that began with the sale of defective rifles to the Union Army. Steering clear of giveaway jargon like "surplus profits" or "labor-added value," my exhaustive compilation of Morgan's schemes and scams spotlighted every odious bit of information I could look up.

For weeks, I lived to hear Mrs. Duffy ask, "Who would like to read their report in front of the class?" When it did, my hand shot up, and, for the last time that year, my history teacher pointed to it. Calmly, I walked to the blackboard and started a strong reading. Midway through my exposé I looked up to see Mrs. Duffy's face actually glowing red, her wide bosom lifting and falling with tiny breaths. Barely waiting for me to finish, she ordered me to my seat without comment or question and called for another report. Happily, no one else was prepared, so she retreated to her desk and recited from the textbook, cheating me out of a class discussion. I had won the round, but the battle was hers with a red "A-" vitiating the paper compounded by a notation about my "bias." But those industrialists really did truly despicable things, and it was Mrs. Duffy's defense of them that was "one-sided."

We both knew that I was the best student in class and that my report deserved an "A." It was a matter of principle, I complained to Mr. Wagner, the kind head of the history department. He had called me to his office, where he paced nervously and avoided eye contact. His meandering lecture, thinly edged with warning, was impossible to understand. Warning me about what? To stop giving Mrs. Duffy a hard time? The FBI, I figured, had been visiting my high school, a suspicion confirmed by my dossier showing both Shawnee-Mission and Germantown High School personnel cooperating. Did that include Mrs. Duffy and Mr. Wagner? The answer lies buried beneath the black strokes filling page after page of redacted names and information.

For the rest of the year, Mrs. Duffy refused to notice my raised hand in class, or even look my way, let alone call on me. Coldly, I handed in all my homework and was rewarded by a final, grudging "A" and my teacher's chagrin when the Soviets beat us into space.

Schoolmates/Comrades

AFTER SCHOOL, MY comrades and I would walk to the intersection of High Street and Germantown Avenue to catch a trolley car clattering east over the cobblestones, past the theater where we had seen Sergei Eisenstein's 1925 landmark film, *Potemkin*, about the 1905 Russian Revolution. Conversations en route to meetings covered Sputnik and Paul Robeson finally getting his passport. Fidel Castro was not a Communist, but his increasing strength was good for the Cuban people.

There was bad news too. The Soviet invasion of Hungary, although necessary, we were told, didn't look good and was unsettling. In another defection, John Gates had resigned as editor of *The Worker* and Chou En-Lai, more attractive than Mao, had resigned as China's Foreign Minister due to divisions there. The Party had finally quit denying the China / USSR split which seemed worrisome, but "The Great Leap Forward" sounded exciting. We discussed these things as if we knew what we were talking about, clueless that the "backyard steel furnaces" would utterly fail and destroy the Chinese economy.

On the west side of town we worked on projects, like the "Youth March on Washington for Integrated Schools," or attended Socialist Youth Union (SYU) meetings. In Center City we filed petitions, distributed handbills, or hawked *The Worker*, a chore I hated, especially during cold weather. Since most people gave us a wide berth, we sold very few. Visibility was the important point, and providing perspective and courage to a few decent people not too frightened to give our ideas a chance. The HUAC was still sending people to jail and the FBI would certainly be lurking nearby taking pictures as they did everywhere we showed up. When the thought crossed our minds we'd strut brazenly for whomever might be watching, just as we'd address remarks to them in phone conversations. "Are you sure you heard that?" we'd ask. At least I'd say it. The FBI could ruin my life but laboring under the illusions of immortal youth, I didn't believe it would happen, and so far, so good. In fact, time and again the FBI has been of invaluable, if unwitting, service to me.

I am grateful for an FBI memo marked "confidential," a reminder that I was active in the SYU, the PYOC (Progressive Youth Organizing Committee), the Philadelphia Chapter of the Fair Play for Cuba Committee, The Philadelphia Social Science Forum Committee, and *New Horizons for Youth*, a new magazine edited by Manny.

"Teens Ahead" began as a discussion group meeting in Nicey's living room until the crowds got too large and we moved to the Germantown YWCA, where the director welcomed us. She liked us because she was open-minded and we were polite, responsible, serious young people concerned with genuine issues who never mentioned Communism, socialism or Marxism. The SYU sponsored monthly social events and programs with titles like "A Free City College in Philadelphia?" and produced shows with musicians, like the young enthusiast, Billy Vanaver, a sweet, dedicated, up-and-coming folk instrumentalist.

Besides politics, there was art and music, music and art. As always, I drew constantly, copying illustrations from books and pictures from magazines. In Kansas City I'd started Saturday art classes, and after we moved back, a sequence of trolley, subway, and bus rides took me to South Philadelphia for classes. As for music, when a group of young singers broke away from the old Yiddish Folk Chorus in Strawberry Mansion to form the Jewish Youth Chorus (JYC), I signed on. Singing songs I loved in a chorus was a delight. Without hearing my own voice, I felt it pour from my throat and immediately be absorbed into the energy of every voice, wrapping me in sweet harmonic sound.

Two girls in my class and I learned the Chordettes' hit song "Lollipop" for the all-school Talent Show. I played the basic four-chord rock 'n' roll progression on guitar and sang the low part. A false start and a few nervous giggles later, we pulled it off to nice applause from the kids in the auditorium. But I preferred performing alone, or with Eliot with our friends.

Sandy was the best person with whom to discuss politics or literature. She had joined the Party mainly to take Manny's exclusive courses. She was always thinking and I admired her probing mind, her clear-headed pursuit of "objective reality." Together we analyzed and interpreted George Orwell's *1984*. No mere fantasy, Big Brother was alive and well, and probably at our meetings. Sandy was fun to joke around with and her love of books led her to *A Raisin in the Sun* before anyone else I knew. It was exciting that Lorraine Hansberry, the young black playwright, was taking off, but we didn't know that she was a lesbian, which would have sharpened my interest.

Lounging on Sandy's bed while she organized a homework assignment on the floor, I read a particularly striking paragraph from *Point Counterpoint* aloud to her. Huxley's narrative was exquisite. But could the same story be told with no narrative at all, only conversation, like the short, powerful farewell chapter from *This Side of Paradise*? "Hey, Sandy," I said, "wouldn't it be a great idea to write a book with only dialogue!" The fine blond head tilted up, displaying her deadpan expression reserved for the imbecilic. She stared at me, her pale forehead wrinkled, her eyebrows arching above the clear plastic rim of her glasses. "That's what we call a play, Alix."

Real/Unreal Loyalties

IN ADDITION TO girlfriends, comradeship offered a selection of trustworthy, eligible young males suitable for dates to occasions like proms. Within the shelter from the storms of teenage dating, respectful boundary lines were clearly drawn and romance was strictly optional.

Joel, a handsome high school senior, lived across town. Dark and gangly, he had a wide smile and a rampaging intellect. More intensely radical than anyone I'd ever known, Joel was the youth section's brilliant rising star. He studied and quoted Marxist theory, questioning whatever failed to meet his Marxist standards. Persuasive and passionate, he began seeking me out, asking my opinions and suggesting we go for coffee. Naturally, I was charmed. In addition to being a True Revolutionary, Joel was a true romantic, escorting me on a private Fairmount Park picnic-for-two, complete with cheese, wine, French bread, and the poetry of Rimbaud. He read aloud to me in his deep voice, clear and soulful, his bony shoulders shifting attractively beneath the crisp white shirt, sleeves rolled to his elbows.

Capping it off was a poem he had written for me, typed neatly on a sheet of typing paper, convincing proof that I could attract a smart, cute boy. So there! If only those popular Shawnee-Mission kids could see me now, reclining on the hillside, soaking up Joel's elusive yet complimentary verse. I gloated in my personal triumph over Kansas City and the loneliness it represented. At the same time, the attention also made me nervous. *Who did he think I was?* I didn't even know who I thought I was. I still hadn't decided if I was a girl or a woman, or even what those words meant to me.

Joel and I were spending more time together, searching each other out at Party functions, having meaningful late night discussions in diners, holding hands at subtitled films, and sometimes even kissing. Was I in love? I should be, wanted to be, but there was no commitment that could overrule the Party. "For life," we all told each other, determined to be the best Communists possible. Plus, for companionship and emotional security, the Party was better than a boyfriend and a lot simpler.

As I remember it, Joel believed that the working class was being betrayed by bourgeois intellectuals, and accused the Party of "revisionism." I recall something about our group "betraying the working class" by not working with a local SWP (Socialist Workers Party) group Joel was hanging out with and getting close to. Challenges to Manny such as these led to a power struggle that escalated into a final confrontation to be resolved by a vote at a meeting where Joel was destined to end up the latest splinter on an insignificant pile, and nothing I could do or say would keep him from it.

Meetings were generally held at Manny and Polly's West Philly living room flat located in Powelton Village, an ethnically mixed student and working-class neighborhood. It was the kind of apartment we were expected to rent with paychecks from the factory jobs the non-students were expected to have.

The room filled as Joel took my arm and pressed me into the relative privacy of jackets hanging in a dim corner. His dark eyes searched mine and I knew he was a goner.

"Alix, I'm counting on your support," said Joel. "Don't let me down." I knew I would, but my response to him was noncommittal. There was no contest between my best friends and a murky relationship with a boy whose main interest was a bunch of theory I didn't always follow with people I didn't know.

More than comrades, my friends were insurance against the stinking life of a fish out of water such as I had recently survived. Even if the Party *did* lack principles and *was* as revisionist as he claimed, my girlfriends came first and no guy, not even Joel, was going to finish in the money. Besides, he'd already proved that I was desired by a boy and worthy of love, which was good enough.

The meeting commenced and Joel made his case. Manny and the Party refuted it, gathering support in a tidal wave of monolithic unity that rose up and came down on my ex-boyfriend, washing him away as my uncle had been excommunicated twenty years earlier. Cross-legged on the floor, with a tinge of sadness, I floated free from the weights of idealized love and its unreal loyalties. Joel didn't stand a chance and immediately disappeared from both the Party and my new, and now simpler, life. The infrequent times when I missed him were theoretical like our romance.

Naturally I hated the FBI, which also represented an oddly comforting continuity, a thread stretching back through my past to Uncle Cecil and Grandma. The Bureau was always there, taking us seriously, validating our Party work. By so doing, they enhanced and honed my self-image. In addition to providing us with a perfect object of ridicule, the "Feebies" could be counted on to pump up our revolutionary zeal. Had they suddenly disappeared, it would have been necessary to invent them.

Their more obvious stoolies nosed around at parties and picnics asking unan-swered questions. Less obvious agents and informers were certainly among us, but we didn't waste time suspecting one another. Arrogant youth, impervious, we strutted confidently on our narrow Party line. *"Subject was not recommended for interview because she is only 17 years of age and there is no indication she would be cooperative if interviewed."*

A Working Girl

THROUGH A BIG shot he knew at the Food Fair supermarket chain, Pop got me a summer job. I got my working papers, joined the Retail Clerks Union, local 1357 (now 1776), and began punching a time card at the Germantown market, two blocks from school. The rest of my family piled into our first new car, a tan hump of a Volvo, and took off for a month on Cape Cod, leaving me alone in the house, an independent, gainfully employed citizen. Five days a week behind the non-prescription drug counter at the back of the store, I sold aspirin and toothpaste, ground customers' coffee perk or drip. Mostly I tried to look like I was earning my $2.13-an-hour union wage, more than twice the minimum.

The Retail Clerks gathered for the annual July Fourth picnic at a park I'd never been to. After lunch, a few of us walked to a gate leading to a pool, where a large uniformed man stopped a couple of my black coworkers. I turned back and protested. "Are you a bigot?" I shot at him, relieved to see that most of our party had stuck around in a united front

"We'll sue you for discriminating!" I hollered through the bars of the gate as people passing through stared at us curiously. If only my comrades could see me now, standing up for justice. Our two black colleagues kept their distance as I continued to yell at the guard who finally turned his back with a shrug, mum-bling about doing his job. Mouthing off made me feel righteous, but it all came to nothing. Did my black coworkers feel supported or more vulnerable? I was afraid to ask, but in a letter to my family I bragged about standing up to the "fat bigot." In reply, my parents commended my stance while cautioning me against using "fat" as a value judgment or insult: a new thought.

Collecting pay envelopes and carrying dollar bills folded neatly in my pocket conferred power. Alone in the house, in charge of my life, making my own plans and earning my own money, I walked naked around the house with the blinds drawn. Not having to tell Mom where I was going or when I'd be back was positively heady. The Party was never named but my involvement was a constant tension between my folks and me, made most apparent when I left for a vaguely defined evening across town, but defying them had earned me greater independence. They lived with my discreet disobedience and I lived with their unspoken disapproval.

By saving from my wages, I moved up from the old Buckaroo with the murderous action to a new, more suitable guitar. Martins and Gibsons were the best, but for more money than two months that at Food Fair paid. An investigation of mid-range instruments led me to a Hofner dealer in a second-floor shop a block from City Hall. Comely and comfortable, the mahogany Hofner lacked f-holes and weighed half as much as I was used to holding. From a dark matte spruce top, its rich folk sound suited me far better than the twang of the big yellow Buckaroo. Gone was the struggle to hold the strings down without a buzz on the fret board. Casting off my lead shoes, I could fly.

Folk Me

WOODY GUTHRIE, THE Weavers and Almanac Singers, John Jacob Niles, Leadbelly, Josh White, Jean Ritchie, Brownie McGhee and Sonny Terry, Reverend Gary Davis, Cynthia Gooding, Oscar Brand, and so many others had for years been sowing the seeds that blossomed into a folk music boom, and no one deserves more credit than the tireless Pete Seeger. Blacklisted from radio, TV, and mainstream productions, Seeger found he could make a living performing for and with children and young people at camps and schools from preschool on up through universities. Singing Seeger's songs bonded and revitalized people of good will working for the common good, and in the late 1950s, the first generation he raised began to come of age. The songs promoted broad themes of peace and social justice, were simple enough to learn, and were known by many. A guitar was portable and cheap enough to buy, and guitar players started popping up everywhere.

Eliot and I fell in with the local folk network, a stronghold of traditional music on the East Coast now swarming with young aficionados and interpreters like us. Folkies from all over Philadelphia flocked to the Gilded Cage in Center City where Ed and Esther Halpern arranged quaint, feeble soda-fountain chairs in a circle for Sunday afternoon song fests. During the first years we didn't even fill the room and everyone got a chance to sing at least one song, but by the end of the fifties, two rooms would be crammed and you'd be lucky to get a single turn.

Beside Leadbelly and Woody Guthrie, we didn't know many "singer-songwriters," but the old songs were plentiful and we all sang them. We liked them because they reflected real lives in other times and cultures and many supported our progressive politics. They came to us through our families, at camps and community sings, from songbooks and records, but mostly from one another. The introduction of an unfamiliar but singable folk tune was an occasion. These "new" songs made the rounds at parties, post-concert gatherings, and Philadelphia Folk Song Society meetings before they passed into the community repertoire. "Blow the Candles Out," a love song and the rage for a few weeks, gave way to "The Gallows Pole" ("Hangman, hangman, slack your rope . . ."), and so on.

Concerts ended in parties, usually held in Carol's living room. They began with dancing and ended with jamming, laughter, and wisecracks. Carol had long, straight hair and a big, pretty smile, and she knew about the Beats before anyone else. Through her, we learned of Jack Kerouac's *On the Road* and later *Howl*, a new and controversial epic poem by Alan Ginsberg. She and I sometimes sat on the stairs to read our poetry to each other.

A number of us had been to Kinderland so camp songs were popular. Eliot and I provided reliable back-up banjo and guitar, Bob brought his washtub bass, and Ozzie played her Irish harp. Among guitars, recorders, and harmonicas, we could pick from an assortment of percussion instruments, and, I recall, an accordion someone played. I can't recall hearing or singing "Tom Dooley" or "Lemon Tree"; rather, we sang a mix of traditional, international, and contemporary music. We sang broadsides and union songs, songs from the Spanish Civil War, or from Scotland and Ireland, including lovely versions of "Kevin Barry." Our music rang through Carol's living room and fortified my repertoire. We backed each other up and shared tips on guitar chords, showed one another runs, exchanged harmonies: "Ah knoooow you rider / gonna miss me when ah'm gone."

Higher Ed

VEERING FROM MY "Academic Track," I signed up for Commercial Typing, a viable skill I hoped I'd never have to "fall back on." The icy teacher and rigid instruction, plus boring business forms and formalities, weighed down a class made even heavier by the pressure of timed exercises testing my speed (good), and my accuracy (terrible).

"What's that 'B'?" Pop half joked. Alone in a sea of A's on my report card, Typing 101 lowered my final grade average, and we needed high grades for a scholarship. But how? And where? Despite a flirtation with Pembroke College of Brown, in the end, art triumphed over music and I enrolled at the Fine Arts College of Temple University, which was housed in the mysterious Penrose Avenue estate bordering Lynnewood Gardens that Steve, Eliot, and I had pedaled by countless times but dared not trespass upon.

Dean Boris Blai had approved my portfolio. My interview was held in his cramped upstairs office in the former mansion. Dean Blai advanced a curriculum based on the same rigorous European traditions that had produced great artists for centuries. Apprentice to the world renown Auguste Rodin, creator of *The Thinker*, Dean Blai often repeated his favorite homily: "Great art," he would declare, "is ten percent inspiration and ninety percent perspiration!"

At graduation I received an unexpected scholarship of four hundred dollars. A month earlier I'd been interviewed for the Widener Memorial Prize and had left the interview thinking there was no chance, so hearing my name when it was announced for the prize at graduation was shocking. "Now I can breathe easier," Pop said in the hall after the ceremony, his face in a wide grin.

To get a car for college, I needed a summer job. Too young to qualify as a counselor at Kinderland, where my age was on record, I subtracted a year from my birthdate on an application to a Girl Scout Camp and was hired. At the end of the summer, during which I was scolded by the camp director for sleeping in the nude, allowing my campers an extra half pint of milk at lunch, and teaching songs not included in the official handbook, I collected my pay and returned home, grateful that a summer spent among conservative stuffed shirts had finally come to an end.

Pop heard about a used black '52 Studebaker coupe for sale and we went to check it out. Thrusting a pointy nose forward between equally pointy headlights, this sleek, peppy car lacked only a propeller. No backseat, but a shelf under the back window and open space from the front bench seat to the end of the trunk. To the driver's right, a round knob poked up on a gearshift rod from the floor. "As is," said the man at the garage. "Perfect," I said.

Tyler

NORMALLY, THE DRIVE to college took fifteen minutes, but I got it down to five, sleeping until the last possible split-second after staying up through the wee hours working at the heavy oak easel Pop had found at an auction he'd begun frequenting.

I liked most of my classmates, from the deeply conventional to the radically visionary. From a conversation with the tall blonde standing behind me in line during orientation at the North Philadelphia Temple campus, I began a friendship with Noelle that lasted beyond graduation.

Paint, brushes, wooden stretchers, rolls of canvas, and everything else I would need were for sale at the Tyler School Store. Black-bound notebooks and pads of paper stacked on shelves ranged from heavy sheets for watercolors to newsprint pads for the five-minute pencil sketches mysteriously called "croakies," when we had to draw the nude (female) or semi-nude (male) models without looking down, or for timed drawings when we couldn't lift our pencils from the paper until the bell sounded. Charcoal and chamois cloths, assorted flat and round camel's-hair and red sable brushes, a variety of elegant sculpture tools, sets of drawing pens, inks, wood-carving tools, linoleum blocks of all sizes, and gelatin rollers were displayed along with everything else a Tyler student might employ. In addition to inspiration and perspiration, making art required a good bit of money, and, jammed into the crowded store with my classmates, I wished we were rich.

Freshman shopping lists included things we had never heard of before, like hunks of rabbit-skin glue, looking like peanut brittle, to be melted down and simmered in a pot of water, cooled off, and frozen in a big mayonnaise jar, then thawed out and painted onto a freshly stretched canvas. I labeled a couple of jars of "glue" and kept them in the freezer.

One day, Grandma, thinking it was stock, used a jar for her special mushroom-barley soup. "Come in here," she motioned to me from the dining room. "Taste this." The strangely unpleasant odor from the kitchen smelled more potent in the ladle Grandma held to my lips. Now I had a story to tell on her, and everyone had a good laugh, especially Grandma.

Decades worth of top-notch senior murals on the walls and ceiling of the ground-floor cafeteria exhibited the social realism of the 1930s onward, the finest works of bygone painting majors preserved in ongoing, organic art history. Would I live up to the challenge when in four years I would paint my patch on the evolving aggregation? And how many years before a new image would cover it?

Art classes were held in sunny studios, rich with silence and concentration, a smocked teacher murmuring advice to students whose heads swiveled back and forth between model and easel, or between model and armature. Raphael

Sabatini, head of the sculpture department, taught us to look for "planes" on the face and body and they would help us understand three dimensions. But planes changed with light and perspective. Now you see them, now you don't. Even when I didn't, the intimate, all-absorbing practice of art was addictive, and the studio, a magnet.

Besides drawing and painting, I studied etching and printmaking, starting with the linoleum block print. Wiry and bent over, Mr. Flory was ill tempered enough for most of us to keep our distance, and skilled enough to have printed Rembrandt plates.

One warning from Karl, my jewelry teacher, and I made sure to pin my long hair back, away from the polishing wheels. I spent a whole semester designing and crafting a silver ring set featuring a carefully tumbled turquoise gem. At the end of the term it disappeared from the display case, the only one taken. Was this a compliment?

Educational Psychology was far too boring to endure, and no way would I survive "Intro to Pedagogy," so I decided I didn't really want to teach and dropped my Education minor, leaving me with only typing "to fall back on."

English class was taught by Gerald Stern, the best teacher since Mrs. Collin, who went on to become a widely recognized, celebrated poet. Knowledgeable, funny, and unpredictable, he reminded me of Ernie Kovacs, loud, rude, and always trying to stir us up. I remember his scratchy, insistent voice needling a devout Mormon classmate from Utah. "Is God in the toilet seat?" he demanded, lowering his head and snorting like a bull. She remained silent, her eyes looking down, regretting her statement that "God is everywhere." "*Everywhere* includes the toilet seat, does it not?" He brushed a bushy mustache with his fingers and squinted at her through thick spectacles.

I loved Gerry. He knew his stuff and didn't care about "normal" America. "You can have a real bird in a real world, and you can have a fake bird in a fake world," he'd declare, shaking someone's composition paper between his fingers. "But you can't have a fake bird in a real world or a real bird in a fake world." Gerry jolted our brains into new thought patterns. His rendition of William Ernest Henley's "Invictus," ". . . I thank whatever gods may be for my unconquerable soul," came complete with upraised fist. But my favorite lines came from Dylan Thomas: "The force that through the green fuse drives the flower . . . Drives my red blood . . ."

Of the three hundred-plus Tyler students, most had been at the top of their high school art classes, the sort of teacher's pet I had looked up to when I compared my forced, awkward style to theirs. Still, I could draw and paint better than some of the students, and felt secretly grateful to them. The handful of legendary artists enrolled at Tyler were more gifted than I'd ever be, regardless of practice. But I was good enough. Plus, I had other things going for me, and as usual, they were politics.

Always happy to see an interested face, advisers to Student Government were on constant lookout for the rare energetic, civic-minded students, hard to find, especially among artists. All I had to do was be respectful, responsible, and show up for meetings. "Secretary of the Student Government, Tyler School of Fine Art, Temple University," added weight to my signature. Singled out more and more as a "student leader," I was happy to use my new authority for the good of Party-approved causes.

When, at the end of the year the president and vice president of the student council both became too ill to produce the Dean's Ball, I stepped in. Weeks later, a commendation from the Temple Student Personnel rep complimented me on having produced "*. . . a fine dance . . . It is not often that a freshman can step into the place of an upperclassman and do so well. The need for a strong leader was urgent. You filled this need and carried the responsibility with a great deal of assurance. I was proud of you!*" In turn, I was grateful to the Party for my self-confidence and initiative.

Everywhere the Youth are Singing

WORLD YOUTH FESTIVALS were a series of Communist-sponsored international cultural/sports spectaculars promoting "Peace and Friendship," the Festival motto. It was important that leftist and progressive young people from every-where around the globe gather for cultural exchange and present worldwide youth support for peace. Toward this end, national Communist Parties from all over the world organized delegations, exhibitions, and performances for this massive biennial event.

The seventh one would be held in Vienna in August of 1958, and a representa-tive from our Youth Section was to be selected. With my credentials as a student official and as a musician who would add to the delegation's cultural contribution, I would also strengthen the chorus scheduled to perform in Vienna where Mattie would direct. She still traveled from the Bronx to Germantown every Tuesday night for our rehearsals and I already knew the material for Vienna.

Although Mom and Pop recognized a Communist front when they smelled one, they also acknowledged a great opportunity and trusted my good sense.

Being selected called for fund-raising, so early in 1959 I began organizing parties where I plied the guests with festival literature and explained why Philadelphia youth should be represented in Vienna. With world peace the issue of the day and "Peace and Friendship" the festival slogan, I found support among progressives. Besides the festival, I'd come home with reports on special tours of the Soviet Union and Czechoslovakia.

On April 9, 1959, as noted in my dossier, passport number 1510122 was issued to me. I would borrow a professional camera to take slides. The round trip to Europe on a student ship cost $400, with more for the tours and expenses on the continent. With the cost of film, it amounted to $1,200. On opening day of the festival, each of the four hundred members of our official American delegation were to wear a suit of blue-and-white seersucker for the ceremonial parade around the gigantic stadium. We'd march behind the American flag, but instead of "The Star Spangled Banner," we'd sing "The World Youth Song": "We are the Youth, and the world acclaims our song of truth. . . ."

Meanwhile, back at FBI headquarters, word arrived from Colonel George T. Pitts Jr. that he would keep track of me from Verona, Italy, London, and Rome, as well as Vienna, and attempt to "*secure additional information regarding subject. . . .*" Was he successful? Blackened pages don't tell.

Across the Great Water

JUST BEFORE DAWN on a day in late June, I left Philadelphia, a backpack slung across my shoulders, a slim, canvas money belt fastened under my blouse, and a suitcase and a guitar in hand. Also in hand was a shopping bag filled with every popular 45 rpm record I'd collected since 1954, which, in my haste to make the Montreal train, I left on a waiting-room bench in Penn Station. The realization struck that evening, while crammed in with twelve hundred students on a dark, rainy Montreal pier, where we'd been waiting for hours to board our ship. So much for the gifts for Soviet and Eastern European youth. Well, at least I still had seventy-five "Peace and Freedom" lapel buttons to distribute.

Of twelve hundred student passengers on the *Irpinia*, thirty-six were festival bound. The others, not counting agents and informers, included American Youth Hostelers, American Friends Service Committee exchange students, guides for an official USA Exhibition in Moscow, and a YMCA group going to study in the USSR for two months. A *New York Times Magazine* correspondent was aboard to research student ships. "Some of the kids are nice," I wrote home, "and some are disgusting 'Golden people' from Yale." For ten days the *Irpinia* rocked and wove across the Atlantic, sending most passengers to hang over the railings or moan in their beds while the rest played shuffleboard, sang folk songs, and engaged in impassioned political debate.

My day began late, ended late, and overflowed with meals, music, and lively conversation about money, politics, religion, sex. A dozen guitars and one five-string banjo were aboard. The ship's newspaper wrote me up when I sang to the kitchen and wait staff who worked sixteen-hour days with good humor. They appreciated my appetite for the extravagant meals. Having steak for breakfast had been, until then, unimaginable, and I enjoyed my first taste of thick-crust pizza. Tea was served at four thirty. One afternoon, a couple of us crashed the First Class dining room, and before being kicked out, snatched a few of their dainty cream-filled cakes to top off our proletarian raisin bread.

A letter to Mom and Pop described my final night on board: "*I met the sweetest guy on the boat. His name is Mark and he's a real doll — we stayed up on deck the last nite on the ship and watched the sun rise over Cannes. Would you believe it?*" Greeting us at Gibraltar, the spectacular Mediterranean sunrise accentuated two American battleships, much to my disgust. The famous rock was smaller than I had imagined. "We were both so overwhelmed . . . so unbelievably romantic, I can't describe it . . . don't worry, there's absolutely no place on board to be private . . . Anyway, I'm not particularly anxious to be involved."

Due to an Italian maritime strike, we docked in Cannes instead of Genoa. Cannes was the most beautiful city I had ever seen, but we stayed only long enough to finish customs before boarding a crowded train filled with American students.

It was two thirty A.M. when we arrived in Genoa. Mark and I parted and I joined two Paris-bound American girls I had met on board. The three of us boarded a seven A.M. train, and as my new companions practiced their French it dawned on me how dependent I was upon them, and by the time we chugged into Paris late in the evening I felt thoroughly helpless and too exhausted to appreciate my first glimpses of Gay Paree. Gwen knew of a two-dollar-a-night hotel, so we checked in, planning to move the following day to one costing only one dollar. Baths cost the same, and we needed them, but not before hunger drove us to the first restaurant in sight. Thereafter I was on my own.

Communist presence was shockingly visible everywhere, proclaiming its legitimacy on large public posters, billboards, and graffiti mostly in the outlying working-class districts around Paris known as the "red belt." Via bus or Metro,

I'd ride to the end of the line and follow a street map, making my way through modest streets and narrow alleys, my eyes wide and my conversation limited to, "Bon jour, ew eh la twa-lett?"

Some afternoons I would sling on the Hofner and busk among the tables singing "Michael Row the Boat Ashore" and "If I Had a Hammer," collecting enough for meals and souvenirs. "Paris is great," I wrote to my parents. "It's sort of like one great big Greenwich Village but there is only French spoken and I don't know a word which is rather inconvenient."

On Bastille Day we danced in the streets and watched fireworks from a bridge over the Seine. I bought postcards from stalls along the bank, and an English translation of *Nina* by Emile Zola. Just before dawn I roamed alone through Les Halles among the hustle and bustle of trucks and stalls in the famous old market that would be destroyed in a fire a month later.

Paris was strike-ridden, services were slow or shut down, and I soon felt restless. Back at American Express, no mail awaited me, but a group of kids had gathered. A boy from New York with a mustache was leaving for Italy the next day and he invited me to join him. A pre-festival week in Italy sounded like a great idea, so the following day Peter and I were on the train back to Italy, where Communists were even more popular than in France.

Arriving in Milan in the evening, we found that the youth hostel was booked up, so to save money we claimed to be married and shared one hotel room. A cheap ring bought on the street turned my finger green, but I wore it through Florence, Bologna, and Venice, my last stop before Vienna and the festival. Thanks to high school Spanish and a good ear, I was able to pick up beginner Italian in short order.

In Florence, we hiked up hills and ambled through churches, museums, and art galleries. Later I wondered how an art student would not know that the Botticelli Venus would be found at the Uffizi Gallery. Tears filled my eyes when I stumbled into her room. The painting was so familiar and iconic that it was like coming across a myth, like crossing paths with a unicorn, too real to absorb at once.

After a hitching a white-knuckled ride through the Alps to Bologna in a tiny car, Pete kissed the sidewalk. To celebrate our survival, we treated ourselves to a four-course dinner. Bologna was a Party stronghold where local CP headquarters turned out to be a slightly seedy palace with a grand lobby and marble staircase. Having lived my life invisible on the margins, the evidence of Communist preeminence in a non-Communist country took my breath away. No matter the language, I could recognize Communist posters when I saw them, and they were everywhere, from handbills to full-wall murals. Peter, a good-natured Kinderland alumni, seemed content to go along when I called on the local Party chief and his lieutenants. They ticked off the many failures of the CPUSA asking me, "Why do you Americans have so many intellectuals and so few workers?"

"We know, I admitted, "It's a weakness and we're working on it." I promised to carry their criticism back to Party leaders in America. If they thought I could have any influence on an issue like that, they had another think coming, but I kept that to myself.

The chief took us home and introduced us to his extended family who, like virtually every person we met in Italy, greeted us enthusiastically, shook our hands, kissed us hello, and hugged us goodbye. I shot pictures of them all with my borrowed camera and we were wined, dined, and showered with pens, prints, candy, and stuffed animals. At their urging, I pulled out the guitar and sang a few songs, and they wanted more, especially repeats of "Coplas" and songs from the Spanish Civil War. Good Communists, we sang an energetic "Bandera Rosa," a tribute to the Red Flag triumphing over all, and they taught me "Bella Ciao," a rousing anti-fascist partisan song.

We were escorted to a street festival with live bands and introduced to many people who came to shake the hand of the visiting young American compañera. The air rang with high spirits, hearty toasts, raised fists, and salutes. "Viva la Revolución!" "Avanti pópulo!"

Today I can better appreciate the magnificence of the golden cathedral domes of San Marco square, but in 1959 I was repelled by the Church's shameless display of wealth when so many peasants and workers were impoverished. In a righteous rage, I refused to take pictures of it, and saying goodbye to Peter, I caught a train to Vienna for the Seventh World Youth Festival.

Festival

BEING AN OFFICIAL U.S. delegate at an international event was downright exhilarating, but, at the first U.S. delegation meeting, our leadership was vigorously challenged. Earlier that spring, at a pre-festival public meeting at Columbia University, a shouting melee had broken out in a mini Cold War between the officially recognized U.S. Festival Committee (us) and the CIA student front (them). We knew that a government agency, probably the CIA, was behind their Committee and that it had been created to take over the U.S. delegation or at least cause trouble for us. Like the Party, the CIA didn't reveal to nonmembers who was really in charge, and we knew that some of them probably had no idea that they were CIA dupes. We also knew that they didn't have a chance against us.

Calmly surveying the scene I spotted the person I was looking for, the smartest, most interesting member of our rival group, Gloria Steinem. Her name was familiar from a photo and article I'd read about the "alternative" committee in which she was prominent. She was leaning against a wall, slim and pretty and looking about my age. I strode over to introduce myself in hopes of unsettling her with cordiality. But, rising to the occasion, she shook my outstretched hand. We sized each other up and exchanged fake smiles. Despite our adversarial positions, I had to admire her poise and charm. Too bad we weren't on the same side, I thought.

We are now, though, and long afterward we chatted over coffee, comparing our corresponding experiences from opposite sides of the political divide of those times. I told her how impressed I'd been when she came out publicly a decade later as having been "misled and duped" by a front group for the CIA, and we laughed about the unexpected and ironic twists and turns of life.

At the festival, however, cordiality was unaffordable. As the sole credentialed U.S. committee, we ran the Helsinki meetings, but at the first one I watched our adversaries strategically positioned throughout the tent, and alarm turned to horror when they began shouting objections and opposing whatever our chairman put forward. It was a bizarre, crazy-mirror image of protests back home, although we were far more polite and considerably less organized. I tried to photograph the troublemakers, but the meeting was thrown into chaos and hastily adjourned. Outside, a group of us huddled together in tears, outraged, vowing not to let them ruin our festival. "What nerve!" we said. But even more infuriating was the biased report carried by the European edition of the *Herald Tribune* in which the disrupters were cast as embattled heroes. "Don't believe anything you read!" I warned my parents in a postcard, as if they would.

But aside from sabotaging our meeting, the CIA posed no threat to festival bosses who were clearly in charge but tried to appear neutral, a posture fooling no one. Clumsy and overbearing as they might be, Soviet bloc Communists knew about fanfare and putting on a grand show of strength and solidarity. And we were eager to be impressed.

Dressed in colorful ethnic costume for the opening-day procession, one national delegation after another paraded around the field of the enormous stadium. The appearance of our group in simple blue-and-white seersucker suits elicited roars of appreciation from the tens of thousands of spectators packing the stands. Lacking government sponsorship or the resources for an elaborate display, we were nevertheless hailed as warriors, heroic resistance fighters from the deadly heart of imperial capitalism. Staying in formation was impossible as we tromped around the track carrying our little American flags, waving and beaming at the crowd chanting "Mir-Eee-Druzbah"—"peace and friendship."

The U.S. delegation was awarded a highly coveted ticket to a performance of the Soviet Ballet. I got lucky and won the lottery, but instead of attending the performance, I was sent to a cot in the infirmary with a case of laryngitis. Two sweat-dripping days and a bottle of Chinese cognac later, my voice barely made it back in time for our choral concert and my solo in "Necessity" from *Porgy and Bess*. Our show was received with wild enthusiasm and the rhythmic applause customary in Europe. Our amateur performance contrasted sharply with the nationally acclaimed acrobats from The People's Republic of China, or the highly polished Soviet Young People's Chorus. The fireworks at the closing ceremony were far more spectacular than those in Paris on Bastille Day.

Touring

AFTER TEN EXUBERANT, exhausting days sampling international culture in Vienna, some fifty of us grabbed a train to Moscow. It stopped for a few hours in Warsaw where I walked the streets gaping at blocks of bombed-out buildings, left as they were, I was told, as a war memorial. Skeletons of buildings rose black in the night overseeing the eerie silence, their deformed walls, twisted stairs and roof pieces making an irregular lace of debris. I would have taken pictures, but it was too dark.

The Soviets had inexplicably cut our tour from two weeks to one. Furthermore, a group of us waited hours at the Czech Embassy but failed to get the visas we needed for our tour of Czechoslovakia, paid for in advance. A refund was, they told us, impossible.

Upon arriving at the Moscow station we were welcomed by a troop of brightly costumed, pretty Russian children proffering flowers. Translators my age guided us aboard special buses for a ride through broad Moscow boulevards to our hotel. As much as our hosts tried to impress us with their modern accommodations, we noted that the cement sills of our windows crumbled when we reached out and rubbed them.

Wherever we went, bewildered children stared, smiling adults offered their hand, and I took their photos. Americans were rare and major celebrities to the

Soviets, who plied us with flowers, cards, and souvenirs. I collected pins depicting Lenin as a baby, as a teenager, as his country's inspirational leader. There were crossed red flags with hammers and sickles, workers with upraised fists, and other emblems exchanged for those I had brought to trade or give away.

Every scrap of Soviet art and culture was infused with the "Social Realist" look. It dominated heroic statues and monuments, was carved into the facades of public buildings outside and on posters displayed on factory walls inside. Rents, we were informed, did not exceed five percent of income, but no mention was made of the housing shortage, with extended families living in one-bedroom apartments.

Books and records promoting Soviet culture cost next to nothing, and although there was next to nothing on shelves in the stores, lines snaked through them and along the sidewalks for whatever was available. Soviet women seemed to spend most waking hours in one line or another, chatting, reading, or just standing, eyes glazed.

The sun was down and, sitting under low, darkened clouds, Red Square seemed to flatten and to stretch for miles into the distance. I stood on the cobblestones at this, center of Moscow's principle tourist attraction with my friend Judy, whose lively, knowing company I enjoyed. She had been at the festival, her father ran the canteen at Kinderland, and we could share our consuming sense of unreality and awe at the historical import of being right there at the heart of world Communism, so different from home, which was looking better all the time.

There was no time to ruminate very long. Honored visitors, we were escorted to the front of a long line of waiting to see Lenin's small neat body entombed under glass on view to the constant stream of admirers. He looked just like the pictures in abundant evidence throughout the Soviet lands.

Our tour included a cruise up the Moscow River where a band played "Moscow Nights" and other popular Soviet tunes. Russians were extremely curious about the United States, and I answered many questions. Yes, poor American students could go to good state universities that cost practically nothing. No, I didn't know any cowboys. I often found myself defending my country in ways I wouldn't have imagined only weeks earlier. "But many white people support integration," I would protest indignantly. The musicians posed for my camera. Glasses of vodka were everywhere in hand and a Russian boy and I exchanged swear words. "*Sukyon sin*" meant "son of a bitch," he said, and "*durak*" meant "shit." The fact that I owned a car impressed him. "How much does it weigh?" he asked. I made a wild guess. "Two tons."

Soviet citizens of every age participated in state-supported national culture, a sharp contrast from the constant hustle for scarce, haphazard funding in America where artists existed on the brink. Our Young People's Chorus barely managed to scrape up Mattie's weekly bus fare between New York and Philly for rehearsals. However, as much as I didn't care to think about it, their art was made to fit within narrow boundaries and I saw no variation.

It went without saying that most Soviet citizens did not eat as well as tourists, and that our royal treatment was meant to convince us of Soviet abundance. When I went home I bragged, but not about Soviet cuisine or opulence. Instead I described generous, friendly people; wide, clean avenues and promenades; lovely "people's parks"; and a profusion of affordable records and books. I told of young children decked out in traditional costumes treating us to flawless singing, and complicated dancing at a "Young Pioneer" camp, and I showed off a book I'd purchased of Mao Tse Tung's poetry translated into English.

My nineteenth birthday passed with songs and hot political debate among my tour-mates as we were jostled and bumped on the hard benches of a troop train from Moscow to Kiev, the capitol of Ukraine. My friend Judy from camp and I teamed up and often speculated about the most likely government agents and informers certain to be among us. Our favorite candidate, a pushy, disagreeable man, was caught at the border with a silver-plated glass holder bearing the inscription of the Moscow hotel in his luggage. A Soviet customs agent unearthed the icon of Eastern European hot tea drinkers.

"But it's a souvenir," whined our prime FBI/CIA suspect. "Everybody does it in America." The agent scowled, saying, "When someone gives you a gift or you buy it, that's a souvenir. When you take it, it's stealing!" We made disgusted faces and tried to distance ourselves from him.

Since the Czechs had canceled our tour, we had ten extra days, so Judy and I decided to hitch across Europe and England. She wanted to see the Westminster Abbey, and an English-speaking country sounded good to me, so off we went, thumbs out. For our first ride we landed a cheery German ex-Luftwaffe pilot who told us, "You Americans made a mistake . . . you should have fought the war with us and together we would have defeated the Communists." Judy and I gazed at each other across the backseat and declined his offer of dinner.

A lonely widower from Belgium picked us up at the French border and changed his holiday plans in order to drive us to Le Havre. Our radio and TV commercials entertained him and he couldn't get enough of, "Who puts eight great tomatoes in that little bitty can? / You know who, you know who, you know who!" We chanted it for him over and over, but neither Judy nor I could recall who put those tomatoes in those cans.

In London we slept for two days in a chilly little flat before summoning the energy to shuffle outside. Sorting shillings from pounds and a quid from a pence was hopeless. All I remember is the bust of William Blake looking wildly out of place at Westminster Abbey, and when the time came to go home, I was ready.

Home, Girl!

SETTING FOOT IN North America, I called home and learned that Pop was only home on weekends and now worked in New York City fundraising for Sidney Glazier, boss of The Eleanor Roosevelt Cancer Research Institute and the man who later staged *The Producers* on Broadway.

"You've *got* to go to Europe," I told them. "You'll *love* it!" Years later, they did.

My romance with Mark resumed on the return trip and continued for a few months thereafter, eventually dwindling down to mutual warm feelings, which suited me fine as I was far too busy with re-entry to nurture a relationship. Besides getting ready for school, I had to report to my club, get forty rolls of film developed, and organize a hundred fifty-slide presentation for my sponsors. I had brought home some new songs too, and when I saw Pete Seeger at one of his concerts a few months later, I taught him the catchy *"Bella Ciao"* with the five handclaps in the chorus. Naturally, he learned it right away.

Joan, a cheery new comrade, enrolled at Tyler in my sophomore year and immediately became my best friend. She lived with her mother and brother in Elkins Park, where, after school, we would dance the Mashed Potato and roll on the floor laughing until tears came. Imitating Dean Blai's "Ten percent inspiration . . ." never failed to set us off.

In February of 1960, some black kids tried to get service at a dime store lunch counter in Greensboro, North Carolina, and were savagely attacked by whites. It made national headlines. Sit-ins rapidly spread through Georgia and Alabama, then went nationwide. The Woolworth store on Germantown Avenue didn't discriminate but they'd be sure to pass our message on to national headquarters. Joan and I talked it up to students and tried to round up enough to make a picket line. Some resisted with, "You can't legislate people's hearts," and we replied, "Maybe not, but you *can* legislate laws and behavior." Many made the bogus claim of being personally "color blind," and some we had to nag for a week, but we rounded up enough to scrunch into my Studebaker for the ride to Germantown. Four or five could squeeze into the elongated trunk and three more could sit beside me in the front seat, although the gearshift with the big knob made second gear particularly challenging. For over a week we kept the line moving in front of Woolworth's doors. No hint of the Party was dropped or picked up.

When Joan began seriously dating a black comrade, her mother became alarmed. But Joan was in love, and rather than breaking off the relationship, marriage plans were accelerated. Dean Blai called me into his office and tried to convince me to talk her out of it. I was appalled and of course refused to attempt any such thing. *Bigotry with a Russian accent*, I thought. The only regret I had about Joan's marriage, which followed shortly thereafter, was that she dropped out of school.

Between the weekly Gilded Cage round robins, jam sessions at Carol's, and repeated listenings to new albums, I was adding to my repertoire, taking in everything from Mahalia Jackson's *In the Upper Room* to songs from Israel, Greece, French-speaking Canada, and the Middle East, as well as folk dances from Macedonia and prison songs recorded at the Alabama State Penitentiary. I learned Puerto Rican anthems of independence and children's songs from records of Bessie Jones in the Georgia Sea Islands. Because I bore easily, a variety of cultures and styles suits me best. I loved singing with a group and the wonderful feeling of community that the music created. Someone had a guitar at least at every party, picnic, and get-together, and we sang a lot. I didn't like all songs, but sometimes learned one because it had a new guitar strum or run to learn, or there was a great harmony that went with it. My most fruitful source of material, *Sing Out!* magazine, was thoroughly studied each month. One evening I sat down to compile a list of tunes I knew and quit from exhaustion at five hundred titles.

Ethel, my beloved Kinderland counselor, knew some rich, unusual harmonies. She had discovered the now-classic album *Le Mystere des Voix Bulgares*, and tipped us off to it. The raw power of traditional Balkan women's singing resonated deep in my Eastern European bones. The low drones and extended dissonances vibrated and danced through me. Although I hadn't listened to it before, the music and even the complicated rhythms felt profoundly familiar. Ethel's musical treatments were so appealing that when I heard her version of "Hughie Graeme" from the Ewan MacColl recording with Peggy Seeger, I pleaded with her to send me a copy, which, after some months, she did. I still have it. On the overcast day it arrived in the mail, I grabbed it and my guitar and dashed to school to try it out on Noelle, working late in the ceramics studio.

As it turned out, the rousing ballad caught the ear of one of Tyler's most notoriously quirky and gifted upper-class legends as she sat in a corner of the converted greenhouse studio. Knuckle-deep in a half-finished candlestick holder, Nancy's attention seemed fixed on the soft clay she molded so artfully in her hands.

Nancy-O

SINGING HAS DELIVERED every serious love interest in my life and Nancy was to be the first. I had seen her around school, a boa constrictor draped across her shoulders. The unique pet was only one aspect of her notoriety. She and I had never spoken, but, like my schoolmates, I admired her work from afar, mindful of her reputation as brilliant and eccentric. So I was shocked and a bit puzzled when, after stumbling through "Hughie Graeme" for Noelle in the ceramics studio, I found myself staring into the pale green eyes of this legendary Tyler eminence. She was, she told me, intrigued by my song and she loved my singing. I couldn't wait to brag to Noelle and Joan.

During those early months, before Nancy came to eclipse even the Party and my comrades, before she grew to be the focus of my entire vision, before I came to hear or know what Billie Holiday meant when she lamented, "Until you face the dawn with sleepless eyes, you don't know what love is," before all that, the one thing I knew for sure was that I had never met anyone like her.

Nancy's talent attracted me, but her looks did not. I was far more likely to notice the darker, earthier types reminiscent of my eighth-grade cheerleader. However, Nancy's reputation and flattery won my full attention, and it was only after several minutes reveling in it that I began even to notice her WASP-ish prettiness. My new admirer's hair was pulled back in a tight ponytail, and her features bore a curious resemblance to Ann Blythe, my least favorite actress along with June Allyson and Barbara Stanwyck. Nancy's cheery smile belonged beneath a straw hat in a magazine ad featuring an all-American farm girl, but my tastes ran more to B-movie, urban sophisticates like Gloria Graham, Ida Lupino, and Audrey Totter, whose images were light years removed from Nancy's rosy exuberance.

Never far from my thoughts, more and more she dominated my days and nights until I found myself in unfamiliar webs of constant longing. It was wonderful and terrible. I ached for her, counting the minutes until we were together again. As she increasingly absorbed my attention, I lived more and more in the moment, deliberately pushing the implications aside, refusing to consider the consequences of my deep feelings.

All the while, there were song-swapping jam sessions with my folkie friends, and I managed to attend to my student government duties and political work. My obsession didn't keep me from political activities with my old Party crowd, nor did I stop partying with my school crowd. As Nancy was neither in the Party nor into partying, I'd go to meetings with Joan and Sandy, and out with Noelle and her crowd to drink wine, play music, and dance, often until dawn. More than once I'd awake on a hard studio floor in the beatnik apartment of an upper-class student. Then I'd make my way home and call Nancy.

As I was drawn to Nancy's talent, she was attracted to my music and thrilled by the Scottish accent I could effect, particularly in those songs featuring her name. How perfect that an abundance of "Nancys" populated the traditional Scottish repertoire with songs like "Hughie Graeme," the vehicle delivering Nancy to me. Ewan had lately teamed up with my longtime banjo-picking hero, Peggy Seeger. For the past year I'd immersed myself in their music along with the equally Nancy-rich Irish repertoire of Tommy Makem and the Clancy Brothers. I loved these "Nanny" songs, as we called them, and I sang each happily, gazing at my beloved, across the room at her easel painting a masterpiece. No presence seemed loftier, no vision so compelling, as when I serenaded Nancy at work on my likeness. Her head bent in concentration, peering at me over her glasses, she cut a fine figure in one of the pair of sleeveless denim smocks her mother had sewn in olive green and blue, with a matching set for me.

Secret looks, phrases, codes, and understandings quickly evolved, and each brought us closer. On romantic strolls through the lush grounds of Tyler's neighboring convent, electricity charged the air between us. Careful to avoid acknowledging our gathering desire smoldering beneath the surface of our friendship, we had eyes only for each other.

"Oh, Nancy, dearest Nancy," I'd intone with more tenderness than I could have ever imagined summoning. In a love-fest of artistic give-and-take, we reveled in each other's abilities. A considerable collection of portraits resulted. One of them was unwittingly left on the trunk of my car, as, deep in the throes of mutual fixation, the two of us packed our stuff for a night at my house. When we discovered it missing we immediately retraced our route in a careful, yet fruitless, search.

Pop bought another, smallish, portrait of my head, which Nancy's white

Manx cat, Baby, had walked across one night while it was set out to dry. A little Prussian blue goes quite a long way, and the next morning Nancy did her best to work the dark tracks into the picture, hence the bluish tinge, lidded eyes, and wild blue-black hair swirling gracefully, forming shapes like stained glass. When Pop offered to buy it, Nancy refused to accept more than one dollar.

I tried to imitate the way Nancy held her ebony pencil in a firm, graceful grip. "There's nothing wrong with being influenced," she would declare. Her own work drew on the whole history of Western Art, combining Rubenesque voluptuousness, chilling medieval solemnity, and impressionistic brilliance. She took from all but painted like no one else, with more natural craft than I could ever hope to duplicate. Nancy made it look easy, and I carefully observed her expert selection of a brush, the way she dabbed at her palette to mix the exact proportion of burnt umber to cobalt blue or golden ochre to alizarin crimson.

"Don't be afraid to put plenty of paint on your brush," she'd instruct in an attempt to redress my habitual frugality. I'd study her flawless strokes, invariably resigning myself to the fact that I would never paint in her universe no matter how hard I studied or how much I learned or practiced. Willing apprentice to the master, I'd scrub Nancy's brushes at the end of her day's work, grateful for the privilege.

"Do you think you're a genius?" I ventured one evening. Her answer came after a long moment's thought. "No. But I *have* genius." How insightful she was!

Springtime Promise

"WHAT'S GOING ON with you two?" Karl, our strapping young jewelry and metal sculpting instructor demanded. He stared at us, his intense dark eyes swiveling back and forth from one to the other. I had accompanied Nancy to his house to drop off some work before stopping at a special pet store to pick up white mice for Crickter, Nancy's boa constrictor. Our rugged, broodingly handsome teacher clearly had the hots for the light of my life. I watched her flirt with him, amused by his strutting.

On a languid evening in Nancy's bedroom, Baby purred and padded across our laps, demanding and then scorning our attention, while Crickter dozed comfortably in his cage, a mouse-shaped lump slowly making its way down his length. Nancy paged through a notebook while I dreamily brushed her long, fine hair. I basked in our closeness and closed my eyes to better savor the moment. A telephone shrilled in the kitchen and I jumped at the sound. Looking down, to my horror, I saw my hand resting lightly upon her breast. It had drifted in a breathtaking accident. Completely flustered, I snatched it away. "Oh, I didn't know. . . ." Our eyes locked and my heart beat furiously. She said nothing. This was important, but what could it mean about our future? I didn't dare pursue the question.

Nancy loved gossip, and I in turn loved her trenchant commentaries on our teachers and fellow students. She'd turn her charm on me, trying to enlist my support for schemes. I resisted participating in her more destructive forays and was appalled by an allusion to an ex-boyfriend's slashed tires. However my passion for her quickly overruled any qualms.

A squeal would telegraph manic inspiration for some dirty trick and my heart would contract at the sound. Eyes sparkling, she'd spin sharply around, lean in, and lower her voice, "Let's have a pizza delivered to Dean LeClair!" Or, "What if we called Alan and told him he won a week's vacation in Las Vegas?" My concerns would be dismissed with an impatient wave and I'd change the subject or try to distract her with a joke.

We enjoyed acting out super-feminine stereotypical caricatures of housewives in conversation. "Oh Jane, I'm *so* excited about that new detergent I saw on TV. It got my wash *really* clean." "Why, Marge, how *won*-derful! My laundry has just been looking terribly drab lately, I'll try it *first* thing tomorrow."

Because none of the men in Nancy's life escaped her private contempt, they didn't feel threatening to me. Why they didn't see through the obvious fakery remained a mystery, until a male friend supplied the answer at a party long after Nancy and I had gone our separate ways. "Explain to me," I asked him, "the reason that guy over there is falling for that woman's phony act." He laughed, "Oh, he just wants to get into her pants, that's all he cares about."

Aha!

Nancy and I each had our spheres of influence. Given her ignorance of current events and utter disinterest in politics, she easily acknowledged my political authority and seemed to value my opinion on a great many worldly topics. She was the only living soul outside the Party to whom I had revealed my membership, with a warning that she never speak of it to anyone. "I could go to jail, you know!" I'd tell her, only half believing it. Many months after this disclosure she told me, "I used to think you were good because of the Party, but now I don't think the Party has anything to do with it. You're good just because of you." *True*, I thought, *my goodness doesn't come from the Party, but I'm a Communist because I'm good*. However, initiating a discussion would have been pointless as the Party meant nothing to her.

On May Day the Soviets shot down and captured Francis Gary Powers flying a spy mission over their territory. He was photographing weapons and bomb plants. Americans acted shocked and said they couldn't believe it, but I had to wonder how anyone could *not* know that our government was guilty. I followed the story, delighted that the United States had finally been caught "red"-handed. But Nancy, whose disinterest extended equally to every government, followed the story only because she had once dated the downed pilot. That girl was full of surprises!

Summer of Love

DURING THAT SUMMER of 1960, the sexual tension budding between us finally blossomed. Early in July, Nancy and I drove to the New Jersey shore to meet her mother for a weekend holiday. That night, as I lay next to Nancy in one of two beds taking up most of the hotel room we shared with her mother, I barely closed my eyes. Electricity crackled in the minuscule space barely separating the lengths of our bodies. The ever-watchful Virginia would be alert to any movement, but none disturbed the stillness of that vast night. Our mounting attraction didn't actually ignite until after my summer job at the Center City YMHA day camp ended, and in mid-August we drove south to visit Nancy's grandparents and four great-aunts in West Virginia.

Years earlier, Nancy's great-aunt Mary had been a dynamic actress with a promising career and a marriage to an equally successful artist. Both were gaining prominence in Philadelphia's cultural circles when one day, family legend went, Mary walked into a church and experienced an epiphany. "Harry," she told her husband, "I've seen the light and I'm going to West Virginia to start my own church. You can come with me, but I'm going, no matter what you do." Harry declined the invitation to follow Mary to the Virginia border, unlike her three single sisters and Nancy's grandmother with her husband, the sole and silent male in the enclave.

The night before we left, I slept over at Nancy's. For some reason, Lionel, the comrade I was dating, stayed over too, so we put him on a bedroll on the floor. Packed and ready to go, we lay in Nancy's single bed as we often had before. But this particular night seethed with the morning's promise of romantic adventure. Refusing to settle for the usual careless brush of hip or toe, my supercharged body tormented my mind with silent debate, *Suppose I . . . what if . . . do I dare?* This would be a turning point in our relationship and by acting I might destroy it, but nothing mattered except to satisfy the unbearable longing to put my arms around her.

Heart in mouth, confounded by indecision yet driven by desperation, I finally made the move. No sooner had my fingertips begun a cautious slide beneath her neck than she was in my arms, clinging silently, as breathless as I. Thought was impossible. My mind whirled in my skull, my heart thundered in my chest, and my entire self pulsed and tingled with flat-out ecstasy. Frozen with elation and horror, I lay motionless until dawn's light, silently reeling in the grip of our embrace. Nancy never moved a muscle either.

Meanwhile, lying on the pallet on the floor, my comrade had spent the night sneezing and sniffling from an allergy to the cat hair that permeated Nancy's room, particularly at floor level. "Poor baby," Nancy cooed over him the next morning. Recognizing her fake voice, I didn't mind the attention she paid him. Her mind, like my own, was riveted on us and our trip, and I knew her heart was mine, just as surely as mine belonged to her.

Sister Mary's band had settled on a two-lane country road on the outskirts of Winchester where five small houses sat side by side in the most beautiful rolling countryside I'd ever seen. But then, Nancy and I were on our honeymoon, and magic gilded everything in sight. Grandma insisted on giving us her room, mostly taken up by a big bed. We glanced meaningfully at each other, barely able to contain our excitement. The following ten days were an idyll exceeding even my youthful fantasies of Jane Powell. "Are you *sure* you've never touched any other breasts but mine?" she'd ask me, doubt creasing her brow. "Don't be silly! Of course I haven't!" I'd swear, taking her in my arms. Beyond that, our mutual delight in touching and cuddling was assumed without question or discussion.

Meals were simple and deeply satisfying. Nancy's grandma cooked mouthwatering country meals from her garden or local markets, and parishioners regularly left covered dishes for the Reverend Mary who shared her bounty. We feasted on fresh eggs, homemade cottage cheese, and home-churned butter. She baked pies and quoted scripture foretelling the end of the world when The Bear (Communist Russia) and The Pope (Catholic Church) unite, improbable as it may have seemed just then. I didn't contradict her, content to be considered a benign curiosity, a "Hebrew," one of "The Chosen People," as she was fond of saying. Nancy and I tried not to smirk.

One evening, my love and I sat together on the front porch swing listening to crickets and nightbird songs, drinking Grandma's special lip-smacking, cool mint tea. Suddenly, Nancy squealed, clapped her hands and leaned in, eyes sparkling. I knew what that meant.

"Tonight when they're asleep, let's cover the hole under the outhouse seat with plastic wrap," she whispered excitedly, and, in the dead of night, keeping the giggles under control, we did. But the next day, to our disappointment, no trace of our prank was left in the outhouse, and both Grandma and her taciturn husband seemed no different, except maybe a degree cooler.

Mornings after breakfast, we'd drive off in Nancy's chunky gray two-door Dodge and explore the hills and back roads. She'd stop the car in the middle of a shallow streambed and park. Squeezed together on the running board, we'd dangle our feet in the rushing water and sketch the soft, graceful trees of West Virginia bent into their lush summer foliage. Assuming her professorial posture, she'd tell me to memorize and draw the negative space surrounding and enclosing objects rather than the objects themselves. An assignment might be a series of compositional exercises using triangle, circle and square. She had me look at a tree, find the core direction, and draw it as a line on the page. "You have to get that right before you can draw the tree," Nancy directed, but it was more difficult than it sounded to define on paper what Virginia Woolf expressed in *The Waves* as "the thing that lies beneath the semblance of the thing." Her instruction helped me to extend my vision and sharpen my attention. Besides my own red blood, "The force that though the green fuse drives the flower" drove every living thing, and you had to train your eye to recognize and then move your hand to reproduce its unique thrust.

Nancy and I sat in the back pew of Aunt Mary's church at a Wednesday night prayer meeting. My sketchy encounters with religion had not prepared me for this denomination, "a cut above snake-handling," someone had told us. People in the congregation went forward to be healed. They spoke in tongues, recalling the nonsense languages Mom and I used to entertain ourselves with. They sang "Leaning on the Everlasting Arms," and "Standing on the Promises of Christ the King."

Aunt Mary's powerful voice never faltered, nor did her charisma. This former actress knew all the tricks and called upon them, punctuating her sermons with "uh"s in rhythmic urgency. "And-uh, the Lord JAY-sus, shall-uh come DOWN among His-uh CHILL-duh-ren-uh . . ." she thundered in sermons that twice weekly brought tears to the eyes of her constituents. I sat glued to my seat, awed by the force of her delivery.

Best of all was the collection, when Reverend Mary would pace back and forth on the platform, clapping out the time and inspiring donations with sharp, nasal phrases that rang out like a bell: "Oh, well, He's WON-der-ful, won-der-ful, Je-sus is to me. . . ." By the time the baskets had completed their rounds I'd learned her routine. Back at Grandma's, Nancy clapped her hands and urged, "Do your Aunt Mary imitation!" I can still do it.

Hot, Hot, Hot!

STARRY-EYED, FLOATING on a cloud, I returned home from West Virginia. Nancy and I presented Mom and Pop with a lovely brown woolen blanket purchased at a Virginia knitting mill. My parents loved the blanket (that now sits on my bed) and the crockery jug with a fancy label Nancy penned in faux-colonial script. Later, when we were alone in the kitchen, Mom said, "You really love her, don't you?" After my panic subsided, I answered, "Yes." Mom nodded her head, and I sensed no disapproval.

Our passion grew, and for the rest of the summer Nancy and I wandered dreamily through the tranquil convent grounds next to Tyler, or lounged around one bedroom or another. With E. Power Biggs blasting Bach on the organ from her record player, we read aloud to each other from *The Story of O*, *Candy*, and *The Tropic of Cancer*, books banned in the United States but smuggled in by a friend who had recently returned from Paris and lent them to me. "Honey pot" and "adorable box" began to pop up in our conversation as did the endlessly hilarious "throbbing member."

Our literary pursuits were not confined to smut, however. We alternately read *Crime and Punishment* aloud to each other, the reader holding the book with one hand and with the other, the listener, her head nestled into the reader's shoulder. When the page was finished the reader would tear it out and drop it on the floor. "This way we can never lose our place," Nancy reasoned, and I was charmed, watching page after page of Dostoevsky's prose casually float down onto the floor in a pile.

Posing side-by-side in front of her full-length mirror, our arms around each other, we'd stand naked, curved, and sleek, examining and comparing ourselves, admiring our sexy young bodies, similar yet very different, each uniquely perfect.

"I want us to grow old together, two old ladies crocheting tablecloths, rocking side by side on our porch," she'd say, and I'd go weak in the knees. We were made for each other, but how possible was that future? I hoped she knew something I didn't.

"You're the best man I know." The first time Nancy said that to me I was changing a flat tire on her Dodge coupe. I believed it meant I was strong, and that she could depend on me. I certainly had no desire to be a man, even *her* man, but I was thrilled that she wanted to be my mate. Nancy's doleful, "Oh Lexy, I wish you were a man," meant, "if only we were a legitimate couple in the eyes of the world." I didn't respond, stymied by the complications.

An old boyfriend had turned up. He was crazy about her. "Let's switch boy-friends," she suggested one afternoon, the familiar glint in her eye stirring the familiar dread in my gut. At the time I was dating Lionel, my clever, aller-gic comrade, and Nancy's boy-exchange idea struck me as weird and unsavory. However, the discomfort I felt dissolved with the promise of enhanced intimacy. My sensible comrade soon quit Nancy's charms, but after a month's dating, her ex-boyfriend fell in love with me and cried when I gently refused his proposal of marriage. I felt touched and oddly powerful in a meaningless kind of way, since it was Nancy I desired.

Jerry was dark, handsome, and well mannered. Grandma adored him, mar-veling at his deep, resonant voice. "You should be an announcer on the radio," she would insist when he came to pick me up. In his mid-twenties, he drove a white convertible Volkswagen bug, and had a bachelor apartment in Center City where, one special evening, he served up a dinner of steak and salad and brought my virginity to as gentle an end as he could manage. At twenty-one, I figured the time was way overdue. But as careful and considerate as this well-endowed man tried to be, it hurt and I hated the whole thing. "It will get easier," he had assured me. Maybe, but at the time it hardly seemed worth the effort.

Nancy claimed to have taken her own virginity on a boy's bike. My own hand, I believed, had claimed mine. In any case, she had given me the go-ahead and expected a full report, so it wasn't like I was betraying her. She herself was already granting full sexual liberties to the rich young Quaker she had met and targeted for marriage, a fact she revealed to me carefully over time with assur-ances that she still loved me and that somehow, nothing would change. The un-examined discomfort about our future grew harder to ignore. Clearly, our path together would surely take a detour, and not knowing what to think, I turned my anxiety aside. My increasingly feckless lover had made a devastating choice but didn't share the heterosexual details I didn't want to hear. In fact, we didn't talk about sex at all. What happened between us was little more than horizontal hugging, cuddling, spooning, and me tickling her back with the lightest of slow, feathery touches the way she liked.

The Fall

"*Ya lieu-blieu*," I whispered softly to Nancy. It meant "I love you," from the lyric of a Russian song I had learned from Ethel. We were huddled tightly together against the bitter wind, walking to my car after a movie in Center City. She squeezed my arm and breathed, "Say it again," into my ear, making me dizzy with desire.

We drove north with her head resting on my shoulder and my heart filled with contentment. This was the life! Suddenly lights flashed in the rearview mirror. I hadn't been speeding and was at a loss. Pulling the Studebaker over, I saw a policeman approach. He glanced in the window and, startled, took a quick step back.

"Oh, sorry . . . I thought, I thought you were a guy and a girl the way you were sitting," he stammered, clearly confounded. "Uh . . . it's illegal to drive like that. From now on, use two hands." He backed away, shaking his head.

Gloom settled over me. "What's the matter?" Nancy asked. "Did he make you feel bad?" Numb with humiliation, I could only mumble, "He thought I was a boy and you were a girl." She waved her hand, dismissing the whole thing, but that couldn't change what I knew about his opinion of us, how queers and lesbians were more reviled than Communists, lower than low. Later in bed, she tried to make love to me, touching me as she hadn't before, but stiff with shame and guilt, I couldn't respond.

On a morning, months earlier, Mom had opened the door to my bedroom while we slept, spooning, my arm flung over Nancy's back. My eyes snapped open and without thinking, I had snatched my arm up in embarrassment. Mom said nothing and I was able to banish it from consciousness. But there was no way to ignore the unmistakable look of disgust in the eyes of the law as the officer had edged away from my car. While our love was beautiful and a blessing, I also knew it was an unacceptable, shameful secret. Even so, it had been our secret, singular and precious, and now we'd been exposed and condemned as shabby and ugly.

Nancy's legendary talent drew students and faculty to her senior show, which was heavily weighed with my image. The main attraction was a bubble-gum-pink, flat, almost one-dimensional nude portrait of me, my dark ponytail in broad swirls framed against an even flatter baby blue background. Despite a slightly Asian cast to my eyes, the style looked more modern Italian to me than "Japanese," but that was how Nancy described her striking departure. Students approached the painting of a Madonna-like figure sitting with downcast look, one knee up, the other folded under. The first glimpse of my exposed breast stopped observers in their tracks. I'd watch them approach, halt, and stare with slack faces, their eyes moving back and forth between me and the painting. "Is, uh . . . that . . . uh . . . you?"

Despite the lack of recognizable features on Nancy's sculpture of two figures lying together, uneasy glances among the viewers zipped between it and us. We paid them no mind and suspicions were soon overcome by admiration for her artistry. Or so I believed. Nancy's artwork impressed my parents, and Mom's best friend, Sophia, bought a woodcut, "Dark Angel," depicting a mythic figure in flight, a woman hugging her back. "That's us," Nancy said, without explaining who was who. No single person close to us, not my parents, Nancy's mother, our friends or fellow students, made an issue of our relationship, but my confrontation with the cop was a blow. Regardless of anything either of us did, he represented the world, demonstrating unambiguous disapproval of my feelings and our love. It caught me off guard and shattered my fragile house of cards, its echo reverberating through the remaining months of our love.

Louise & Lesbians

MY VERY FIRST lesbian friend was Louise Fishman, a slim, fair-haired, curly-headed senior who radiated a compelling aura. Her air of purpose intrigued me, and I was drawn to her handsome features, her wary, wired energy. A gifted, serious painter with a wacky light side, her thoughtful face might instantly break into a sharp burst of laughter. She came into my life around the same time as Nancy, and over time we became friends. My parents were taken with her authenticity, her intelligence and good heart. And they admired her work. "I paint my inner landscape," she said about the tormented bones and flowers: still-lifes reminiscent of Rouault and Soutine. Dedicating herself to her dark, solemn canvases, she was on her way to non-figurative abstract expressionism.

Louise was the first one I knew to learn the Twist and I loved watching her dance. We enjoyed hanging out together, going to museums and exhibitions. She got us appointments to view the mostly private Barnes Foundation on the Main Line. Luminaries such as T. S. Eliot, James Michener, and Le Corbusier were turned away by Alfred Barnes for reasons he alone understood. After ten years in the courts, the *Philadelphia Inquirer* finally compelled the foundation governing the arguably greatest private art collection in America to admit the public two days a week.

Once inside, Louise would discreetly direct my gaze to Violette de Mazia when she appeared, her pale face decked with tinted glasses topped off by a halo of wild red hair. Rings flashing and gossamer dress billowing behind her, Violette was European, a teacher, a character, and a fixture. Thirty years Alfred's junior and his reputed mistress, she had been named perennial director in his will and was frequently seen navigating the world of masterpieces cramming the walls in a millennia of Western European art.

Hung close together throughout, one hundred and eighty-one Renoirs, fifty-nine Matisses, forty-one Picassos, and a couple of Titians crowded a healthy smattering of Modiglianis, El Grecos, and Soutines. Crowning the collection were sixty-nine Cézannes, Nancy's primary inspiration. *She is a credit to him*, I thought, but didn't say, fearful of seeming overly favorable.

Louise and I didn't lack for conversation and discussed Violette, the collection, theories of art, school, our families, and her parents' fearful attitude towards her lesbianism. She was my introduction to the Philadelphia lesbian bar scene, which was both attractive and unsavory. In her presence I felt confident and strong, partly because of my heterosexual superiority complex, but mostly because she herself was tough and grounded. I trusted her, cared about her, worried about her. She was always having woman trouble.

After my relationship with Nancy ended, I told Louise that we had been lovers. She was surprised. "I didn't think you had the guts to actually do anything," she said. Of course we hadn't done that much. On the other hand, many years after I had come out, Louise heard me mention having been "straight," and remarked, "You were never straight, Alix."

Maybe not, but I was certainly nothing like that crowd of women with whom Louise hung out. Their world seemed gray, shadowy, and wounded: a world where saloons provided common ground and alcohol was currency. Finding a multitude of differences between me and lesbians, I was grateful for the discomfort I experienced. *Some of the women looked so rough and mannish, not attractive at all*, I thought to myself, seizing on dissimilarities. It was my psychic shield and I polished it vigilantly.

Through my friendship with Louise, I became acquainted with a scene encompassing some of Philadelphia's most diverting mavericks and misfits. I liked to tag along with her to lesbian parties, feeling both thrilled and strangely disconnected from the sad, chaotic, crisis-ridden lives I perceived around me.

Like Communists, lesbians were outcasts, but these women fell even lower on the social scale, carrying secrets deeper and more intimate than ours. Communists might be jailed for what we believed, but lesbians were a target because of who they were. My heterosexual privilege protected me. On the other hand, I felt lucky to be allowed entry into Louise's lesbian social circle and to share in their freedom and bawdy, rowdy fun, their ease with each other and edgy, often sexually laced humor. After Louise, my favorite lesbian was Mike. Her humor entertained me and her playful flirtation flattered me.

Louise had met Mike downtown at the Museum School—now the Philadelphia College of Art—where Louise had studied before transferring to Tyler. They loved each other and all had gone well until Louise was betrayed by a counselor who reported the romance to Louise's mother, who in turn panicked, locked her daughter in her room, and threatened to have Mike arrested. Mike's parents weren't much better. Their own families, I realized, had proven more dangerous to these girls than the FBI ever had to me. Their lives could be disrupted and ruined at any moment. Police raids on bars were frequent, and they could be arrested and find their name and address in the morning paper. Outside, they might be beaten up or killed. There was no safety for lesbians anywhere.

From time to time I joined them for coffee at Day's Deli on Spruce, the Harvey House on Broad, or The Oak Lane Diner, back when it was open all night. These women, along with an assortment of writers, artists, and lefties, frequented the South China restaurant in Chinatown where my family and friends also enjoyed an infrequent dinner out. And when Philly's first Middle Eastern restaurant, The Middle East, opened, we all went there too. For Italian food the girls convened at Dante and Luigi's in South Philly.

A handful of downtown art students and other young lesbians, bonded into a fierce, drama-prone band, who partied and sometimes vacationed together, successively loving, then betraying, cherishing, and abusing one another in wracking succession. Decades later, Mike recalled their crowd: "We loved each other, but we had such a terrible, terrible time with each other. We were cruel one minute, loving the next, and we were bed-hopping the entire time. It led to a lot of anxiety, a lot of sadness, and sometimes physical confrontation. It was a teenage thing, but in our day, you couldn't suffer out loud. So we built our own family, and it was the only family we could suffer with. We suffered together."

This family celebrated the holidays and birthdays, frequenting clubs like Pepe's and the Blue Note, where they'd go to see Nina Simone or a famous Philly native, Billie Holiday. When Billie died in 1959 they took it hard, meeting together and mourning as a family would. Nina Simone's music was familiar to me, but Louise first got me to listen to Billie, the tragic icon who touched this hard-boiled, volatile community of lesbians the way Judy Garland affected their gay brothers.

Both boys and girls flocked to see Jeri Southern, a "cool" jazz stylist, Chris Connor, and Frances Faye ("Gay, gay, gay" she'd add), another popular entertainer who performed her playful routines on the homosexual club circuit of the day. Frances Faye records could be found in the collection of every gay man in Philadelphia. She wore heavy pancake makeup and, Mike recounted, "looked like John Wayne in drag with a voice that could flatten the redwoods."

Lesbian culture fascinated me, highly seasoned as it was with worldly in-jokes, codes, and bawdy wisecracks. No party was complete without a tale of local characters like "Little Gin" or "Big Gin," who was so drunk one night that she sailed over the top of a car on her Harley and tore up her leg, which was why she limped, laughing about it afterward. These women laughed, always on the edge, always at risk.

Mike described another mythic lesbian character, a big, tough, Italian, bleached blonde named Rusty, who slicked her hair back in the customary butch "Duck Tail." Rusty ran the infamous bar bearing her name but actually belonging to the mob. From Mike I learned that during that time, a mysterious series of Center City fires ravaged Philadelphia's lesbian and gay bars, and Rusty was burnt out more than once at more than one location.

She was operating on a small side street above a restaurant on the night Mike and her lesbian friends first walked in. The maître d' spotted them right away and, hissing, "Go around the corner," shuffled them outside and pointed them to a side entrance and staircase.

"He knew just what we were looking for," Mike explained, "and he didn't want us in his place. At the top of the stairway you were stopped by Dee, a very, very tough dyke, good looking but very nasty, with the typical DA haircut, white T-shirt, rolled-up sleeves—and the cigarettes were in there—black chinos, and penny loafers, and she made it very hard to get in. Dee would scrutinize IDs with one eye on the bathrooms and would leap up to bang on the door and yell if she saw more than one woman at a time going in.

"Everyone would turn to see who would come out looking very sheepish, fixing their hair," Mike recalled. "You see, women would go there and meet someone, and it was instant love that had to be consummated right away. Of course the men could do whatever they wanted to in their bars, the more, the merrier . . . that Dee was 'a real tough cookie.'"

Rusty's longtime, role-playing butch and femme clientele didn't exactly welcome the youngsters with open arms. Alcohol-driven violence routinely enforced a socially ingrained butch-and-femme canon in which fights were commonplace and women roughed up women. The more relaxed ways of the newcomers didn't go over very well with the old-timers, and Mike herself was once beaten up by a disgruntled butch. The culture was slowly changing: sometimes an all-women's band would play live music, and there were vague rumors about a couple of women's country music bands.

Despite aggressive threats that discouraged cruising and loud music that drowned out conversation, the young lesbians kept returning to Rusty's. They went back for cutting-edge dance music and for alcohol. And because it was the best place, sometimes the only place, for lesbians to be together.

I did not look kindly upon anyone mistaking Nancy and me for lesbians. Clearly we were not. We had boyfriends. Plus, the lesbians I knew were nothing like me. So when Pop repeated my old friend Steve's offhand comment that maybe Nancy and I were "more than friends," I hit the ceiling. "That is SO insulting!" I declared, believing it.

Yet, my introduction to women who made their lives with other women was stunning, enthralling, intoxicating. Louise knew a lesbian janitor who had once worked at the convent next to the Tyler campus. She had, she claimed, slept with every sister there. "To me," she grinned, "there is nothing more exciting than a pile of black-and-whites at the foot of the bed."

I met lesbians at parties and art openings where certain female professors were pointed out to me. Two in particular had lived together as a couple for years, a vision catapulting me into new dimensions of reverie. They wore well-tailored wool suits, flat shoes, and stockings. One had bangs and glasses with tortoiseshell frames, while the other twisted her hair into a dignified bun. Overcome with longing, I imagined their perfect lives. Images of respectable, happy lesbian couples embedded themselves into my brain as an ideal, and into my heart as an unattainable dream, a hopeless fantasy far beyond anything I could imagine for Nancy and me.

For one thing, Nancy's mind was set on marriage, and, for another, I was nowhere near willing to compound "Jew" and "Commie" with "queer!" But mainly, I liked heterosexual privilege and delighted in flaunting it.

"You should try men," I advised Louise, who had never been with one. We'd just finished eating at the Oak Lane Diner. Having watched my friend's heart battered over years of tormented, unsatisfying love affairs, I was genuinely concerned for her as I walked her to the Broad Street bus stop, as full of myself as I was of the meal we had just finished.

"Women are too easy," I said as she stepped up to pay her fare, "whereas men are a challenge." She seemed unimpressed. "I'll think about it," she replied.

But in fact, finding women was much harder than finding men, who were plentiful and had clear agendas. Most girls could pick and choose from any number of them, whereas choices of women were few and far between. As Louise remarked later, "Back in those days, when you met a lesbian, you slept with her!" Exaggerated or not, it made the point.

My own lesbian love life—although I never would have called it that—wasn't doing much better. For the past year, Nancy and I had been growing apart and she'd landed her young tycoon with his fresh Harvard MBA. Unfailingly cordial, he would chitchat pleasantly with me before whisking her away in his white MG convertible.

"I'm going to marry him," she had declared in the bathtub after their second date, and I heard her wedding bells toll the death of our love. What happened to the two of us, sitting and crocheting on our porch? I had yearned for that with my whole heart while knowing how unlikely it was for us. So when Mr. Toad appeared, I knew to resign myself to the inevitable, just like I had done for fairy tales with their unhappy endings.

Herb

MEANWHILE, MY COMRADES and I had gotten used to seeing Herb at events run by one or another Party front. A nerdy rotund guy of our generation, he seemed so nosy that we suspected him of being an FBI informer, so whenever we spotted him we kept our guard up and our mouths closed. Never could I ever have imagined Herb starting me on my career, but he surely did, and I am grateful. But back in the spring of 1961 I knew him only well enough for an occasional cool nod of recognition.

The Second Fret, for decades a nationally recognized coffeehouse and premier commercial folk club, brought national folk acts to Philadelphia. Before that, the less durable "Kabuki-American Teahouse" had opened its doors on Walnut Street. So, late in the autumn of my senior year, when Nancy's marriage campaign finally paid off with a proposal, my attention re-focused, and the disappointment faded into lightness and anticipation. Herb called, I was ready to listen to what he had to say, and what he said changed my life.

The Teahouse, a new folk club, was about to open in Center City and Herb was booking it. Would I like to make thirty-five dollars singing on the weekend? "Crazy," I said.

Just as we suspected, Herb had been keeping track of of my doings, but for personal reasons. He genuinely appreciated my music and over the years proved his strong belief in me.

My vivid and no doubt romanticized memory of that first professional performance, was, thanks to loyal family, friends, and comrades who flocked to the narrow Teahouse and showered me with wild enthusiasm, a magnificent success. An enthusiastic introduction for "Philly's own," belting out a rousing "Coplas," "Viva La Quince Brigada," and making it through "Eppie Morrie" without losing my breath or falling off the short riser amounted to a head-spinning, triumph. It would take me a few years to provoke the same response from an audience of strangers.

"How would you like to make a hundred and fifty dollars a week after you graduate?" Herb and I were standing at the back of the room between sets. Could I believe him? Impossible to tell, but he promised that for the rest of the school year he would book local gigs for me, set up sessions with performance coaches, introduce me to movers and shakers, and, when I finished Tyler, launch my career.

Such a thing had never entered my mind. A hundred and fifty dollars a week was big money. And singing professionally for an audience? I was fond of telling people, "Anyone can get a guitar and learn three chords." Soon I'd be saying, "I can't imagine doing anything else for a living."

I decided to take a chance and see what he could do for me. I never regretted it, for, in the following years Herb earned his 20 percent fee with mostly solid advice and hard work on my behalf.

My first priority was my career, and everything else took a back seat, even politics. There was no doubt in my mind so I just went ahead and grabbed the opportunity because if I didn't I would regret it forever. No comrade ever said a word about it. Herb supported me and made good on his promises. His ambition to be an important showbiz manager by filling his stable with musicians he thought worth shepherding into the Big Time worked for me. He believed that to sustain a career it was important for me to build on my strengths and ground myself in tradition, so we searched out unfamiliar, out-of-the-way neighborhoods where odd, colorful pieces of an exploding folk mosaic were hidden. Frank Profitt from North Carolina, one of many folk treasures passed over by the mainstream, seemed happy to share an original song or two with appreciative young people, and we were grateful to listen. Traditional singers like Lonnie Johnson and others welcomed us in sad, gray tenements and hotel rooms. I had grown up listening to Lonnie's recording of "Mean Old Bedbug Blues," and when I played his guitar riff back to him, the bashful, old, musician was astounded.

Bleecker Street, Buzzards Bay, and Onward

A SONG ON one of several albums recorded by the noted folksinger and radio show host Cynthia Gooding had inspired me to learn guitar, and in the first of many negotiations undertaken on my behalf, Herb convinced her to take me on as a private student. I would have been satisfied with eye contact and a handshake. Worldly and accomplished, with an urbane cult following, she was "A folksinger's folksinger." A serious musician and scholar, dignified and unmarried, Cynthia was a reluctant teacher, as unaccustomed to the role of private coach as I was to private coaching. However, since she'd be part of the distinguished staff of performers and scholars leading a week of intensive traditional folk music classes and workshops at Pinewoods, a folk music camp on Cape Cod, she might agree to coach me, if my audition impressed her enough.

On a spring day, Herb borrowed his parents' sedan and we drove to Cynthia's Bleecker Street apartment. No one answered the buzzer in the lobby, so we called her from a pay phone down the block with the same result. Back in the lobby we parked ourselves on a hard bench and waited. The minutes crawled by. The afternoon lengthened.

To break the tedium, we wandered across the street and down a few blocks and peered into a club undergoing renovation. New management had changed the name from The Cock and Bull to The Bitter End, and I couldn't decide which name was worse. Music issued from the interior, and we stepped into the dark entrance. A burly, spectacled man with a big mass of white hair was studying two guys with beards on each side of a tall blonde as they rehearsed. They were new to me, but I liked their rich, layered sound, like The Weavers revisited. Edging around the disorder of construction, I made my way beside him to listen. After a couple of songs, without turning to me, he said, "Well, what do you think of them?" I said I thought they were great.

He introduced himself as Albert Grossman and said the trio was Peter, Paul, and Mary, whom he had put together and was grooming. "They're not quite ready, but when they break out they're going to be huge," he said, and I believed him. *Would I be able to compete with such a professional sound?* Herb and I went back across the street to wait some more and just when we decided to give up, Cynthia arrived. Having completely forgotten the appointment, she was surprised to see us but could spare a few minutes.

Massive bookcases covered some walls, while on others hung rugs, hangings, and exotic artwork from Turkey and the Middle East, all of it contributing to an exotic atmosphere. Her great height added to the quiet force of the woman's wisdom and experience, intimidating me, but I pulled out my guitar and did my strongest material. Only "Eppie Morrie" interested her, and on the strength of the tune learned from my taping of a Ewan MacColl and Peggy Seeger concert at the University of Pennsylvania, I became her first student. Like so much of Scots and Irish tradition, the a cappella song calls for a vigorous delivery, which I managed without running out of breath and collapsing.

On the first day of my studies at Pinewoods Camp on Cape Cod Bay, I knocked on Cynthia's cabin door, with a notebook in one hand, my guitar case in the other, and no clue about what to expect. Once inside, I stood before her, drowning in insignificance, and lowered the case to the floor. She lounged on the pillows of a white, wicker sofa, the smoke from her cigarette curling lazily between us.

"What kind of woman are you, Alix?" I had no idea, and thought about the kid in Chicago asking me if I was a girl or a woman, a question I still hadn't figured out.

"Are you quiet? Passionate?"

"I dunno. Passionate, I guess." Ignoring my self-conscious confusion, Cynthia requested a song and I chose "Old Blue" about a good ol' dog. An extended howl in the chorus made the tune a great hit in folk circles. The E string was lowered to D for the deep, resonant D-chord sound we all loved, and I was proud of the arrangement, my version of the one developed by the Boston folkie Tom Rush, but it failed to sweep Cynthia away. She had me play it as slowly, then as fast as I could. Next, she had me experiment with emphasis and phrasing.

We worked on "Mrs. McGrath," an angry, Irish anti-war song. Being fiercely against war, I infused it with great conviction. We took it apart and experimented, phrase by phrase. Cynthia advised me that no matter how often a song is sung, each performance requires a conscious, fresh view, and I was to visualize every image in the song. "If you close your eyes when you sing, you shut the audience out. Open up and acknowledge them," she instructed, and now, even with lights in my eyes I still seek eye contact with the audience. "Do you care about what you're saying? Then pronounce each word clearly!" Mom and Pop had told me the same thing.

Dreary Buzzards Bay weather didn't dampen ten days of concentrated study or nightly jamming and song-swapping. My appreciation was sharpened for British folk tradition with its Child ballads, Robert Burns songs, and the repertoire of William Dyer Bennett and John Jacob Nyles. The ability to hold my own among the Pinewoods heavyweights encouraged me to take myself seriously as a musician and a performer.

Small groups gathered in one or another cabin every night, and from those song swaps I took home several excellent songs and rounds. A young couple sang and harmonized "Jovanno," which had to be one of the three most beautiful songs I'd ever heard. The first one had been an instrumental Macedonian wedding tune on a Folkways album, and I hadn't yet discovered the third. I couldn't wait to sing "Jovanno" to Ethel. As I'd come to expect from my former counselor, she learned my version, then tracked down a more authentic one.

Throughout the Pinewoods Camp session, I watched middle-aged women swoon over John Langstaff, a highly respected longtime staff member whose deep, resonant baritone and several recorded albums of traditional ballads enhanced his charm. Naturally I admired the darkly handsome idol, but didn't join the swarm of women seeking his attention and had no real conversation with him.

Weeks after camp ended, I received a call from John. Not having imagined that he'd noticed me, I was shocked. In town overnight, he wanted to see me, and would I meet him at an apartment near the University of Pennsylvania? Indeed I would. Upon my arrival, we immediately climbed into a single bed and enjoyed nonstop, energetic sex until morning. Jerry had been right. Sex was fun, thus verifying my heterosexual core, a basic belief about myself that, although beleaguered, I had not abandoned. Unconnected to the genuine center of my being, my love for Nancy had been a singular aberration, now in decline. On the other hand, John was a celebrity, a grown-up adult man whose attention and fervor was added proof of my own maturity. I was, yes, a passionate woman, I realized as I walked to the subway the next morning, inwardly savoring my badge of the insignificant burn between my legs. Cynthia should see me now!

Entry-Level Showbiz

TRUE TO HIS word, Herb booked me into several of the fly-by-night joints popping up and closing down throughout that summer. He arranged shows for me at University International House where students from India, Africa, and the Philippines sat quietly and applauded politely. He also introduced me to Philadelphia's jazz scene, and took me to nightclubs like the Showboat and Pepe's Lounge, where we saw the great African drummer, Olatunji, on his first U.S. tour, and singers like Anita O'Day and Peggy Lee, who appeared at those venues.

Besides escorting me to cool hot spots during my senior year, Herb booked me into clubs with Bill Cosby, three years my elder and a fellow Temple University senior whom Herb thought was exceptionally talented and "commercial," meaning "saleable" or current, rather than "ethnic" or traditional. Comedians were automatically "commercial," and I was a mix of both. Herb got us work at the Cellar Bar of the Underground, a room humming with life. The all-black crowd really wanted Bill, but got me as part of the package. For five dollars each we opened for acts like Moms Mabley and Redd Foxx. Cowed by the presence of these exalted talents, I felt even more self-conscious in my pale white skin. Rather than taking insult at the steady hum of inattention and the clinking of glassware during my brief warm-up set, I felt grateful for the audience's mild curiosity and polite response. Some of the women actually applauded and smiled cordially at me. I returned my warmest smile. Of course they loved Bill with his early versions of the Noah/God conversation, high school Spanish, and stories of his Philadelphia youth.

As student government VP, I was able to hire Cosby to entertain at our Tyler senior prom, along with Lonnie Johnson. Bill was cordial to me, but a bit aloof, and we didn't converse much. The excitement of the show and my share of a bottle of cheap red wine sent me to the bathroom sink. The next morning I woke up with my first hangover.

Meanwhile, Back on the Block

IN THE EARLY 1960s, Philadelphia real estate interests targeted our lower-middle-class neighborhood, trying to "break the block" by putting a bar on the corner and pressuring residents to sell low so the investors could re-sell high to African American families trying to upgrade their housing. Profiteers encouraged "white flight" and influenced City Hall to change zoning laws and bring in bars and liquor stores. Mom collected signatures for petitions against it. A block filled with "for sale" and "sold" signs induced panic selling, but Mom discovered a city ordinance restricting "sold" signs to nine days. She'd haul my sister Julie around in the Volvo to document the first appearance of a sign, and when the time limit expired, she'd complain to the Board of Realtors. Her calls prompted the city to finally outlaw all such signs, a ruling lasting forty years. In spite of her and others' efforts, the neighborhood ultimately fell victim to the real estate sharks.

My four years at Tyler was winding down fast and, with a summa cum laude, it was time to answer the call of show business. As maid of honor at Nancy's wedding, I wore a pink satin dress with a square-cut neckline, my broken heart well on the mend.

The Folk Biz

What good is originality if you can't crank it out?

—CALVIN, *in It's a Magical World: A Calvin and Hobbes Collection*

TO CELEBRATE MY bachelor's degree, Mom and Pop presented me with a snappy white leather suitcase, lending a touch of class to my flight from the nest. By a stroke of luck, one of Pop's colleagues was out of town for the month of July and her apartment on East Seventy-ninth Street was available. A world away from Sixty-eighth Avenue, it was only a few subway stops from the Greenwich Village of *Wonderful Town* and my Midwest fantasies.

The Eighth World Youth Festival had again rolled around, this time in Helsinki, Finland. In what was to be my final Party work as Cultural Coordinator for the U.S. Festival Committee, I was responsible for the American delegation's cultural program. By day, during those first weeks in Manhattan, I traveled to the Festival office at 460 Park Avenue South, then down to the Village, returning at night to the Upper East Side.

A Party member at-large attended no meetings and had no one to answer to. Though a scant one hundred and twenty miles away, Philadelphia and the Party, Nancy and art, seemed more and more like ghosts swept back into the past. Being disconnected from my comrades uncoupled me from the political culture of my student years, and unlike my parents, I had not become disenchanted with the Party, but rather enchanted by my dream coming true: the Village and entry into its exciting folk scene. Meanwhile, instructions came down from FBI headquarters that "Philadelphia should immediately attempt to develop further details concerning subject's proposed travel plans."

My plan was to travel with our delegation to Helsinki and work with the artists to set up the exhibits I had solicited and organized. According to pages of documents stamped and initialed a dozen times, the moment I applied for a passport, an assistant attorney general sprang into action. While being a Communist was not against the law, the State Department, alerted by the Bureau, stepped in. *"Subject has not been identified as a member of the CP since the passport sanction of the ISA (Internal Security Act) of 1950 went into effect"*; nevertheless, a *"Passport Violation under Internal Security Act of 1950"* was invoked.

The government wasn't going to get me to sign anything, let alone *"a sworn statement regarding present or past Communist Party membership."* I was also warned that I *"may possibly come within the provisions of Section 6 of the Internal Security Act of 1950. . . ."* While outrageous and unlawful, this obstacle served my purposes since *"two months abroad for travel"* would be time lost from my real focus. With Mattie directing the Young People's Chorus, and first-class musicians like Ethel, Mattie, the guitarist Jerry Silverman, and the jazz pianist Archie Shepp—the program would run just fine without me. Once again aiding and abetting my career, the government designated me a "security risk," thus freeing me to see to my career. Plus, dollars not spent on the trip would come in handy settling into the Village of my dreams.

Exiting the subway early in August, I caught the terrible headline "Marilyn dead!" Time stopped and my heart recoiled. I'd adored Marilyn Monroe in *Gentlemen Prefer Blondes*, *The Seven-Year Itch*, and *Some Like It Hot*, and her performance in *Bus Stop* had touched me profoundly. Marilyn had always struck me as kind, funny, and approachable, a good person I would have liked as a friend. Also steadfast. About Arthur Miller she had declared, "When Mr. Miller was on trial for contempt of Congress, as a certain corporation executive said, either he named names and I got him to name names, or I was finished. I said, 'I'm proud of my husband's position and I stand behind him all the way,' and the court did too. 'Finished,' they said. 'You'll never be heard of again.'" Marilyn had won that one. A wave of loss washed through me and the world seemed lonelier.

Me in my buggy (with union leaflets?).

Me and Grandma.

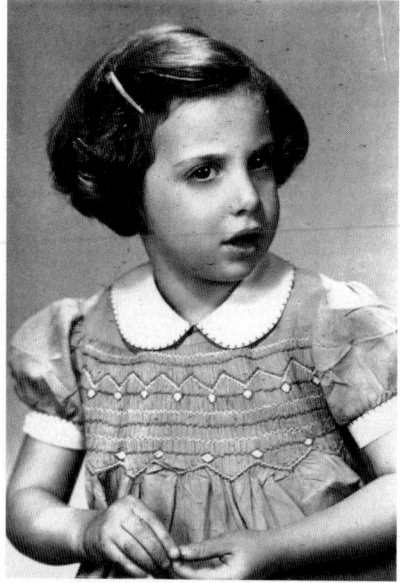

1946, waiting for a bus.

Above: In one of those dresses that most five-year-old girls wore in 1945.

Right: Mom and me.

Mom and Margie.

1947, (L to R), Carlie, Grandma, and me in Wellfleet, Cape Cod, MA

Uncle Cecil (third from Left) in Spain with his comrades.

Left: 1952, (L to R), Steve, me, and Eliot in Lynnewood Gardens with our maroon Packard at the curb.

Above: 1951, in the park off Riverside Drive.

Left: 1954, the family minus Pop, who took the picture in Kansas City.

Below left: Playing the Hoefner at home in Philadelphia. *Below right:* 1954, writing back home to the kids, trying to beat the heat in Kansas City.

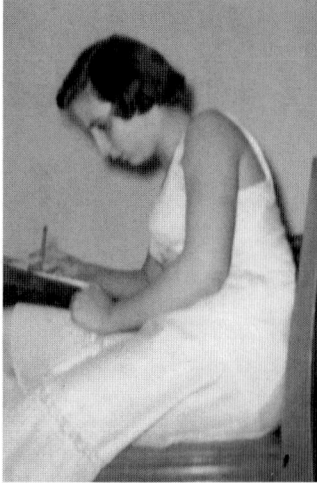

1954, on Micki's front porch in Strawberry Mansion.

1954, flannel shirt, dungarees and all.

Above left: Promo shot with finger picks and capo. *Above right:* 1964, Betsy Klein, me, and a kitty belonging to Lena Spencer, offstage at Caffe Lena, Saratoga Springs, NY.

Chester's Children

Looking wistful in Fairmount Park for my first promo shot. Photo by Murray Weiss.

In front of my posters in Ft. Lauderdale, FL at the Catacombs Cafe, summer, 1963.

Above left: Wedding party at the Dom (L to R) Pop, Sam, Mama, Papa, me, Mom. *Above right:* On my honeymoon when I water-skied for the first time and loved it.

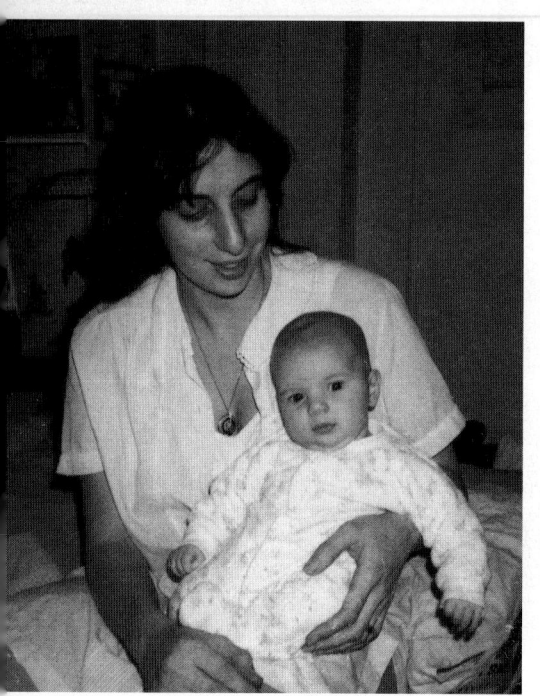 

Left: 1970, Madonna and child. *Above:* Happily married in Miami.

My Village Folk Scene

MY GENERATION LEARNED to champion civil rights, social justice, and peace through singing together, and in less than a decade after rock 'n' roll fractured the music industry, an even more accessible subculture of do-it-yourself musicians began to emerge.

In the early '60s, it seemed the whole world was learning to play guitar, banjo, mandolin, harmonica, and bongos. The attraction of folk music was not limited to those raised on Pete Seeger, Woody Guthrie, The Almanac Singers, Leadbelly, Josh White, or The Weavers, but that's who started it. Just beginning to feel its strength, early 1960s folk music was preparing to reconstruct popular culture and turn pop music on its ear just as rock 'n' roll had in the 1950s. Ready for a great ride on the tidal wave, I needed to log more stage time and earn my chops. What better place than Greenwich Village? East Coast folk musicians flocked to Philadelphia, Boston, and D.C., but mecca was located within a few lower Manhattan blocks where three showcase clubs, The Gaslight, The Bitter End, and Gerde's Folk City, marked an irregular district serving as folk central.

Jazz musicians had lived in the Village for decades, as did lesbians and gay men, all drawn to the bit of acceptance those streets had historically provided. Writers like Dawn Powell had lived and worked in the Village, and before that, Walt Whitman and Edgar Allan Poe had claimed the rare, safe space for creative originals and other misfits. The old neighborhood families, accustomed to the unconventional, put up with the new nightly folk invasion and the abundant tourist dollars they attracted.

Washington Square defined the northern edge of the world's major folk district. It was the site of regular Sunday afternoon jams and a magnet for swarms of kids and enthusiasts cruising through the arch at the foot of Fifth Avenue. They clustered around the circular fountain to listen or join in with music styles ranging from jug band, ragtime, original topical and union songs to old-time country and traditional ballads, both pious and bawdy. Bluegrass alternated with tragic Scots ballads and Irish drinking songs or the blues, now and again punctuated by arrangements right off the latest Kingston Trio or Joan Baez record.

As darkness fell and the music faded, the crowd thinned, drifting in a southwesterly direction toward West Third Street where the Village "Pain" Shop— the "*t*" long gone from the sign showing a can pouring paint over the world— pointed down MacDougal toward the Folklore Center and the clubs. Performers threaded through the multitudes and passed baskets for tips at "basket houses" like The Fat Black Pussycat, The Why Not, The Café Wha?, and The Id, several of which opened and folded regularly. Managers, bookers, agents, promoters, producers, photographers, journalists, techies, cooks, bartenders, club owners and managers, waiters, dishwashers, spouses, and groupies congregated, gossiped, hustled, and forged a breezy, transient community.

Among the neighborhood shops, chess houses, Italian butchers, funeral homes, and jewelry and news shops, pedestrians might purchase fresh Caribbean piña coladas and Argentinean empanadas from storefronts opening onto the street. The sweet aroma of sizzling onions on grills tempted passers-by stopping to watch an upright rotating leg of lamb roast slowly in plain sight of anyone suddenly hungry for souvlaki. Halfway down the street, The Gaslight hunkered down beside The Kettle of Fish bar. Directly across the street, the time-honored Rienzi Café did business next to the equally venerable Minetta Tavern half a block from where Pop had lived during the Great Depression.

Nestled among the food stands, jewelry stores, boutiques, head shops, and souvenir joints south of The Gaslight, Izzy Young's Folklore Center drew musicians, fans, and curiosity seekers from far and wide. A steadfast supporter, producer, and folk advocate, Izzy was too generous to turn a profit in his shop, which often resembled a hostel. "Frets and Frails," his regular *Sing Out!* column, kept track of the latest folk gossip a few pages from Pete Seeger's "Johnny Appleseed."

Tourists flocked from New Jersey, every borough and beyond to sample the latest "groovy" thing. Through The Café Borgia and the Figaro, back and forth across Bleecker Street, they flowed, consuming nonstop espresso and paying too much for anemic sandwiches and continental pastries. Legendary songwriter Fred Neil consecrated this fabled crossroads, his basso as profundo as Paul Robeson's: "Standin' on the corner of Bleecker and MacDougal, wonderin' which a-way to go. . . ."

And many were the ways to go. The Hip Bagel opened shortly after I arrived on the scene and was where I was introduced to the delight of post-midnight breakfasts. Just after the last bow of the closing act, when the last penny had been counted, the last chair upended on the table, and the last key turned in the lock for the night; when the stragglers would be on their F, D, and A trains back to Brooklyn, Queens, and the Bronx; when the New Jersey license plates would have left our streets empty and hushed, The Bagel was a fine place to cap a night.

With deep cultural roots reaching back before the folk boom, The "World-Famous Gaslight Café," sat at the center of a street alive with colors in motion as multitudes window shopped, walked off a rich Italian meal, or made their way down the steps of 116 MacDougal to the home of Ginsburg, Kerouac, Ferlinghetti, and other Beat poets before they beat paths west.

The previous March during our senior year, Herb had driven Cosby and me up the New Jersey Turnpike to MacDougal Street. We'd made our way down one of two parallel staircases leading to the cramped basement lobby of The Gaslight. A thick black curtain was pulled aside to reveal an aisle leading back through a rectangular room to a modest stage at the rear wall. After introducing us to the only one in the room, a languid man who claimed to represent John Mitchell, Herb explained how smart it would be to hire us, young cutting edges of the hot new thing. I sang a couple of songs and Bill did some jokes. The man barely opened an eye the whole time, and, unacquainted with the look of a stoned person, I thought he was bored, so when he told Herb they had a deal and to bring Bill and me back after graduation, I was shocked.

Herb, Bill, and I and reported for work in early July. Ducking into dark silence, we could barely make out the shadowy figure seated at a large round table of the front booth, which, I learned later, was generally reserved for large parties, VIPs, or Gaslight regulars. An older, sleepy-eyed man sat alone in the empty basement. It seemed that shortly before or after his friend and Herb shook hands, John Mitchell had sold the business to Ed and Penny Simon and was rumored to have skipped to Spain a step ahead of the law and the mob. John Moyant then bought the Gaslight with Harry Fry and brought Papa and his youngest son, Sam, up from Lake Wales, Florida; established them in a Village apartment; and threw them to the folkies.

Originally from Mississippi, Clarence E. Hood Jr. knew as much about folk music as he did about our booking, which was nothing. Surprised when Herb explained why we were there, he invited us to re-audition, saying that if he liked what he heard, he'd hire us. Eyelids at half mast, he lowered himself into a booth and listened quietly. He was completely taken with Bill doing his *"Grande es el burro, el burro es grande"* commentary on learning Spanish and other childhood recollections, and he liked me well enough to make a deal with Herb.

Except for Tuesday night, when noted bluesman Dave Van Ronk hosted the weekly "hoot," three or four performers rotated forty-five-minute sets for two shows during the week, three on weekends. At times I thought well of my abilities, but I also felt raw and ragged compared with those I considered veteran performers. Most of us were kids in our twenties, more or less starting out together, but it was a thrill to see my name on the sandwich board at the top of the steps alongside Van Ronk, Tom Paxton, Len Chandler, Ramblin' Jack Elliott, Josh White Jr, and Carolyn Hester. Comics like Cosby, Flip Wilson, Richard Pryor, David Fry, "Uncle Dirty," Biff Rose, Lord Buckley, and Hugh Romney (who later became Wavy Gravy), (Bill) Greco, and (the always agree-able Fred) Willard regularly tried out new material and kibbitzed from the Gaslight stage.

But folk singing ruled, with featured talents like Judy Mayhan, singing with heartbreaking sweetness, Judy Roderick belting out mellifluous blues, elegantly stylized Hal Waters, Jackie Washington, David Blue, Jim and Jean, Osborne Smith, and Richie Havens, dripping sweat and driving relentless rhythms, his giant mitts making the guitar look like a toy. Personable, witty Artie Traum cracked wise with Happy, his brother and good-natured straight man. Both brothers picked home-spun guitar and crooned melodious old-timey numbers. On some nights, John Sebastian could be spotted slipping gracefully through knots of tourists, an ammunition belt loaded with harmonicas strapped across his chest. Good-hearted, soft-spoken John was getting ready to form The Lovin' Spoonful and write some of the best popular music ever written.

Native Americans Buffy Sainte-Marie and Peter LaFarge, along with song-writer Patrick Sky, earned wide respect for bringing to the scene a consciousness of the original American genocide and continuing oppression of their people, as well as a passion for their heritage. A nasal twang and self-deprecating laugh enhanced Pat's boyish charm and belied his cynicism, which I teased him about. "If it ain't as good as 'Rye Whiskey,'" he'd say, "then it ain't worth listenin' to."

During that gilded era, city and country blues pickers were drawn to the Vil-lage and legendary blues men like John Lee Hooker could be seen at Gerde's and The Gaslight, as could Bukka White, whose classic recording of "Stealin" had been worn out on my record player in Philadelphia. Some nights, Mis-sissippi John Hurt, his fedora perched on his head, rocked back and forth on a chair gently rendering lines of "Oh, Babe, It Ain't No Lie," "Salty Dog," "Candy Man," and his other classics. Although they picked his brain at every opportunity, not even John Sebastian or the Traums could have predicted the profound influence of Mississippi John's playing style on country blues pickers forever after.

On other nights, Brownie McGee plied his guitar behind the raspy vocals and wailing harmonica of Sonny Terry, on "Diggin' My Potatoes," and "Step It Up and Go." A decade earlier they had performed at Town Hall Hoots along with The Weavers, Martha Schlamme, Leon Bibb, Elizabeth Knight, Earl

Robinson, and comedian Les Pine. I'd listened to the legendary duo on my favorite Hootenanny album for years, and now we were on the same bill! While I felt comfortable in the casual atmosphere of that time and place, every so often it would hit me how extraordinary it all was, how outstanding these people were, and how lucky I was to be right in the thick of it.

I sang under my breath along with the blind Reverend Gary Davis and his virtuoso guitar on "Keep Your Lamp Trimmed and Burning" and "Just a Closer Walk with Thee," songs I'd learned from the issue of the *Sing Out!* with his picture on the cover. When he was led off the stage—a cigar sticking out of his mouth, its plastic holder set at a jaunty angle—I made sure to keep a safe distance from his wandering hands.

On any given night the creative sparkle on the streets reflected lights such as Buzzy Linhart, Phil Ochs, Paul Geremia, The Greenbriar Boys, Eric Anderson, and Charlotte Daniels with Pat Webb, who, on a snowy weekday night, inspected a sparse Gaslight crowd and remarked, "Hell, I been *married* to more people than this!"

According to the FBI, I was now *"fairly well known as a performer in Greenwich Village,"* and, by circulating between The Gaslight and Gerde's and out-of-town clubs, I was mostly able to pay my bills. When bookings were scarce, the Olsten Agency found me temporary secretarial work and I appreciated those awful typing classes.

The Bitter End/Gerde's Folk City

FOLK MUSIC HAD become big business and the Village was crawling with talent and talent scouts. The slicker commercial acts generally showcased at The Bitter End, which attracted more high-end agents and bookers than the funkier Gaslight or the raucous Gerde's. Bitter End regulars included formidable artists like Judy Henske, Bob Gibson, and Hamilton Camp, and groups like The Rooftop Singers, The Big Three with the great Cass Elliot, and Eric Weissberg and The Tarriers. Before forming the Blues Project, Danny Kalb played The Bitter End regularly, as did comic David Steinberg and the brilliant singer/songwriter duo from Canada, Ian and Sylvia. From time to time, Woody Allen's managers could be spotted in the audience taking notes as they groomed him for stardom.

Equally at ease in cocktail lounge or coffeehouse, Jo Mapes often took the Bitter End stage. Accompanying herself on guitar made her a folksinger, but her jazzy style made it difficult to fit her into a neat category, and Jo's managers, not knowing what to do with her, booked her back and forth between The Blue Angel uptown and The Bitter End downtown.

Sooner or later, everyone passed through Gerde's Folk City, where Bob Shelton wrote the *New York Times* review in which he described Bob Dylan as "Resembling a cross between a choir boy and a beatnik . . . bursting at the seams with talent," and launched Dylan's career. The Italian pasta bar was run by Mike Porco, a local businessman who recognized the vitality and profitability of folk music early on. After agreeing to let Izzy Young and a partner run regular Monday night "hoots," Mike became a strong force in the community. Unlike attentive coffeehouse audiences, the bar's clientele created a rowdy environment for live music.

From the small, high stage, performers could peer through the lights and thick plumes of smoke, over tables and partitions, to watch themselves in the mirror while customers schmoozed at the bar. The walls were hung with photos of Gerde's veterans like Freddy Neil, Brother John Sellars, Billy Faier, Dave Van Ronk, Jean Redpath, Lisa Kindred, Cisco Houston, Muddy Waters, and even me, among others who shuttled between The Gaslight and Gerde's. Tom Pasley, José Feliciano, and John Hammond Jr., as well as bawdy balladeer-scholars Ed McCurdy and Oscar Brand, performed regularly. Both of these men stuck to tradition and knew their stuff. Oscar and I shared the bill many times. Always respectful and encouraging to me, he sometimes plays my music on his syndicated WNYC show, the longest continually running program on the radio.

His face and the faces of Hedy West, the Clancy Boys with Tommy Makem, The New Lost City Ramblers, Emmylou Harris, Sonny & Brownie, and Mississippi John graced the red-flocked walls. Others who performed on that stage Lightning Hopkins, Gil Turner, The Rooftop Singers, The Greenbriar Boys featuring John Herald's sweet lead vocal, Lynn Gold, and Logan English. The ambiance of a class reunion sustained the uniquely talented acoustic artists and acolytes who filled the informal folk venues of the time with our enthusiasms, rivalries, support, humor, and ambition mixing in with the ubiquitous smoke from our Marlboro cigarettes.

Soon after my arrival in New York, Herb arranged an audition at Folk City, and Mike hired me for my first two-week job accompanying myself on my new Guild guitar. Because of Gerde's liquor license, membership in Local 802 of the American Federation of Musicians was required, so Mike deducted eighty dollars in dues from my first week's paycheck. I filled out an application at the Local's midtown office and walked out a card-carrying union member, a pro, complete with anxiety dreams about trying to find venues or losing my finger picks while impatient audiences fidgeted and walked out.

At Gerde's I met Suze Rotolo, who could have been a Kinderland bunkmate, I felt so comfortable with her. The imaginative, thoughtful creator of Mike's flyers, Suze liked me and my work, and, until Tom Pasley complained, placed my name first in the publicity, even when I was just the opening act. Cute and bright, she was Bob Dylan's girlfriend. "My gal Sue," he called her.

Elmer, Neighbors, Friends, and Other Characters

"THE IDEA IS to establish me as a regular, keep me around after it's no longer a fad," I explained in a 1963 interview. To that end, Herb signed me up to study with a performance coach whom I immediately adored, the breezy, limp-wristed gay boy Elmer Jared Gordon. Sam and Papa got a kick out of Elmer and comped him whenever he came around. Their affectionate teasing was designed to bring out the queenly manner that they found highly amusing.

Dark hair slicked back, slim, dapper, and seemingly fragile, Elmer dressed impeccably in short-sleeved, monogrammed shirts under a jacket and tie. A twinkle alternated with sleepy-eyed disinterest behind black horn-rimmed glasses. Whether exploding into high-pitched giggles or making a point with a faultless Jewish-yenta accent, his studied flippancy and sharp criticisms never bothered me. Always in character, he'd begin a sentence, "So leee-s'n dahlink. . . ." A serious bridge player, his daily *New York Times* folded to Goren's column, Elmer often traveled to play in tournaments. No insults were made within my hearing in regard to the queerness of the first obviously gay man I had ever known.

Caroline, a neighbor to a client of Elmer's, had just lost her apartment-mate, so the connection was made, and by the fall of 1962 my move to the folk heartland was accomplished. A telephone listing and checking account completed my independence. Confident and eager to meet the future, I still sometimes felt the old tug of unworthiness and a fear of not measuring up to the bright talents around me, but this didn't slow me down. For my room at 190 Waverly Place I bought a nearly-double bed, hung my clothes in the closet, and arranged some of my paintings along with framed cartoons Mike had given me on the bedroom wall.

My roommate and I led our separate lives cordially and cooperatively, sharing an entryway and living room, a cramped bathroom, and a tiny kitchen where cooking seldom occurred. The FBI kept track through a *"Greenwich Village cafe habitat* [sic]" who advised [blacked-out] that I *"had a continuous succession of*

Greenwich Village cafe performers as co-residents of [my] *apartment.*" Did the Feds know that for us, putting people up for the night was a way of life? Most days you never knew who might be sprawled on Herb's couch or curled up on his office floor. Ellen McIlwaine and Judy Mayhan lived there for extended periods, as did José and Hilda Feliciano. Jesse Colin Young, his sweet voice singing of heartbreak and preaching peace and harmony, camped there from time to time with his wife Susie and a Youngblood or two from his group five years before his classic "Get Together" would become the anthem of a generation.

Around the corner, "The House of D," the Women's House of Detention, a dreadful facility by all accounts, dominated the intersection of Greenwich and Sixth avenues. Inmates shouted down to friends, families, lawyers, and passers-by who stretched their necks up to the high, barred windows. When you walked by, the women yelled, "Hey, honey . . ." and "Look up here!" Noisy verbal exchanges continued at all hours.

The building next to ours housed a venerable old bar and, as I discovered years later, a notoriously gay one. Walls and fixtures were buried in cobwebs and inches deep in soot that appeared to have accumulated over decades, giving the place its nickname, "Dirty Julius's." Their burgers, served on rye toast, were the tastiest since Mom's salt-fried ones.

It had taken six long years for my Kansas City fantasy to become a Greenwich Village reality. My neighbors were as eccentric and colorful as any character from *My Sister Eileen*.

Varda, a singer, dark and expressive, lived upstairs. When she bought a sewing machine, we made dresses (my bright orange frock looked awful). Another time a woman knocked on the door selling electrical boxes with suction-cuplike attachments guaranteed to vibrate the fat right off our thighs while we were watching TV. Varda's enthusiasm overcame my reluctance and I chipped in, but we lost interest and returned it. Vibrators were not yet on the scene and the whopping orgasms a certain type might bring on was beyond imagination.

Guitarist Barry Kornfeld taught his craft downstairs, and up-and-coming, gruff young blues singer and guitarist Dave Van Ronk lived up on the fifth floor with his wife, Terri Thal. Tall, lanky, extremely bright and direct, Terri wore dark bangs, cat's-eye glasses, and an incipient sneer. Dave's snarly voice, large presence, and lumbering gait likened him to a big bear. When he sang, his shaggy head snapped up and down, slapping long straight hairs across his face. Neither he nor Terri had time for phonies, but treated those they liked with warmth and generosity. I numbered among the fortunate ones, but not at first.

"I used to hate you," Van Ronk informed me after we had become friends. Accustomed to his gruff manner and bearing, I knew that he hated most people, but not that I'd been one of them. "You were always so, soooo . . ." Searching for the word, he waved his hands and at length growled, "*Nice!*"

No matter, the upgrade was a relief as Dave's and Terri's opinions were important to me. Unapologetic Trotskyites, the daunting pair were too smart and way too much fun for ideological differences to come between us. We agreed on fundamentals, like holding capitalism in deep contempt, scorning the ruling class and their lackeys, and championing the workers. One afternoon, upon spotting two lesbians walking down the street, Dave remarked, "I feel like an unemployed worker looking at a closed factory." I chuckled uneasily. My mixed feelings of attraction and repulsion regarding lesbians wasn't anything I wanted to think about.

It's unlikely that I revealed my Party membership either, but during more than one heated political exchange I was branded a "Stalinist." Together, we fumed at Kennedy for playing with everyone's lives during the October Missile Crisis. "Those bastards!" we said about the Bay of Pigs invasion. With a greedy thug of a neighbor only ninety miles from their shores, Castro and the Cuban people were having a hard time trying to run their own country.

The Hoods

MY LIFE QUICKLY became populated with characters of all sorts, not the least of whom were my employers at The Gaslight. Family legend had Clarence making and losing a million dollars three times over. From Mississippi he had relocated his family to South Carolina, then Northern Florida, where at one time he had owned lumber mills and logged the forests. The last time Clarence—known to all as "Papa"—went broke, he accepted the offer from his son-in-law to forsake Central Florida and run the club.

In addition to a colorful past, Papa had a slow, deliberate drawl, a sharp beak, potbelly, and a taste for Kentucky Tavern bourbon. Shoulders hunched, he'd peer with slitted eyes over he rim of his newspaper to pass judgment. When sober, Papa was focused and humorous, but otherwise cranky, testing with calculated questions and pointed remarks. Decades earlier in Mississippi, he had courted and wed the beautiful, smart Janie Linfield Jones. Mama's sharp tongue and clever asides delighted me, and I savored her references to Papa as "old goat," in frustration mixed with fondness. A wonderful cook and gifted, self-taught painter, Mama didn't miss much. Between sets one night, Buffy Sainte-Marie leaned over the front desk in a low-cut blouse. After she left, Mama quipped, "It's a good thing there wasn't a hungry baby on the other side of this counter."

Lynn, the oldest Hood daughter, had been born weighing eleven pounds and was presented to Mama, who took one look and waved nurse and baby aside declaring, "This is *not* my baby . . . this baby is at least three months old." A beauty like her mother, Lynn moved with feline grace, attracting male gazes wherever she went. More than forty years later it's still true. A cool demeanor belied warmth and kindness, and from disparate worlds, our lifelong friendship began.

One morning, when Sam was an older teen sleeping off a big night, Mama ran into his bedroom and shook him awake. "I know what's wrong with you," she declared to her hungover son. "You're Chinese . . . it says in the paper that every fourth baby born in the world is Chinese, and you're my fourth," and from then on, every so often she would refer to him as "my Chinese baby."

A husky nineteen-year-old with a football scholarship to Florida State, Sam helped Papa set up the Gaslight operation, then left to go back to school. When he returned to The Gaslight, he lit up the basement's natural gloom with vitality and lighthearted banter. Everyone seemed to like Sam, but despite his robust energy and playfulness, I thought he was stuck up. It took weeks for him to notice me and longer before we greeted each other with more than a nod.

Unprepared as they were for the hip Village folk life, Sam, Papa, and later, Mama made a place for themselves, winning everyone over, young folkie and old Italian alike. Barely out of their forties and totally out of their element, the older Hoods may have been new in town, but deep roots in the genteel Southern culture of proper etiquette and colorful euphemism charmed Village elders, while young people responded to the couple's parental eminence.

After resisting temptation through four children, the Hood parents named their fifth Robin. The youngest Hood, a chipper, wide-eyed teenager resembling the first bird of spring far more than she did her swashbuckling namesake, traveled from school in Florida during holidays to help out at The Gaslight.

A veteran of Mississippi politics, Papa was well acquainted with graft and corruption, and he quickly adjusted to the cost of doing business in the Greenwich Village of 1962. One summer evening, a large man ducked his head under the entrance and walked in. He was from "Empire Protection" and had come for his monthly fee. Robin piped up, "What are you protecting us from?" and Sam stomped on her foot, muttering, "Pay him!" from the side of his mouth.

In addition to payments to the mob, the Hoods had been left with the residue of John Mitchell's adversarial relationship with the city health and fire departments. An inspector would arrive and Papa would ask, "What brand of cigar do you smoke?" A "big" cigar cost one hundred dollars, and a "medium" cost fifty. Either was preferable to "none," meaning a real inspection and a big fine, since there was no way that kitchen would pass. Most nights, city officials showed up to write out violations, and most mornings, Papa trudged down to the city courthouse, rain or shine, for his temporary waiver.

On Thanksgiving, the Hoods opened the club, and volunteer staff fed neighborhood strays, street people, and kids away from home with nowhere else to go. Cooking with the women was fun and the donated food was delicious, with me dishing out cranberry sauce between Mama and Lynn while hilarious comments flew back and forth between them.

Papa booked Mississippi John Hurt at The Gaslight and the two hit it off right away, discovering that beyond having been raised in the same town, they had, as children, witnessed the same lynching. When Mississippi John came to town, as he often did, he and Papa would embrace fondly. When Mama was in Florida, as she often was, Mississippi John and Papa slept in the same bed.

Sam & The Gaslight Regulars

THROUGH MY WORK on the folk circuit and my relationship with Sam which developed later, I enjoyed a special entree into folk society. When he returned from Florida to help Papa run the Gaslight, Sam was welcomed back by the regulars. Dylan took him to a shoe store, advising Sam that if he wanted to be cool he should buy the extremely hip, pull-on brown desert boots with elastic at the ankles, a style Sam wore for years afterward.

Ken, the Gaslight host, was a young actor whose major film credit was a part in *The Wild Women of Wongo*. Handsome and dark with a wicked sense of humor, he was ready to do or say almost anything for a laugh. He and Sam teamed up for gags, like thumb-tacking a box of Marlboros, which they both smoked, to the front counter.

Len Chandler took Sam under his super-hip wing. About as manic a fast-thinking, fast-talking being as I'd ever met, Len knew what was happen'n, how, when, where, and why. More often than not, he would turn up with a new song, ranging from the serious "Turn Around, Miss Liberty," and "Keep on Keepin' On," to a children's song about putting beans in your ears. His intensity never slackened, and his company never failed to stimulate. His wife, Nancy, had a loom in their living room and wove beautifully.

Len, like Phil Ochs, another of Sam's intimates and composer of many activist anthems such as "I Ain't Marchin' Anymore," hailed from Ohio. But unlike Phil who had studied journalism, Len's major was music and he'd earned a masters degree from Columbia University. Smooth, streetwise, and black, Len got a huge kick from mentoring a white Southern kid, especially a bright one with an open mind and healthy sense of humor. He introduced Sam to hip terminology, played head games with him, coached him on being cool, and might have been the one to introduce Sam to marijuana. It didn't take long for the two to become close friends.

One evening they strolled down MacDougal Street and Jimmy, the beat cop, walked toward them. Everyone liked the smiling young Irishman, who greeted the pair with "How are you?" Sam, a big smile on his face, replied "Hi" and continued on. The moment Jimmy was out of range, Len leaned into Sam and whispered frantically, "Oh my God, Sam! Do you know what just *hap*-pened? Jimmy asked how you *were*, and you said, 'Hi!' I can't be-*lieve* you actually said that, *told* him you were *high*!" Spinning on his heel, Sam made to sprint back and explain that he only meant "hello," but Len grabbed his arm and held him back. "*Dig* yourself!" he said, breaking into giggles, and they both cracked up.

Months later, on our first actual date, Sam took me to Donnie's Bar, where, shy and silent, we sat at a table writing cryptic, suggestive notes on beverage napkins we pushed back and forth across the table. His voice was deeply resonant; his hands, strong and classically formed. We smiled into each other's eyes and lit up the air around us.

Not long after coming to the Village, Sam had wandered into this very Bleecker Street bar, he related, and was enjoying a nightcap when he saw a man hit a woman. The sight triggered Sam's gallantry. He sprang up, punched the man in the face, and knocked him down. When the dust settled, Sam learned that the place was a favorite of the "boys" and that he had slugged a local hitman. Luckily, the stunned fellow apologized to the woman and bought Sam a drink. "From now on," he said to the bartender, "whenever our hero comes in, put his drink on my tab!"

"I had no idea who that guy was," Sam laughed, and beneath the fetching chivalry I recognized a determined defender of justice. Minutes later I was surprised to find us arguing about the morality of dropping the second atomic bomb on Nagasaki. As far as I was concerned, it was wrong to drop the first one, let alone the second. But like his father, Sam remained loyal to Harry S Truman, insisting that the decision had been necessary to save American lives. That such an intelligent person could actually believe such a thing puzzled me. Later Sam claimed to have been playing devil's advocate, a game his father also enjoyed. They both teased, but when Sam needled or flirted, clear signs of a sweet nature and heroic soul glimmered beneath the self-assurance.

Undereducated but a quick study, he was bound to overcome his political deficits with an analytical mind that worked rapid-fire, like Papa's. But the father's unforgiving steel was tempered in the son's generous nature, and getting to know him, I found myself increasingly drawn to this attractive country boy, three years my junior, who made me laugh. By the time Vietnam began creeping onto front-page headlines, Sam—like everyone else with a brain and heart—opposed the U.S. military policy, its origins in the administration of none other than Truman himself.

Mom and Pop came to see me on the bill with Tom Paxton and Bill Cosby, who were unknown to them. They'd heard my stories about Bill and knew that I thought he was funny. After the show Sam and I walked them up the steps and we lingered in front of The Kettle. The night was balmy and I was filled with goodwill. Mom looked anxious to get home. "What did you think?" I asked. Tom was very good, "But that Cosby!" Pop shook his head. "He doesn't have what it takes. He'll never make it." Years later, Pop and I laughed over his prediction.

One night, Bill flew into The Gaslight raving about a comic he had just seen at the Apollo Theater in Harlem. He couldn't believe this guy, Flip Wilson, and for the next few weeks, Bill praised Flip in his sets and even repeated some of his jokes. When Flip started coming down to the Village he won many friends and fans. Gentle, kind, and always amusing, he, like all good comics, was also smart. The more I got to know him, the more I valued his friendship and enjoyed his buoyant company. In all the time I knew him, I never saw Flip become cranky with anyone, particularly his fans. After his great TV success, he gave Sam and me a ride from D.C. to New York in his limo. As we were about to pull away from the curb, some preteens spotted him and ran up for his autograph. He had the driver stop and got out to chat with them for a few minutes. "Gotta take care of the young ones so they'll support me in my old age," he explained when he'd climbed back in. "I want my fans for a lifetime!"

Known and admired for his fervent "protest songs," the talented, tormented Phil Ochs demanded attention and hit it off with Sam, who admired Phil's creativity and nimble mind. Tom Paxton first journeyed to the Village from

Oklahoma, and he seemed so straight and all-American that everyone thought he was an agent until a couple of all-night drinking sessions with the guys convinced them otherwise. Tom treated me kindly, like an amiable big brother would, and I was fond of him and his wonderfully singable songs full of wit and social consciousness. Like Len and Phil, he turned them out with dazzling regularity, charming audiences with a down-home personality and corny humor. Tom's classics like "Bottle of Wine," "Ramblin' Boy," and "Can't Help But Wonder Where I'm Bound,"were first heard on the Gaslight stage. In a widely supported boycott, he joined many who refused invitations from ABC-TV's *Hootenanny* because Pete Seeger had been blacklisted.

Jo Mapes was a frequent and popular guest on *Hootenanny*, the second most popular TV show in 1963. Previously, she and Pete had met in Los Angeles at a folk jam session. Jo never learned why she'd become known as a "people's singer from San Francisco" or why she was invited—along with Ronnie Gilbert, Will Geer, and other mostly West Coast folkies—to an original "hootenanny" at Butch and Bessie Lomax Hawse's home. Jo sat at Pete's feet, gazing up at him as he sang some songs. Then he looked down and in his characteristic way, said, "Why don't you do one?" She froze, but managed to get through a tune and they became friends.

Asked to appear on the controversial show, she wrote to Pete to explain that she wanted to support him, but was a poor single mom raising young children. "Do it!" Pete wrote back. "The more of us who get on the networks, the better!" But, with fewer responsibilities and greater resources, Bob Dylan, Joan Baez, Barbara Dane, Jack Elliott, The Kingston Trio, and The Greenbriar Boys, like Paxton, stayed off the show.

Community Life

AS SAM'S GIRLFRIEND, the privilege of housekeeping during his select afterhours Gaslight poker sessions fell to me. Quite a bit of money passed across the big round table, which I was happy to clear and supply with fresh beer and clean ashtrays. It was fun watching the game from the perimeter. "Chicks" did not participate in the virile amusement, and sitting in on the high-stakes Gaslight game was unthinkable.

Nor were we invited upstairs to the room that had been wired from the Gaslight stage where the boys hung out, played poker, and where Dylan lived for a while. At the downstairs games, Sam, Ken, Paxton, Van Ronk, Peter LaFarge, Flip, Elmer, and assorted guys drank, smoked, and joked their way through dealers' choice of five- or seven-card draw and stud until the sky lightened. Len Chandler didn't play cards, but occasionally came by to stand around and play the guitar, improvise lyrics, and kibbitz. But mostly I remember periods of dead silence alternating between sharp laughter and low groans. A skilled player, Sam often won, swelling his image along with the thick roll of bills in his pocket. Vince Martin reported seeing him tear a deck of cards in half when he lost a big hand. "He was a strong guy!"

When Dylan showed up, it didn't take long before he was shifting restlessly in his seat, his foot kicking, his attention fixed on cards he continually rearranged. They didn't let him play too often due to the length of his deliberations and the crazy bets he liked to make, such as the number of times a Hummingbird flaps its wings between Los Angeles and Indonesia, or the speed of thought. Phil Ochs sometimes showed up, anxious beneath a bouncy exterior, too manic (or depressed) to sit in very often. Although tightly wound, Elmer held his own. Ken got somber and usually lost, whereas Tom played concentrated poker and often went home a winner. After Sam and I married and moved to Miami, Tom wrote "The Name of the Game Was Stud," a mock-cowboy ballad memorializing those games and starring my husband. Dylan idolized Sam as a shrewd Mississippi gambler and incorporated a bit of Sam's style into the folk-hero mix he was cooking up for himself.

No community escapes conflict, but I felt that those of us in the folk scene generally operated with cooperative, supportive values. Thanks to Pete Seeger and the progressive folk music of the 1940s and '50s, folk music had a social conscience, and to one degree or another, most folk musicians favored the working class over the ruling class, supported unions, integration, and peace, and shared a general sense of progressive ideals. The biggest controversy was "ethnic" versus "commercial," which I considered a phony, overblown division. Some singers stuck to tradition while others went for a popular sound, and there was room for both approaches, provided they put on a good show. Sometimes I spouted off and came on pretty strong, and from time to time Sam and Ken referred to me as "Big Al from Philly." That was fine with me, but rarely did I connect with my hometown or my comrades in the Party, both now totally supplanted by my new identity in my new world.

If so many of my peers didn't share my opinion, I would suspect myself of romanticizing those few brief years that seemed to go on forever, when, if you craved lo mein or sweet and sour ribs at one A.M., you could always share a cab down to Mott Street where restaurants like Hong Fat and Sam Wo stayed open all night.

Sometimes, when Jim and Jean Glover were between tours, Sam, Ken, and I would visit them in their Leroy Street apartment. If Flip was around he'd join us to watch late-night movies on their small TV and turn the sound off so that he and Ken could improvise hilarious dialogue, leaving us doubled up and weak, pounding the floor.

My friends were good company for an early morning trip to Chinatown after the last show, or a cab to Harlem and Welles Restaurant for the chicken and waffles Sam especially loved. Every so often we'd take in the show at an all-night Forty-second Street theater playing double features of second-run and B movies, where bums slept in the seats and escaped the weather. Keeping our distance from unsavory characters wasn't difficult in the cavernous, virtually empty old theater. Early one morning we were sitting up front in the orchestra when, from the balcony, we heard an outraged male voice bellow, "*Sorry?* You *piss* on my *wife*, and you're *sorry?*" a line appearing in our conversation for years to come.

Don't Think Twice

WHEN I ARRIVED in New York in the summer of 1962, Bob Zimmerman had already landed there, changed his name to Dylan, and met his idol, Woody Guthrie, during Woody's last months on earth. Bob wrote constantly and tried out his new songs on every Village stage that would have him. Bobby's joking and spontaneity were well known and unpredictable, and people were starting to pay close attention to the shy, nervous boy with the sly, cutting humor and quirky songs.

Dylan's ticks and jerky movements mimicked Woody's symptoms of advanced Huntington's chorea. Along with his nervous disorder, Guthrie's authentic, straight-talking, country style found a new host in young Bob Zimmerman, who was then constructing his waif-hobo-outlaw-poet-loner persona. I first saw Dylan at Gerde's, then bought the self-titled, just-released *Bob Dylan*. I lit candles and played the album over and over, pondering this raw kid my own age. Although I was warned that his singing was terrible, he won me over. His covers and original songs were unusual, to be sure, and while some may have considered the raspy, half-talking style sloppy, he hit every note squarely and sang with authentic feeling, at times even sweetly. After the first playing of Dylan's record, I was impressed, and after the third, hooked. His insistent, straightforward harmonica captured me, but his ragged "Pretty Peggy-O" took some getting used to before I was able to appreciate the wit and originality of his charge through the old chestnut. His versions of "Fixin' to Die" and "See That My Grave Is Kept Clean" cleaved to the traditional tunes I had listened to repeatedly on my Bukka White album. Peter, Paul, and Mary's recording of Dylan's *"Blowin' in the Wind"* was shooting up the charts, and it was plain to see that, as he often said himself, "Bob Dylan is gonna be really, really BIG!"

Months before Robert Shelton wrote his pivotal *New York Times* rave, Bobby practically lived with Terri Thal and Dave Van Ronk and spent many a night on their couch. The couple encouraged his work, put up with his quirky moods, and generally looked after him. Terri managed his career before Albert took over. Dylan's first album hadn't sold well, but his second, *Freewheelin'*, featured more of his own songs and it caught on. His raw, poignant rendition of "Corrina, Corrina" crushed my heart while "Honey, Just Allow Me One More Chance" made me laugh. I adored the cover picture of him and Suze in the Village, walking close together, huddling against the cold winter air.

Bobby cycled in and out of the after-hours crowd. In a game stretching over months, he and I took turns treating each other to lox and eggs at The Bagel, teasing each other about whose turn it was to buy.

After *Freewheelin'*, Bob got himself a small upstairs flat just off Sixth Avenue, where he'd invite me over to hear Robert Johnson and Big Joe Williams records. "Listen to that, man, listen to that," he'd mumble, eyes half closed, a cigarette held between graceful fingers, his foot swinging. "The greatest singer that ever lived."

Dylan's limbs were in constant motion and his mind never still beneath the wild, wondrous hairdo. "It opens up the head," he explained to me in his conversational chant, ". . . lets in air around the brain . . . lets ideas breathe." In the days when all men cut their hair short, Bobby's big afro was extraordinary.

One night Pop visited The Gaslight, a group of us went to The Limelight after the show. He sat across the table from young Bob, decked out in a blousey, black, long-sleeved shirt with white polka dots. Pop quietly took in the scene. My folks were great fans of Dylan's work, and I couldn't wait to hear what my father thought about sitting with him in person. Later, the group lingered on the street and Pop took me aside. In a low voice he asked, "That one with the polka dots, who *is* she?" I laughed. "That's not a *she*, that's Bob Dylan!" Pop sucked in a breath and shook his head, saying, "Oh, boy!"

On another night, Dylan swung by The Gaslight to try out a song he had just written and launched into "A Hard Rain." Sitting in the front booth on this slow weeknight, Van Ronk and I listened to the apocalyptic prophecy in doleful

waltz-time. "I saw guns and sharp swords in the hands of young children. . . ."
The hairs on the back of my neck stood at attention. *That's right*, I thought, *that's going to happen!* One more timeless classic from the mouth of the visionary.

Dave leaned over. "Gifted little bastard, isn't he?"

A great thing about Dylan was that you never knew what he would do or say.
Leaping light years ahead of us mortals, Bob's line of thought could be tricky
to follow. On certain occasions, with the boyish charm turned on and the grin
peering up from under the corduroy seaman's cap, he was irresistible. Dylan's
genius, however, didn't always extend to the social skills that he switched on
and off. Once during the wee hours, a few of us were sitting around a table in
a coffee shop off West Broadway when we noticed a teenaged girl, obviously a
fan, heading toward our table. Dylan took notice and perked up. Conversation
stopped. "Excuse me," she said under her breath. "I'm looking for Dave Van
Ronk." Dylan cocked his head to one side, eyes squinting against the smoke
curling off the cigarette on his lower lip. His eyes, more hard than playful, swept
over her. "Why aren't you looking for me? Do you know who I am?"

She laughed nervously. "I just wanted Dave Van Ronk's autograph."

"My name is Bob Dylan, and you should want *my* autograph!" Foot going,
he leaned back in his chair and looked away. An awkward moment of silence followed, during which, shocked and embarrassed at this unfamiliar side of my friend
Bobby, no one spoke. The eyes of the mortified girl searched for help, and from
the head of the table, Dave motioned her over and identified himself. "Don't mind
him," he said and signed her paper, shooting a cautionary sideways glance at Bob,
slumped next to me. The girl left and silence reigned until someone broke it with,
"Jeez, Bobby, what's your problem, man . . . she just wanted Dave's autograph."
"Yeah man, dig yourself," from another voice, a reproach Bobby sometimes used.
People put up with Dylan's rudeness and made allowances in deference to his brilliance. Yet, more often, he showed a playful, silly side.

One dark, winter evening snow had buried parked cars on streets now
magically quiet with few pedestrians and fewer vehicles moving about. At the
corner of MacDougal and Third, I ran into Bob and Suze coming toward me,
snuggled together, clearly in love, looking exactly like the cover of *Freewheelin'*.
We converged in the middle of the empty intersection. Bobby was expansive.
"We just got back from shoppin' uptown." He was being adorable. "We got
Suze a coat, some dresses, six pair of shoes, ten scarves . . . uh . . . a mink stole
. . . uh . . . ," Bob drawled away, adding to the fanciful list in flattened, prolonged vowels, " a diamond tiara . . . a white Buick convertible . . . an island in

the Caribbean," and so on. "And I got a comb for me," he laughed. Suze and I smiled patient smiles and rolled our eyes. "Yep, a f i-i-i-ne comb!"

Suze kept Bob's feet on the ground, but counterpressures from his accelerating career eventually split them up. On the night he said he wrote it, Bob sang his brand-new "Boots of Spanish Leather," on the Gaslight stage, in my opinion a truly deep and nuanced love song. Knowing that he had written it for Suze, who had recently departed for the Continent, I sympathized with them both. It was a heartbreaker as only Dylan could write and sing them.

Booked for a concert in Philadelphia, Bob told me he was nervous about going alone to an unfamiliar city, so I volunteered to be his guide. Once there, the most convenient spot I could think of where Dylan could rest undisturbed before show time was the Center City apartment belonging to Pop's ex-boss and the father of the twins. He hadn't recognized Dylan's name when I arranged the brief stopover, so I took him aside, saying, "Remember this because someday soon, Bob Dylan is gonna be a *big* star!" Our host aside, Dylan's legend had, by then, escaped few in the know. Safely in my charge, Bob allowed me to escort him to the venue, and afterward to an exclusive jam session where I shared him with a select group of Philly folkies. As he sat, unusually relaxed, the center of attention in someone's living room, I studied the classic profile sharply etched in shadow, and marveled at the breathtaking beauty in the jagged contours of his face. Suddenly it dawned on me that he looked exactly like myfriend Louise.

On another evening, in between sets, I was lounging at the top of the Gaslight steps when Bob rushed up and grabbed my arm. "C'mere," he whispered, and led me down the stairs into the darkness. During that period, Bobby informed me more than once that I was his "favorite female singer," a title that I believed I held for the better part of two years, unaware of other singers he buttered up to sing his songs. But he came across as perfectly authentic and so offbeat in his own universe that he may have been sincere. It was flattering, whatever his motives.

Sliding into a chair at the round table by the back curtain, he said, "Here, listen. I just wrote this song and I want you to sing it. It's perfect for you!" He handed me a book of matches, and one at a time, I held a small flame over a spiral notepad while he scribbled down the words to "Don't Think Twice, It's All Right." Tearing them out, he handed me four pieces of paper guaranteed to be worth a fortune. "You gotta sing it, it's perfect." I checked to make sure he had signed his name, and there it was, scrawled on the last page, "Bob Dylan—Flyin' by, shot out / Passin' thru, Watch out!" Someday it would be worth money but

I'd never sell it. (Unfortunately, it was lost along with most of my possessions in a flood in 1980.) I did sing it, accompanied by my version of his guitar arrangement. But as well written as they were, the lyrics didn't sit quite right and I was uncomfortable with the passive-aggressive tone beneath the irony. Van Ronk was fond of repeating, "I can tell a lie, but I can't sing one," and the more I sang the tune, the more I knew it wasn't right for me. An interview of the time had me saying, "I sing songs I like," with my variation of Dave's epigram, "I won't sing a song unless I live it a little bit."

When I told him about my decision to pass on *Don't Think Twice*, Bob was not pleased. In subsequent weeks when he stepped onto the Gaslight stage, his intro went something like, "It's a hard song to sing. I can sing it sometimes, but I ain't that good yet." He'd complain crossly, "'Course, *some* singers don't want to *sing* this song. *Some* singers say it ain't *right* for them," and so on.

Of course, I loved Dylan's songs, and at one time or another, many of them made their way onto my set lists. Thirty years later I told this story to my sensible daughter and independent Dylan fan, Adrian, who advised me to put "Don't Think Twice" back into my show, which I did.

Months after we met, Bob traveled to London where the folk crowd at Cecil Sharp House rejected and dismissed him. Nevertheless, he absorbed centuries of solid tradition, and like his mentor, Woody—who bragged about stealing tunes and employed Leadbelly's "Good Night Irene" many times—Dylan listened carefully, and from good tunes, fashioned even stronger ones. I was not alone in recognizing the melody of "Nottamun Town" in Dylan's "Masters of War," "Patriot Game" in "With God on Our Side," or "Scarborough Fair" in "Girl from the North Country."

I hadn't seen him for several months when he appeared with Joan Baez in The Kettle of Fish. He motioned me over to their table and introduced us, but she didn't seem impressed and barely raised her eyes. That was when she and Bob began touring and he stepped completely out of my world into the universe of advanced stardom where our paths were unlikely to cross. Naturally, she performed and recorded "Don't Think Twice." Clearly, my "favorite female singer" title had been passed on.

Chick Singers

NO ONE, INCLUDING me, ever questioned the conventional wisdom of the time that said, "two chick singers back-to-back is bad programming." I heard and spoke that exact phrase many times myself to justify whole evenings of nothing but Jack Elliot/Bob Dylan-wannabes-with-guitars. We played the same clubs but not at the same time.

Jo Mapes was an inspiration from the moment I heard her in 1962 from a side booth at The Second Fret. She walked on stage, a classy blonde, and perched on a high stool. All I knew about her was that she had just come East with friend and sister Californian Odetta and was causing a stir. Instantly banishing any expectation of rivalry I'd carried with me, Jo's tasteful arrangements and sleek, jazzy guitar absorbed my complete attention as did her casually clever banter between tunes. Her treatments of "San Francisco Bay Blues" and an over-the-top version of "The Race Is On," stretching the country hit to the extreme of parody blew me away. And she could sing "Take Me Out to the Ball Game" back-phrasing one beat behind the melody.

The show ended and I climbed the stairs to the second-floor dressing room feeling strangely awkward and insecure. Upstairs I was greeted by a receptive, friendly Jo, just a few years older than I. She put me entirely at ease, and thus began our lifelong friendship. She had worked with many greats, including the groundbreaking Lenny Bruce, a stand-up genius who was sickened and hounded to death by U.S. government officials.

The songs Jo wrote—contemporary reflections about her life on the road, missing her kids, and aging—were grounded in a strong female point of view which resonated beneath consciousness. I had never heard any song content like her self-reflective, thoughtful lyrics. They were highly personal and forthright in an entirely new way, at least to me, and later, I performed "Come on In," a song of hers welcoming back an old lover. Jo's disarming, offbeat phrasing in "The Young Girl's Lament," about a girl suffering from gonorrhea and her unsentimental treatment, brought the tragedy to life. Jo's vivid picture of a dying young woman on the street of an old Western town gripped my heart each time she sang it. In due course, and with her blessing, I arranged a version to add to my song list.

Carolyn Hester worked at The Gaslight and Gerde's and over time we became friends. Carolyn's big smile and blue eyes dazzled while the fetchingly soft Texas twang charmed. Gifted and popular, she could hit the highest note on the East Coast, and listening to Carolyn's pleasing soprano trill made me a believer. In California, she had married and divorced Richard Fariña, who cheated on her and then married Joan Baez's beautiful sister Mimi.

Bob Dylan's recording career was set in motion when Carolyn invited him to lay down a harmonica track on her first album. Her producer, John Hammond, the larger-than-life senior Columbia producer, walked in and heard Bob play. Known for recognizing great talent, John signed the young harmonica player, just as, in the past, he had signed Billie Holiday, Bessie Smith, Duke Ellington, and Count Basie, and in the future would sign Aretha Franklin and Bruce Springsteen. Carolyn's crystal voice, magnetic beauty, and hard work earned the tiny blonde universal high regard, and a sharp mind combined with generous ways made her a pleasure to hang out with. Our apartments were within blocks of each other, and when we were both in town we'd meet for breakfast and a matinee.

Hailing from different parts of the country, Jim & Jean (Jim Glover and Jean Ray) brought their eclectic repertoire; clear, strong arrangements; and rich harmonies to the Gaslight stage. Jim, a classically handsome, solid musician and guitar player, had introduced the pre-eminent topical songwriter Phil Ochs to politics when they were college roommates in Ohio. A good-natured fellow, Jim seemed to live in perpetual wonder. Luckily, Jean—complete with turned-up nose and straight, long, shiny hair—had her feet on the ground. In addition to wholesome good looks and a knock-out voice reminiscent of Ronnie Gilbert of The Weavers, Jean radiated California sunshine and a sweet, open spirit. We admired each other's work and became close, but as it happened with other performers, our schedules rarely brought us together for long.

With Herb's other female client, Buffy Sainte-Marie, I admit to occasional feelings of competition, yet I admired her shows and looked forward to running into her. Despite the calm presence she summoned for personal chats, her big energy could fill a room. I remember a time in Philly when Buffy was coming through after a tour, I was on my way to Detroit, and we sat on the floor trading gossip and stories of the road. Being with Buffy was electric, like being next to a perpetual generator. It was hard to resist the bright smile, and it was hard to deny the natural talent of my passionate colleague. Strong performances and songs like "Codeine" and "Universal Soldier" were attracting well-deserved attention, and I was genuinely happy for her successes. Her attitude toward me was friendly and warm, her talent was unique, and she wrote about important issues in people's lives. When in the city she'd often sleep in Herb's uptown office, sometimes with her on-again-off-again boyfriend, songwriter Patrick Sky. I observed their tortured relationship and tried to be a friend to each while keeping a distance from the drama when it surfaced.

Singers Charlotte Daniels, Judy Mayhan, Lynn Gold, Lisa Kindred, Koko Taylor, Judy Henske, Janis Ian, Judy Roderick, Norma Tanega, and the sisters

Carly and Lucy Simon passed through the Village from time to time, but on the circuit, one "chick" per show was the limit.

In certain places and genres that's still true, but in the mid-1960s, the exceptional successes of Joni Mitchell, Emmylou Harris, Linda Ronstadt, and Bonnie Raitt only proved the undisputed rule that male singers were the standard. Yet, somewhere in this exclusive world, I found my niche and held it. Before the phrase "world music" had been coined, my international repertoire, which included songs in languages from a variety of cultures, helped me carve a place within the slim margins of working female folksingers.

Polishing the Act

HERB, IN CHARGE for 20 percent of my gross, was overseeing my career. He had posters printed headlining "Miss Alix Dobkin." With a name like mine, "Miss" was requisite. "Songs of . . ." was followed by a list of the fourteen countries represented by songs in my show.

Immediately upon graduation, I'd contacted Murray Weiss, a fine photographer and Nancy's former instructor at the Museum School. From the contact sheets of a single outdoor session in Philadelphia's Fairmont Park, Herb and I selected two photos that we used for years. One horizontal worm's-eye shot has me singing and playing against a background of flowering trees. My dark hair falls in loosely gathered waves over my shoulder, while the guitar angle and my easy stance suggest the youthful confidence and vigor of spring itself. In the vertical shot Herb selected for my poster, I lean against a tree, starry-eyed, my new Guild F-30 cradled in my arms.

Months after I had moved to New York, Herb decided that we needed a more glamorous set of photos to balance out the innocent, folky ones. "For contrast," he explained and set up a date with a New York photographer. Coyly posed on seamless white paper, wearing a white shirt with three buttons open—provocative for then—with my hair piled artfully on top of my head and loose strands hanging casually at the back, we attempted to project the oxymoronic image of a sexy but urbane folkie.

The first series had been unposed, without cosmetics, and they looked vital and animated compared with the stiff, self-conscious studio takes. Yet I rarely went without daily makeup, and piled it on even more at night. It didn't occur to me to go on stage without it, and besides, Elmer wouldn't have had it any other way. Showbiz glamour didn't come cheap. Many dollars, not to mention hours, were devoted to cosmetics. For the better part of an hour, six nights a week, I'd eyeball my bathroom mirror and apply foundation, eye shadow, eye liner, mascara, blush, lip liner, and lipstick, and squeeze a final curl into my eyelashes with the fascinating, chilling instrument designed for that purpose. I bought tubes of Erase to lighten the dark shadows under my eyes, and little brushes to outline the fullness of my lips. Elmer shared his expert advice and tips. The allure of makeup lasted a couple of years before becoming deeply tiresome.

No priority overruled career development. For graduation I had been given the book *Acting: The First Six Lessons*, and during those first months in New York, I studied the text and followed Richard Boleslavsky's exercises designed to help tell a convincing story.

Most important however, was Elmer's coaching. We held our sessions at Herb's office on East Fifty-fourth Street where I learned tricks of the trade, like how to open big, close big, vary the pace, and keep the program moving. Cuttingly sarcastic with a languid world-weariness that I loved, Elmer stood me in front of a mirror and showed me how to stand, how to move, how to hold my head and where to look. He made up my early set lists, taught me to sing on the vowel, and to relate to an audience through the brightest of bright lights. In due course I learned how to present my public self, project an image, and generally keep an audience interested.

After a session we'd adjourn to a booth at the Waverly Restaurant down on Sixth to smoke and sip coffee for hours. Guided by Elmer's notes, we'd start by analyzing my last performance and finish with my assignments. Then, we'd catalog our latest likes and dislikes, review who was interested in, sleeping with, or cheating on whom, and crack wise about whose act was any good and whose wasn't.

Daylight hours were devoted to study, guitar practice, learning new songs, and working out potent arrangements. I sampled one singing lesson from an earnest European diva in a charming West Village town house, and two from an old queen wearing an ascot who instructed me in proper singing technique at the notorious Ansonia Hotel uptown. It was hard to tell if I was doing it "right" or not. Each teacher claimed exclusive knowledge of correct vocal production, none of which made any difference in my singing, so I gave them all a pass.

The first time I heard my voice was on a tape of a radio interview. I listened in horror to the dreary, unrecognizable drone pronouncing the same words I remembered speaking earlier. My voice seemed so resonant, so much more expressive, and far more colorful to my inner ear than did the flat monotone issuing from a clunky tape machine. Apart from all that, how often did I signal uncertainty with, "and–uhhh . . ." between phrases, and how many "ya know"s did I let drop in a sentence? I lost count. There was so much to improve on. My singing voice, thin and cursory, was only slightly more bearable than my speaking voice, but following Elmer's guidance, I forced myself through grueling reviews of performance tapes, a critical yet disagreeable task necessary to correct subtle lapses that audiences barely sensed but which blazed like neon to Elmer and me.

With the exception of the Balkan and Eastern European pieces with their different, oddly comfortable modes and time signatures, I lacked the pipes and the vocal ease of Joan Baez, Judy Collins, or Carolyn Hester. Hyperalert to maintaining pitch, I had to struggle for my voice and only rarely could relax and sing out wholly unrestrained. Although I had found my particular guitar sound, my playing qualified as little more than simple accompaniment. With limited natural ability, my career would rest on other elements.

The great Ella Fitzgerald made singing sound so easy that her brilliance had always been a given I took for granted. Instead, my role models were Dinah Washington, Etta James, Pearl Bailey, and my top three: Anita O'Day, Billie Holiday, and Carmen McRae. During repeated listenings I compared their individual treatments of the same jazz standards. When and how did they stray from the melody, take breaths, cut a word short or prolong it? Where and how did they place emphasis, and what was the emotional impact of their phrasing? How did Anita come up with that imaginative wit, or Carmen exploit a phrase to yield maximum irony, or Billie maximum despair? But mostly I studied how they kept it interesting, and each approach revealed a universe of possibility.

Far more men got away with it, but only a precious few notable female singers lacked conventionally "pretty" voices, proving that a vocal deficit could be offset by creativity and focused delivery. It took interesting material laced with challenges and metaphors calculated to heighten interest. "You've gotta have a point of view about a song. Direct identification. Or be a storyteller. Or a sympathetic onlooker," I said in an interview, adding, "You've got to establish some sort of intimacy with a song. Otherwise you can't communicate. You're a machine."

Along with the unwritten law of "no-two-chick-singers-back-to-back" was the universal prohibition of a female showing both strength and independence on stage. Down to the marrow of our bones, every one of us understood that a strong woman had better make it immediately clear that she was sexually available to men, and it was years before I realized that "the important people" in the audience were the men. Within the limitations of that script, I was about as removed from the submissive ingénue type as it was possible to get. Playful confrontation, Mae West style, seemed the way to go, and with that persona, I charged ahead, blissfully unaware of the discomfort a forward, self-identified female can visit upon some men. On the contrary, I believed that a super-heterosexual luster on stage would be the perfect shield, so I was shocked when Irwin Silber called me a "castrator" in a 1965 review for *Sing Out!* In a subsequent issue, Irwin apologized for insulting me and Dave Van Ronk, whom he'd also blasted in a review of the same Town Hall concert. At least I was in good company.

My Tyler fencing and dance teacher, Shelley, and his wife introduced me to a friend who'd opened a small boutique from which she sold her strikingly original clothing line. Ruth's shop, called Gussie and Becky, was located on St. Marks Place at the heart of what was destined to become the East Village. Ruth became my clothier, and to show off my figure, put together scoop-necked, thigh-high, linen cocktail dresses in a series of rich, bright colors. Matching two-inch heels underscored the sophisticated image I was going for, whether fashionable in folk circles or not. I wasn't going to look like a slob or fit the beatnik stereotype!

"People think if you're skinny you're sensitive," I declared for a July 1963 *Miami News* article. At twenty-three, my definition of "beat" was "a very young person." My vocabulary was laced with terms like "crazy," "groovy," "hip," and the like, as well as abbreviations like "three and a half" for "three hundred and fifty." But I was not a hippie! Hip slang identified me as in the know and set me apart from the squares. Or so I imagined. "I try not to get in the habit of beat talk. I try to use it when it's most inappropriate," I said. My "advice to young folksingers," or "kids," as I called them, was, "New York's the Apple. Maybe because it's got more worms in it with the toughest competition, the most so-phisticated crowd . . . if you make it in New York, honey, you got it made." The Damon Runyon touch amplified the truth.

Repertoire

THE SONGS I liked covered a wide spectrum of lesser-known, often quirky tunes in a hodge-podge covering the globe and heavily seasoned with Scot-tish and Irish along with American history and culture. From this cacophony, Elmer helped me construct programs that moved naturally towards the great-est impact. My career would be built with choice, offbeat material in a certain order, tunes like "McPherson's Lament," a stark, Scottish death-row number first heard on Ewan and Peggy's *Classic Scots Ballads*, source of many songs in my program.

From Peggy's solo Folkways album, I learned "Whistle Daughter Whistle," a tune making light of a young girl set on getting a man, the theme of an entire genre. "The Old Maid's Song," in a similar "light" vein, caricatured the despair of a woman desperate for a mate. The refrain: "Don't you let me die an old maid, but take me out of pity." All in fun, of course. But married life was no picnic either, as in "I wish I was a single girl again," the refrain from "When I Was Single," and in "The Housewife's Lament" an ironic view of an equally bleak landscape. One of Elmer and my preferred openers, a defiant "Katie Cruel," catalogs a woman's lack of options: "Oh were I was what I would be / Then would I be what I am not / Here am I where I must be / Go where would I cannot." The verses suggest a tragic, public fall from grace. To me she was heroic.

My programs were a mix of traditional material and original songs from the likes of Woody, Pete, The New Lost City Ramblers, Shel Silverstein, and Malvina Reynolds, whose "Little Boxes" and "The Vegetable Song," another send-up of conformity, had been supplied by *Sing Out!* magazine. So was "The Handsome Cabin Boy," in which an adventure-seeking English girl masquerades as a boy, takes to sea, and finds a surprising outcome.

Tommy Makem and the Clancy Brothers contributed "The Bold Tenant Farmer," "Jug of Punch," and my favorite of many versions of the romantic fantasy "Gypsy Davy." Crooning the spirited "Finnegan's Wake" with as authentic an Irish accent as I could manage, I let loose with, ". . . THUN-um an' JAY-sus d'ya think oi'm dead?!" It was Mom's favorite.

Since leaving Philadelphia I had not participated in any political action nor kept up with my old comrades. Cut loose from the Party's activism and focus, I felt politically adrift but tried to keep the faith by punctuating each set with "protest songs," as they were then called. Fortunately, Dylan was turning out good ones. Months before Peter, Paul, and Mary made a hit of it, "Blowing in the Wind," as well as "With God on Our Side," "Oxford Town," and "The Times They Are A-Changin'," together with Buffy Sainte-Marie's "Universal Soldier," appeared on my set lists.

The salty old reliable "Coplas," Pop's favorite, became an international anchor, as did "Jovanno," the haunting Macedonian love song I'd learned at Pinewoods. The third, "Eppie Morrie," was popular with my audiences but taxing to sing. Ethel, my camp counselor, taught me "Ochi Maya Daragaya," representing a fetching side of peasant Russian culture. She also introduced me to the recording *Music of Bulgaria*, a pirated French radio broadcast of Philip Koutev leading a powerful national women's folk chorus, and I was desperate for a copy.

However, despite crystal-clear instructions to buy the Nonesuch album, Pop instead came home with an A. L. Lloyd and Alan Lomax field recording on Columbia. When my fury and disappointment subsided—as it had after he'd bought the wrong *Kiss Me Kate* album—I began to appreciate the value of his gift. On one cut, a Bulgarian folk hero, Markko, is memorialized with the most powerful, flat-out vocalizing I'd ever heard. Listening to the traditional women's Balkan solo singing over and over, I tried to memorize and reproduce the sound as faithfully as I possibly could. When I sang it to Ethel, she thought a moment, then said, "I never heard that version before."

Furthering my global credentials were an Argentinean song from the Pampas, a macho French drinking song, and a Greek number I learned from a Theodore Bikel album. Like "Jovanno," the time signature was 7/8, but this was a lighthearted account of a girl who falls down a well and a boy who extorts sexual favors in exchange for her rescue. I sang "Yerakina" the way it was written, going for the cheap sex innuendo and making fun of the girl's dilemma, playing it as a slightly naughty joke.

Writing Songs

AMONG THE ALBUMS I'd hauled to New York was a Folkways edition of traditional Macedonian, Croatian, and Serbian instrumental music. Haunted by one track in particular, a heart-tugging Macedonian wedding dance sustained by a deep, liquid bass line, I drank it in, again and again. All it needed were some lyrics and a little noodling, so, by flattening every ornamentation and short-cutting through complex phrases, I simplified the melody. The first time Jo Mapes sang "Over the Banks," she restored every note and trill I'd dropped. "I couldn't help myself," she laughed. "It must be my Rah-zhin blood."

For lyrics, I searched my Scots book of ballads to find something that fit the hypnotic Macedonian melody line, which explains the odd reference to "heather" in the first verse. Barely enough time had passed to afford a comfortable distance from the emotional whirlwind of my relationship with Nancy, but by distilling memorable peaks of delight and depths of longing, and combining them with an obscure melody from halfway around the world, I fashioned my first whole song. With it, I put a period to all-consuming first love, and, I vowed, my first and last lesbian experiment.

At the end of August in 1963, I rode a bus to Washington with Fran for the great civil rights demonstration. Under the hot sun, we joined the masses of people walking together past rows of parked busses on our way to the Lincoln Memorial. Despite the temperature and inconvenient toilet situation, the day was invigorating and joyful. There were so many of us! We filled every inch of Independence Mall as far as I could see and beyond. Looking across the reflecting pool at the Washington Monument and up to Abraham Lincoln grandly seated in the distance was thrilling. This was what the best of America was all about! Beneath Lincoln's gaze, The Reverend Martin Luther King Jr. proclaimed his dream, his voice resonating over the multicolored crowd, filling everyone with solidarity and determination. The folk world was well represented. Len Chandler was there, along with Judy Collins, Joan Baez, Dylan, Odetta, Josh White, and Harry Belafonte, as well as Hollywood stars like Burt Lancaster and Charlton Heston. We were too far away to see them on the podium, and also missed Judy Garland, Shelley Winters, Paul Newman, and Marlon Brando. "Now you can tell your grandchildren you were there!" we all said.

From Waverly Place, I moved into three tiny rooms and a kitchenette on Bedford Street at the invitation of a Gaslight waitress named Karen with whom I had become friends. Considering its state, the seedy tenement should have been depressing, but that's not how I remember it. Those high times, generously seasoned with music and parties, proved to be not only exciting but also fruitful. Creature comforts were not a high priority, but practicing and studying were, and my song writing took off.

One night Tim Hardin came by with some friends. Sitting at the small table wedged under a dirty window in our middle room, he sang "If I Were a Carpenter" long before it was a huge hit. Tim's voice rasped agreeably, like a little boy's. I played and sang a tune and Tim commented that I had "girl's time." When I asked what that meant, he explained, "You're a chick, and chicks don't live in regular men's time." Putting aside my resentment of Tim's misogyny, I later bought a metronome and worked on keeping a steadier beat. However, that night I slipped back to my tiny room and lay down on the bed. The sound of Tim playing in the next room inspired "And Then Some," a blazing response loaded with double meanings and playful, edgy metaphors that were terrific fun to write:

> *You're not meetin' me where I like to be met*
> *You're not treatin' me right and I'm gettin' upset*
> *You're not shapin' up to the scene that you set*

Now, go add up your score, cover your bet,
And then some

and ended with:

You can come back when you've paid your dues
When you've learned your lines and you know your cues
When you can fill the bill, and you know the score
When you can rise to the occasion, a little bit more
And then some.

It seemed to me that anyone who could speak a sentence could write a song, and eventually I wrote several, both tender and defiant, about love and lust, men and disappointment. It wasn't as if I had any complaints about my personal sex life, because I didn't. However, the minute I figured out that my frustration with politics and inept politicians could be translated into disappointment with male sexual performance there was no stopping me. After all, it was the '60s, when the aura of newly chic, assertive, sexual women seemed to cast safe space for a woman to show other strengths.

Dylan had written, "If I Had to Do It All Over Again, I'd Do It All Over You," following the same standard ragtime progression Buffy used in "Don't Call Me Honey When Your Mama's Around (Ya' Know It's Gonna Drive Her Wild)," a ditty she wrote for Sam about Mama. The rakish good humor of both songs appealed to me and I was impatient to include one in my show but knew neither lyric. Frustration drove me to write my own rag. I lay in bed and saw my refrain staring up at me: "If you're gonna eat your crackers in bed / You're gonna have to sleep with crumbs." Three spiky verses followed, all aimed at failed masculinity. Flinging good-natured sexual challenges left and right, "Crackers" became one of my most popular numbers. Soon afterward, Jo introduced me to her old friend, the writer Shel Silverstein, who went on to write several children's books and articles for *Playboy* magazine as well as quirky songs, one of which I performed. He wanted to hear my songs, he said, and Karen was working, so he came up to the apartment and seduced me. Afterward, we sat naked in the bedclothes and I played "Crackers" while Shel listened. He particularly admired the lines, "You put me up-tight, and I'm not gonna take it / You're a bad, old habit, now just watch me shake it." I liked those lines myself.

My first major review appeared on May 18, 1963, when the *New York Times* ran a small piece by journalist Robert Shelton reviewing a Town Hall program featuring young folk singers, ". . . whose abilities exceed their recognition." Shelton led off with Van Ronk, "a sensitive singer and guitarist whose leadership in the city white-blues coterie is well-deserved." About me, he wrote, "Alix Dobkin used a basically warm, pleasant soprano to good effect on international folk songs. Her Spanish material gave her the greatest opportunity for unleashing the considerable color in her voice." An endorsement from a powerful critic boosted my morale. The "uncertain microphone technique" Shelton noted would be corrected. I worked on singing more steadily and directly into the mic.

A columnist reviewing a set at Gerde's in the *Village Voice* noted, "Six months off the Village green and she's experienced an astonishing growth." Six months later a reviewer for the *Michigan Daily* opened his review with, "Wow!" and ended with, "Don't miss her." In between, he wrote: "The audience is hers from the moment she begins, and they stay that way. . . . There is no pretentious crusading, or assumed emotion, nor is she of the overpolished highly commercial and sterile school; Miss Dobkin sings songs she likes, and sings them naturally and beautifully." He continued to report on my "natural ease, talent," and "consummate charm."

My labor was paying off with an improved performance and the ability to sing through rudeness and interruptions. A soft delivery would usually quiet talkers and a quick, "If you wanna be in the show, come to rehearsal!" would silence most loudmouths. My worst run-in with hecklers occurred at Gerde's. Four men at a front table appeared polite and supportive at first, but their mood grew more raucous as the night advanced, and by my third set they were howling. The bartender, after one attempt to calm them, had abandoned the effort and it was all I could do to keep the beat and remember my next line, my eyes fixed on the mirror across the room above the bar. One fellow in particular wouldn't quit. "Smile . . . you should smile," he boomed up as I ploughed on with *Mrs. McGrath*, where no smile belonged. "Say something funny," I countered after the song, but my set had been pretty much ruined. By the end of it, shaking with anger, I marched downstairs to the basement storage room that performers shared with rats and jumbo-sized cockroaches outfitted with a table and two chairs. I threw my guitar in its case and flew back upstairs.

The men at the front table were getting ready to leave, so I hurried over and asked, "Which one of you felt it necessary to make those comments during my show?" "I did," a shadowy figure sang out, actually sounding proud of himself. I turned around and slapped him hard across his cheek. The man rocked on his heels and the remaining audience members applauded politely. With a nod of acknowledgment I hoisted my guitar and strode out the door, my honor defended.

A year out of the Party, and the FBI imagined I might be ready to talk to them. However, "*. . . special Agents* [redacted] *interviewed the subject. Subject advised these Agents that she did not want to discuss anything with the FBI, and refused to engage in any additional conversation,*" noting that I had been "*uncooperative when approached for interview on 2/11/63 . . .* [redacted, redacted] *. . . and in [blackout] opinion she would not be receptive to an interview by the FBI.*" They continued to track me on frequent visits to Philadelphia for picnics with my old comrades or parties with Tyler kids and Noelle, who had dated one of our more interesting and talented classmates named Bob during the last year at school. I had admired his work in printmaking class where he excelled, and his agreeable looks reminded me of Marlon Brando in black-rimmed glasses.

"Louise is a good painter, for a woman," he once told me, "because she paints like a man." He couldn't explain what that meant any better than Tim Hardin could explain what "girl's time" was. Months after Bob and Noelle broke up, he and I started seeing each other. He was easygoing, funny, and fun to be with, and during visits to Philadelphia between tours I'd stay in his Germantown Avenue apartment. Sam was disdainful, which I took as a compliment.

On the Road

HERB WAS BOOKING me throughout the East and Midwest, but travel and housing arrangements were my responsibility. If I couldn't find a drive-away car to deliver—the cheapest transportation—I'd catch a bus and ride long nights watching quiet houses slide by outside the window. Traveling had always felt like a blessing, but as a professional it seemed downright divine. Of course, there was no escaping the bad gig or situation that can accompany life on the road.

During one booking at The Blue Dog Cellar in Baltimore, a call came in from the local mental institution requesting a show for their patient entertainment program. Sure, said George, the Club's proprietor, and negotiated the details. When the day came, some local folksingers and I piled into a car with our instruments and followed directions out to a suburb. Arriving ready to play, we drew a blank from the administrators, who hadn't heard a thing about it. "But we got a call inviting us to come here," we explained. "Oh, that must have been Bryan," said the head nurse matter-of-factly. "He's a patient. He's does that sometimes." The attendants nodded confirmation. "Sorry you had to come all the way out here for nothing."

Late in the spring of 1963 Herb arranged two weeks for me at The Retort, a club in Detroit. Sharing the bill was newcomer José Feliciano, currently dazzling everyone on the circuit with his snazzy guitar playing and fingers that moved faster than the human eye could follow. He'd throw his head back, crack dumb jokes and puns about being blind, and was likely to say any wild thing to get a laugh.

Pete, the club owner, introduced me to his best friend, a good-looking blonde named Judy. Because she was a model and constantly being hit on, she carried cards with her name printed in the center and "*NO!*" in each corner. A single mom raising two young daughters, Judy was a streetwise survivor, and like Jo, she became a lifelong friend. Driving around Detroit and over to Canada to eat fresh-baked bread, her girls begged us to tell them what "Faloorum" meant in the Scottish song, "He's Got No Faloorum," and we'd tell them, "When you're older," which, when they got older, they figured out on their own.

With my ever-present guitar and suitcase, I grabbed a bus west to Chicago and settled in with Mom's friend Selma, one of my very favorite people in one of my favorite cities. Selma was interested in my opinions and treated me as an adult. We smoked and chatted for hours.

For my two-week booking I traveled north by bus to Evanston and a new cavernous folk club called It's Here, with a high stage and state-of-the-art sound and lighting. Instead of chairs, fat pillows surrounded low tables in faux-beatnik/Japanese teahouse style. Eddie, the owner, liked me and my raunchy material. He started booking me there regularly and invited me to his home for barbeque with his family.

The earlier, more suburban schedule of It's Here served me well. When my last show ended I'd still have time to make it to Old Town, center of Chicago folk action, and there was plenty! I'd head to where Jo was playing. Ginni Clemens mostly stayed put in Chicago, where she had a following. Bob Gibson with Hamilton Camp, Josh White, or Judy Henske might be headlining at the Gate of Horn, Midwest folk mecca, where supermanager Albert Grossman started out.

From there, I flew to Miami with enough cash to rent a cute white convertible for my four week booking at The Catacombs coffeehouse. Cruising north to Fort Lauderdale, I felt on top of the world. On nights off I visited Grandma in Miami Beach in the comfortable garage apartment belonging to a family whose young children she watched in exchange for rent. I stayed at a small, comfortable motel near the club, and straightaway found myself a boyfriend. And a girlfriend.

Audiences were receptive, the management pleasant, the weather perfect, and the lifestyle highly congenial. When the last show ended I'd walk my dark beauty, a waitress at the club, to her house. There, with a large pillow crushed between us—a mutual defense system protecting us from possible lesbian-like contact—we'd stretch out on her bed, whereupon I, sophisticated woman-of-the-world, would warn her of the pitfalls of lesbian life. "It's a sad gray, world," I confided, imagining that I could discourage any impulse she might have had in that direction. The pillow served until the first glow of morning when we'd separate, chaste and unsatisfied, proud of successful resistance.

At midday I'd awake, have breakfast, and take a walk before meeting the blond beach boy I'd picked up. Chuck lived with an older man who supported him. In return, he ran errands, shopped for groceries, did chores, and performed other unnamed services. While the old man took his afternoon nap, Chuck would sneak me into his bedroom and we'd try to keep the noise down during hours of nonstop athletic romps that certified our heterosexuality.

Nerves

MY FOUR WEEKS at the Catacombs was coming to a close. In the shower, two days before my flight to St. Louis, I noticed a tingling on the soles of my feet as if they had fallen asleep. No matter how I scrubbed, rubbed, or flexed, the sensation continued, and the next day it had spread to my legs, which felt number by the minute. With little feeling left in them it was hard to keep my balance and not bump into things, but I managed to get onto a plane to St. Louis and The Laughing Buddha where I was booked.

Clearly, there was no way I'd be able to make it through a set, let alone two weeks of performances, so after my sound check I hobbled to a phone and called Pop, who told me to fly back to Philadelphia that night. For ten days I lay in a hospital bed subject to every neurological test they could think up. My affliction was migrating up my torso and out to my hands, where it lodged. Feeling no pain or anything else, my hands moved like a pair of mittens that could not button a button, zip a zipper, tie a knot, or strike a match. The hospital ran out of tests and I was discharged. The doctors didn't have a clue and settled on "peripheral neuritis." Until I recovered, independence was impossible, so I moved back in with my family.

Everyone was busy. Mom was busy cramming for her finals before her eight-years-in-the-making music degree. Pop was busy organizing for the High Holidays fund-raising dinner, and my brother Carl had started playing cornet as he finished his senior year of high school and got ready for college. Julie had started flute lessons and kept herself occupied cutting junior high classes and getting into trouble. Meanwhile, I kept busy smoking a million cigarettes, mooning around the house feeling sorry for myself or hanging out with Bob and friends.

Each morning I'd awake and paw the covers crying and flexing fingers that felt the same as they had the night before. They could hold a steering wheel but they couldn't play guitar, or type, which was the work that supported me. Nerves, I was told, heal at a rate of one millimeter per day, and although my body soon regained normal sensation, my hands seemed stuck in numbness forever. But even in my worst moments I knew I'd recover, and finally the feeling started to return. At the end of two months, with a couple of guitar strings lowered to a modal tuning, I could manage to make a few crude chords with two fingers.

The "A" Word

AS TIME WENT on I was able to get out more and more, and one weekend Bob and I went to a friend's converted barn in the country. On Sunday morning I awoke staring at my diaphragm. With sinking heart I realized that my partially numb fingers had failed to place it properly the night before, and it had made its way up to the pillow. I knew there wasn't anything I could do until I missed a period, and anyway, I had a more immediate concern: money. My guitar playing was, I figured, passable enough to get through a set, so I called Herb to line up some work and waited.

Weeks later, my period was nowhere to be found, and a visit to a local doctor confirmed my worst fears. Within days, I would be setting off for Council Bluffs, Iowa, for my first booking in many months. I'd work two weeks, rest a week, and work two more in Oklahoma City. Bob was distraught but could contribute little practical help, and my few abortion leads led to prices higher than I could have afforded even if I had been working. Having a baby was out of the question, but I had run out of ideas and resources. On top of that, Carl had been feeling sickly, and the day before leaving for Iowa, I sat across the dinner table and saw him droop, his skin and eyeballs yellow. My heart sank in my chest. As it turned out, an overdose of prescribed sulfa drugs had brought on a case of hepatitis, hospitalizing and nearly killing my little brother.

In no way would I saddle my parents with another worry, but where would I turn? Desperate, I called Herb. He'd find someone, he said as I leaned on the side of the phone booth blocks from my house, and soon after, he located a woman who used a sterile technique to induce miscarriages. She was cheap and all he could find, but she claimed to be a registered nurse, so I would be safe. Bob offered to pay half and I would earn my part (besides actually going through it) in Council Bluffs. An appointment at Herb's office was set up for the week between cities. The gravity of the situation weighed heavily on me, and I was frightened, but youthful invincibility sustained my spirits and, setting my course, I stayed on it.

First, Council Bluffs and the luxury of anonymity. Shuffling between a tacky motel room and a tacky lounge, I performed my act and seemed to satisfy polite, lackluster audiences. Reading and smoking my way through two weeks, I pondered an uncertain future. On my final night the club manager counted out my fee in dollar bills. I caught a cab to the airport and returned to Philadelphia, where Bob met me at the airport, and we drove north to New York City. Herb had cleared his office out for the occasion. The self-proclaimed nurse arrived and I lay spread-eagled on the couch. She inserted a long plastic tube into my uterus and packed it all around with gauze. I don't remember feeling anything but determination that it would work out. After yards of gauze had been unwound and stashed, she said to leave the tube in for two days during which time enough air would be allowed into the uterus to kill and abort the fetus. Or so she assured me before taking the ninety dollars and slipping out the door.

We were back in Philadelphia that night, and from then on I had to lay low, ducking down in Bob's car whenever we approached my old neighborhood. Carl had come through the hepatitis, but after almost losing him, Mom and Pop didn't need to find out about my pregnancy, and they never did. Hiding out at Bob's apartment, I smoked, read, and waited for the fetus to drop. Sometimes Bob's friends visited. Before sleep, Bob and I would read poetry aloud, a candle burning by the mattress on the floor. I'd get through this as I had the neuritis, but after a few days with no sign of miscarriage I thought that maybe I'd need help. At the drug store, among an impressive collection of Humphreys' Remedies for every known ailment and fetchingly packaged in consecutively numbered little glass tubes containing a stack of pills, "Humphreys' no. 11" claimed it would induce menstruation. But it didn't induce mine. Nor did an afternoon on horseback. Or running up and down flights of stairs. Nothing worked, not even leaving the packing in for two extra days.

During this time, a paperback edition of *The Feminine Mystique* on a drug-store bookstand caught my eye. I skimmed through Betty Friedan's landmark volume, which I bought and read. Her political analysis resonated and made sense, and maybe someday I'd look into it. But there was no time for that now, and besides, I wasn't a housewife.

Forty-eight hours before my departure to Oklahoma City, I sat on the toilet unpacking the lengths of bloody, slime-soaked gauze. Hours later my reward was thick clots of blood and killer cramps that doubled me over, but nothing resembling a fetus appeared.

Bob and I were hanging out with another couple when a news flash interrupted the music on the radio. JFK had been shot. We looked blankly at each other, shocked. The news was inconceivable, monstrous. We turned again to stare at the radio until the announcement that he had died in the hospital. First Marilyn, now Kennedy. Despite the staggering news, my mind kept snapping back to my own precarious situation and the unknown course of my pregnancy. The next day my cramps and the bleeding subsided, and that night, another doctor pronounced me still pregnant. I left his office in a daze, and flew to Oklahoma City the following morning.

The Laughing Buddha, well established for years, had been grooming a knowledgeable, loyal, appreciative audience. A large apartment up the street housed out-of-town performers who called it "Heartbreak Hotel." I opened for The Dillards, a popular bluegrass band, good musicians and decent guys whose laid-back attitude and lack of ego made them congenial housemates.

When in Council Bluffs, I had become friendly with Mike and Sandy Brewer, a sweet young couple who lived in Oklahoma City. Within three years, Mike, a gifted singer/songwriter, would reach the big time with a string of Brewer and Shipley hits like "One Toke over the Line." Every night after the Buddha show closed, the Dillard boys, Mike, assorted local folkies, and I would jam in the big living room until dawn in the Heartbreak Hotel tradition. As wonderful fun as this was, my thoughts never strayed far from the little life now threatening to lay mine to waste.

Then, on the last night of the first week of the booking, during the last song of my last set, halfway through the last chorus of "Jug o' Punch," the floodgates opened up. I had been spotting blood for a week and still wore a pad, for which I gave silent thanks. Praying that this was finally it and that I'd make it to the end of the show, I finished the song. Losing neither beat nor smile, I bowed, departed the stage, walked briskly to the dressing room, packed up my guitar, and smiled good night to some folks on my way out. "Enjoy your night off," we told each other.

Once outside, I high-tailed it to the blessedly empty apartment as fast as the puddle between my legs would permit. When the boys returned to begin the nightly party, I was installed on the toilet. The big gush had abated, and, feeling a bit more in control, I sponged myself off, put a fresh pad in place, and eased into the living room and took a spot on the floor. No one had noticed anything amiss. I picked up my guitar and joined in, counting the minutes until they all left. Every ten or fifteen minutes I'd slip away to the bathroom and check myself out, but not much was happening. Back and forth I went, until the room emptied out, and I was alone at last.

Back on the toilet and knowing there would be no sleep that night, I paged through a tattered copy of *Goldfinger*. Before long, the sensation of something peeling away from my uterus wall snapped me to attention, and seconds later, I looked down at a balled-up figure about three inches long floating in the bowl. I scooped it up and stared into my cupped palms. Minutes passed before I could bring myself to rinse it off. Then I lowered myself back down onto the toilet and studied the figure for a long time.

The tiny form was perfection itself, unlike anything I had ever seen, with teensy hands and fingernails. I wanted to wake the boys and shout, "Hey, look at this!" but of course I couldn't. I wanted to memorize the image of this breathtaking miniature being from another world, and I did. Heavy with sadness for what and who it would never be, I simultaneously felt an enormous weight lift, along with sadness that there was no one with whom to share the tiny miracle in my hands.

A songbird greeted the morning, and, unable to think of a meaningful eulogy, I said goodbye to the little false start and flushed it away with a small pang of regret beneath the huge wave of relief. From a drugstore pay phone, I called Bob with the good news. "I love you," he said and asked me to marry him. This was a first, but was it love or deliverance? I said I'd think about it. I'd lost a lot of blood, and my next call was to Mike and Sandy. Feeling weak and light-headed, I explained what had happened and asked if they could recommend a doctor. Alarmed, they sped to the apartment, rushed me to the hospital, and checked me in for a dilation and curettage.

A nurse injected me with sodium pentothal and shaved my pubes. The next morning, a boyish doctor carefully sat himself on the bed and introduced himself. He listened sympathetically as I recounted my story. He frowned and told me that I had taken a dangerous risk and was lucky to be alive. "It took me forty-five minutes to clean out the mess in there." He shook his head disapprovingly. "If you'd waited any longer you might have died." Dying seemed far-fetched, but I promised never to take such a chance again, adding that I hadn't had time to mail my paycheck to my New York bank, so would he accept a postdated check? Taking pity on me, he agreed, and that night I took the stage to begin my final week at the Laughing Buddha.

Return to Life

ON MY WAY back to Philadelphia, I stopped off to visit Louise, now working on a postgraduate degree in painting in Champaign, Illinois. After the low of pregnancy, the reunion was a high and I felt heady with my reprieve. My shaved crotch appalled her and then we laughed because it looked so stupid.

Although we loved each other, Louise and I had never been lovers, despite one electrifying kiss back in Philadelphia. Now, during this visit, we shared laughs, sweet kisses, and agreeable incidental sex, which we knew wouldn't change the basic facts of our friendship—even though the kissing left all the kisses with boys in the dust.

Back with my family in Philadelphia, I found Carl recovering from his brush with death and, with an extra-light heart, I joined in the good spirits. Bob and I celebrated by arranging to go with two of his friends who were buying a pound of weed in Germantown. We gassed up the car at thirty cents a gallon, drove down a cobblestone street to the address, and trekked upstairs carrying one hundred dollars. The deal was done and because they all thought I was the least suspicious looking—true, compared to them—I picked up the suitcase and carried it to the car while they followed me at a distance looking out for narcs.

Bob wanted to move to California, which might have been interesting as a concept, but marriage and California were for a distant future. I was far from ready to leave my folk community in the Village or the professional, independent life I'd so recently re-engaged, and I secretly felt more relieved than sad when, months later, Bob called it off. In a marriage, he explained, the man should be the primary breadwinner, while I would probably be earning more money from show business than he could make from art. He just couldn't live that way, he said. It was the perfect subject for a lost-love song, so, using the foolproof "La

Bamba" progression, I went for it. The result was "For the Love of Him," with the refrain, "my lamp will burn, and my world will turn for the love of him."

Sad, yes, but if this was all there was to the anguish of thwarted romance, it wasn't all that bad. Plus, it was terrific material. "For the Love of Him" closed the Bob chapter and became the first song of mine to be recorded when Canadian folksinger Bonnie Dobson chose it as her album's title song.

The FBI had a hard time keeping up with me during my travels. *"Subject is a missing Security Index subject of the New York Division. . . . The name of specific location of subject's place of employment in Cleveland could not be determined. . . . Cleveland has requested to attempt to determine where subject might be booked in that city, and any information pertinent to her. . . . A photograph of the subject is enclosed. It need not be returned. . . . Cleveland Federation of Musicians, 2200 Carnegie Street, advised that he could find no record of subject's employment in CV nor any membership in the union. He advised he wished to be notified if the subject were located in CV as non-union members were not allowed to work in the CV area. . . . Observation of females which could fit the description of subject as furnished in Cleveland . . . but no certain identification was possible. . . . On 3/16/64 pretext calls were made to ALL theatrical booking agencies in CV."*

No one I knew used theatrical booking agencies and everyone I knew played at Le Cave, the established folk institution in Cleveland, advertising in local papers for years. The people in my world could have found me in an instant, but the FBI lives in a another universe, and it wasn't until many pretexts later, when my booking was about over, that they hit pay dirt.

"On 3/21/64 [redacted] *subject was a member of Musicians Union Local 802, NY, and that she was finishing her tour . . . and was going immediately to Hazard, KY for a 3 Day tour."* Having forgotten the dates, I was happy for the dossier to refresh my memory. Pages headed *"Conference, Hazard, Kentucky, 3/26-29/64 sponsored by students for diplomatic* [sic] *society, a committee for miners, Appalachian Committee for full employment"* are completely blacked out, as is the rest of the report because disclosure, *". . . could constitute an unwarranted invasion of the* personal privacy of others [my emphasis]."

In the hills of Appalachia, the striking miners and their families were having a terrible time. The heirs of authentic country music tradition needed all the help they could get, and a big benefit concert was put together by the Committee [see FBI report] at The Village Gate. Pete Seeger was there, of course, and so was I, along with Tom Paxton, Carolyn Hester, and Bob Dylan.

Pete had popularized the five-string banjo and championed all kinds of music in Washington Square Park and folk gatherings far and wide. As legendary banjo picker Eric Weissberg told *Sing Out!*, "Pete was the real driving force behind everything. He advocated everything. He tried to put a little bit of everything in his show—politics, Appalachian, blues, real country."

The sharp glare of the stage lights bathed Pete in brilliance. From the wings I watched his lanky silhouette dance on the back curtain, his long neck straining upward, chin bouncing as it led the packed house in chorus. Next to it, the long neck of the banjo angled out and bobbed up and down to the beat. Sparkling beads of sweat sprayed upon the front tables like a blessing. St. Pete, incandescent archangel, urged the room into harmony like no one else on earth.

That and other benefit concerts succeeded in raising a bundle for the miners, but they needed more than money. To demonstrate wide national support for their strike, the committee arranged for a few of us to drive down to Hazard, meet the miners and their families, and put on a concert in solidarity. So Tom; his fiancée, Midge; Carolyn; and I packed into Tom's Volkswagen Beetle and drove down to the mountains of West Virginia. After winding around sharp turns in the black of night, having no idea where we were on steep, foggy dirt roads where I came within inches of backing off a cliff, we somehow arrived at our destination and were greeted by the roomful of miners, their families, UMW organizers, and even some press.

Introductions made and hellos exchanged, the four of us sat and listened as the miners resumed a discussion of their situation and strategies. Compared to the coal companies, the union's resources were minuscule, but their intelligence and spirit were mighty. The full hall seemed to appreciate our songs and sang along with us. To this day the coal companies continue to be as covetous and dishonorable as when The Almanac Singers began singing the very same union songs we sang together that night.

These people, I realized with a jolt, didn't need some punk Commie kid coming down from New York to tell them about the class struggle. They knew exactly who was doing what to whom, and how. What possible "vanguard" role could I play here, and what could the Party offer that they hadn't already absorbed through common sense and hard experience? Furthermore, the Party had nothing to do with the life I was living, and continuing in it made no sense. In fact, since leaving Philadelphia I had barely given the Party a thought. Clearly, it was time to quit. Back in the city, I called Manny, recently promoted to a national position, and we arranged to meet at Horn & Hardart. He was sitting at a small side table where I joined him, carrying a sturdy white cup of hot chocolate upon which tiny yellowish bubbles floated in their richness.

I informed the man who'd recruited me six years earlier that I was leaving. My commitment to the Party had been primary, but in six years my life had changed and was taking me in a different direction. Manny wasn't happy to hear what I had to say, and it was not an easy conversation, but thinking of how irrelevant the Party was to the people in Hazard kept me firmly on course. It had been almost a year since I'd been to a meeting and I rarely saw my old comrades. The Party years had been worthwhile, but it was over for me.

The Hawkes

NOEL STOOKEY, A Gaslight regular, had run the Tuesday hoots before Albert scooped him up, named him Paul, and put him together with Peter Yarrow and Mary Travers to create the hottest act in the biz: Peter, Paul and, Mary. Albert's success inspired in Herb a vision of an all-girl trio to consist of me; my roommate Karen Harvey, a lively redhead with a sweet voice; and Debbie Green, a long-legged, blond California girl who was dating songwriter Eric Andersen.

Coming up with a good name for a band is no easy task, and by the time Herb informed me that we'd be called The Hawkes, I was sick of constantly trying to come up with something that fit the music and our blonde-brunette-redhead image. The extra "*e*" in "Hawkes" would set us apart, said Herb. Regardless, "The Hawkes" needed an act. Like me times three, I imagined. Our music would be offbeat-traditional with a commercial touch, "the all-girl Peter, Paul, and Mary."

Herb hired a musical director, Felix Pappilardi, a multitalented, classically trained guitarist/bassist/keyboard player I had met at the Gaslight when he worked with Lou Gossett who sang and played guitar. Wiry and wired, with dark, curly hair, Felix was passionate about music in general, and crazy about rock 'n' roll in particular. Mom would have approved the unexpected baroque touches he wove into arrangements. Working with Felix was inspiring, plus, he listened to me, admired my work, and valued my ideas, like using dissonances and unresolved chords. Musically in tune, we worked well together, often into the wee hours after the other two girls had gone off. They had lives and we had The Hawkes' arrangements. But after frustrating months of moderate success, just as our sound was starting to come together, our individual lives took different paths, and the Hawkes disbanded, a victim of too much work for too little payoff.

Again, I was broke. My solo career had to be revived as soon as possible, and until then, I earned money by posing in the nude—a job my mother had also taken, I learned only later from her friend Selma. My sculptor complimented my body and treated me respectfully. The job paid a little more than office work and was only slightly more boring.

Pages from Mississippi

HAVING SPENT MUCH of my twenty-four years afraid that I'd miss something, there was no way to pass up an invitation to sign on with the Folk Music Caravan in August of 1964 to go to Mississippi for "Freedom Summer." Starting in May, a massive voter registration effort began as a response to the escalation of violent attacks against civil rights workers who were jailed, beaten, and murdered. Thousands of mostly young people from northern cities converged on Mississippi to work with the Student Non-Violent Coordinating Committee (SNCC) and the Congress of Racial Equality (CORE). My decision was made on August 4, the day that the murdered bodies of three young civil rights workers, Andrew Goodman, Michael Schwerner, and James Chaney were discovered. One day in June they had driven off from Philadelphia, Mississippi, to investigate a church burning and no one saw them again until their bodies were discovered buried in an earthen dam. The previous year, the entire country had been horrified by the murder of Medgar Evers who, with his wife, Myrlie, had opened the first office of the NAACP in Mississippi.

Every person I knew stood squarely for civil rights and against racism. Bob Dylan was showcasing his stark "Oxford Town," and Phil Ochs was singing, "Here's to the State of Mississippi" at The Gaslight, while a few blocks away, Nina Simone was rocking The Village Gate, with "Mississippi Goddam."

The Southern Christian Leadership Conference (SCLC), SNCC, Freedom Schools, and voter registration drives were hot. Bob Cohen, director of the Folk Music Caravan for Freedom Summer, along with Gil Turner, Len Chandler, Julius Lester, and Jackie Washington worked to bring performers to Mississippi. Gil and Len recruited me as well as Gaslight regulars Peter LaFarge, Tom Paxton, and Eric Andersen. Theo Bikel would be there, and, of course, Pete Seeger. The idea was that during the day, Judy Collins, Barbara Dane, Phil Ochs, Jim & Jean, and the rest of us would visit local people for one-on-one conversations about black culture and its hidden history. We'd tell them of the wide support they had up North and share stories about the Underground Railroad and heroes like Harriet Tubman and Sojourner Truth. Nights, at rallies and gatherings in churches, community centers, and Freedom Schools, along with gospel favorites, we'd sing songs of artists like Leadbelly and Big Bill Broonzy.

This was something new under the sun. Nothing like it had ever been attempted anywhere. That summer, over a thousand American kids, black and white, transformed into freedom fighters, helped register voters, taught in the "Freedom Schools," and organized the "Freedom Democratic Party" to challenge the legitimacy of the exclusionary Democratic Party. They met and learned from people like the legendary grassroots organizer Fannie Lou Hamer, and together they changed the deep South, letting black people know that there was hope for citizenship and signaling the white establishment that change was coming. That change landed later in the month when the fateful 1964 Democratic National convention rolled around, and the white, racist Mississippi delegation was challenged by heroes like Fannie Lou Hamer, who exposed the voter fraud and intimidation that was keeping corrupt Dixiecrats in power. TV showed the whole world the racism of the Dixiecrats and the Democratic Party, which was forced to change.

History was being made and I was grateful to have a chance to play a part, so, in the final week of my twenty-third year, I flew to Jackson, Mississippi. At a downtown hotel Carolyn and I met Gil, who showed us to our room. We were feeling wired and a bit nervous, but mostly curious about the adventure awaiting us. I perched on the chenille spread at the foot of a twin bed and faced my friend, now in partial shadow, sitting upright in a chair with wooden armrests. The last bit of sunlight beamed in from the tall window behind her and highlighted her long, straight hair.

Texas had conferred upon Carolyn a charming, soft twang, as well as personal knowledge of the South and its ways. But it was all news to me. Except for the two numbing years in Kansas and one bliss-filled week sequestered with Nancy in West Virginia, I'd spent my entire life in the Northeast and been raised in a family very much aware of violence, Jim Crow, and racism in the "Deep South." I'd read books and seen movies about the South, but nothing had prepared me for the impact on my senses beneath a high ceiling fan, breathing the mythic atmosphere, immersed in the romance and decay of it. The dank humidity lay over me like an uneasy weight. Flashes of *Cat on a Hot Tin Roof* and stories from Eudora Welty and William Faulkner came to mind, bringing with them an uneasy sense of being watched by distrustful eyes, much like my own. In my view every white person was immediately suspect and in their world, I, too, stood accused.

The wake-up call Carolyn had requested at the desk came at 6 A.M. She picked up the phone and heard, "Okay, time to get up, niggah lovuh." We packed our bags, and on our way out, we saw that someone had scrawled "KKK" in red letters across the outside panel of our door. Serious and sobering, we agreed, but no surprise. Naturally, the Klan would know about and dislike our presence here in Jackson. Of course those bullies would try to scare us away from their domain. And this respectably seedy white hotel had to be riddled with them.

Every single black person here and elsewhere endured far greater, even life-threatening, risks on a daily basis. A nasty wake-up call and a vandalized door were nothing compared to being shot in front of your own home as Medgar Evers had been. Our small presence became a drama in which to finally activate the heroic role I was born and bred for. Here was a chance to do the right thing, to deepen my insight and strengthen my convictions. As it turned out, the notice from the "KKK" proved more validating than intimidating, and the graffiti proved a powerful credential, my red badge of courage, proof that we had put ourselves on the line.

Feeling righteous, indignant, and edgy, we waited for the elevator, then rode down to the lobby, strode to the desk, and eyed the clerk suspiciously. His cronies, lounging silently behind him, eyed us back. Static animosity crackled silently above the once-grand carpet between us and the door. Carolyn checked us out, and, with measured step, we turned to walk toward the sunshine beckoning outside. A venomous "Y'all come back now" followed us out into the fresh air.

Thankful to be out of the hotel, we beat it to headquarters and our people, where black, brown, and white hands reached to shake ours, the contrast as dramatic as life is to death. COFO (Council of Federated Organizations) was the umbrella for SNCC, CORE, and a host of civil rights groups, and had brought us all together. After the hotel's brittle silence, a warm, rich cacophony of voices treated our ears.

Inside, I remember a whirlwind of movement, swirling activity amidst pamphlets and papers, books, and booklets stashed on shelves, heaped on tables, people speaking intently into phones, a casual exchange here, an intense discussion there, a few pieces of funky furniture haphazardly arranged throughout a series of small dark rooms. Women activists, equally at risk as their male counterparts worked as much and as long, but with lower profiles. "If you want something answered, call a man," they said. "But if you want something done, call a woman."

While darkness and urgency prevailed inside, outside a lazy morning sun beamed down upon a multicolored mix of small, relaxed groups: organizers and supporters, students and young volunteers, making plans and exchanging information. We spotted Gil, who welcomed us in his typically warm, slightly distracted way. Len bounded up to us, his volcanic energy slightly more contained than usual. They introduced us to other SNCC workers and we met Bob Cohen, who pointed to a line of cars parked across from the storefront. An unmarked sheriff's car was followed by one with a Justice Department deputy and finally a Jackson police car. They were photographing everyone. I didn't care. I was used to it.

We walked a few blocks to an empty car parked at a curb and squeezed in to huddle with the veterans, who brought us up to date. Intent upon the task while staying alert to movement outside, they exchanged knowing looks as Carolyn and I described the phone call and the red "KKK" on our hotel door.

We were given our itinerary covering Moss Point, Biloxi, Hattiesburg, and Meridian. There were general instructions. Traffic laws were to be strictly obeyed, no one was to travel alone, and someone was always to know our whereabouts. Carolyn and I would be transported and escorted through rural Mississippi. Only a very few elite, highly trained, and experienced organizers ventured into the Delta where the violence had been particularly intense. In one part of my mind I was intrigued and challenged, but happy to stay away from there. People got murdered in the Delta. Slowly we cruised the neighborhood, coming to a full halt at every stop sign, signaling for every turn, always mindful of activity, especially in front of hangouts like bars and gas stations where men liked to congregate.

Our backwoods tour commenced with visits to one community after another. The last thing I wanted was to appear condescending or ignorant. Fearful of committing an unconscious offense, I looked for any opportunity to express the admiration and respect I felt for our cheery hosts who fussed over us and eased my self-consciousness. The women served spectacular endless courses consisting of crispy fried chicken and ham, buttery mashed potatoes, candied sweet potatoes, corn, black-eyed peas, greens and beans cooked with chunks of salt pork, biscuits, gravy, and unfamiliar chitterlings and okra, which I sampled and praised politely.

The two-lane paved and one-lane dirt roads we traveled led to churches, schools, and comfortable houses on the outskirts of small towns along with isolated, decaying wooden shacks stuck way out in a lonely field. We chatted with people about the importance of voting, and how their vote would make a difference in their lives. I vividly remember standing in front of a mailbox listening to a resolute old woman with glittering eyes say, "Nothing is going to keep me from putting that ballot in that ballot box on election day!" She nodded for emphasis, turned, and, leaning on a cane, painstakingly made her way down the narrow, potholed dirt road. How many more breathtaking old ladies were there? A truly responsive government would not only control the savage racism that daily threatened their safety but also provide services for them and pave the roads in their neighborhoods.

Some people were reluctant to register. We didn't press, just asked them to think about it and left a card in case they had a change of heart, wanted more information, or needed a lift to the polls. Children sat quietly attentive, like little jewels peeking out from around a doorway or through their mother's legs. Every last person treated us kindly and warmly. Many handshakes and hugs were exchanged, and there were many times we squatted down to have a word with beautiful barefoot children, each endangered like the four girls killed the year before by a bomb in the basement of a Birmingham, Alabama, church. I asked and answered questions about their lives and my own, let them strum my guitar. Sometimes a gentle touch passed between us to affirm the extraordinary occasion.

Particularly vulnerable before or after a meeting or rally, we practiced more vigilance than usual when coming and going. As many as a dozen of us would climb into cars and follow each other to the night's housing. Once there, people came by to meet us and to thank us for coming. Their lives in constant jeopardy, our invariably genial hosts welcomed neighbors, relations, community activists, and newly signed-up voters into their homes to meet us. A lookout would be dispatched to watch for trouble outside, while inside we hooted at funny stories and quieted down for sad or scary ones. Here were genuine heroes with their brave, upbeat attitude, and we quickly formed a mutual admiration society.

Most couples insisted on giving us their bed for the night. Otherwise, we slept on couches and floors, often within feet of a loaded shotgun propped up behind a door. Being in the room with loaded firearms was a new experience for me, both comforting and alarming.

Keeping safe meant keeping on the move, so we'd say our thanks and good-byes early in the morning and push on. It wasn't always possible to avoid driving at night along dark, deserted dirt roads, and a couple of times, cars filled with white men followed us for long distances. Once our battery died, but a friendly minister gave us a jump start. We'd fill up the gas tank, make grim jokes, and pray against a breakdown or flat tire. A couple of our guides had recently been beaten up and jailed. In March, seven months later, civil rights activist Viola Liuzzo was shot and killed driving on those same roads.

The Mississippi countryside, although menacing at night, proved exhilarating by day. In four years of fine arts training I'd never beheld such greens. A rich palette was layered throughout the neat fields and acres of woodlands separating towns with their white neighborhoods where live oak trees reached high to form a canopy, shading smoothly paved streets utterly different from the places where we had come and where we were headed. Like most of the world, I reflected sadly, this exquisite country was controlled by racist thieves and murderers. Luscious greenery streamed by the window and accented raw injustices, past and present.

Besides encouraging people to vote as part of the statewide campaign, we were there to entertain and to let people know that their voices were being heard and that their struggles were being widely watched and supported. By registering to vote, black Americans could unseat the Dixiecrats and break their decades-old hold on local and national politics. Our days were devoted to nonstop traveling, meeting, talking, singing, eating, and laughing in small and large groups of new people every day.

We gathered in dim churches and bright community centers, listened to eloquent speeches and plainspoken testimonies. Occasionally we crossed paths with others, like SNCC organizer Bob Moses, or musicians like the Freedom Singers with Bernice Johnson. After marriage to Cordell, the group's leader, she became Bernice Johnson Reagon, distinguished Smithsonian scholar and later the founder of the celebrated a capella group Sweet Honey in the Rock. So impressed was Bob Dylan when he first heard her sing that, when he returned to New York, he informed me that rather than his "favorite female singer," I was now his "favorite *white* female singer."

My program included "The Times They Are A-Changin'" along with "The Jug o' Punch," "Coplas," and "Vegetable." In Mississippi we were celebrities simply for making the trip. I wondered how the people related to my performances, and chose to believe that their appreciation and enthusiasm extended beyond politeness. I had come to sing for the people, but what I remember most is singing with them. "Singing," Bob Moses said, "is the backbone and balm of this movement."

Despite my diehard, lifelong aversion to religion and its symbols, when the people sang songs I knew—thanks to Aunt Reverend Mary's West Virginia church—I joined in, heart and soul. This community was organized and sustained through the church and I respected this, and understood that the words to a song might be gospel, but their meaning was "Freedom." Civil rights workers adapted the union songs that had traditionally served as "spirituals" for the community I was raised in, and as I joined in with the familiar chorus of "Which Side Are You On?" I felt an evolutionary circle revolving within me, leaving me more strengthened by my past, and more deeply connected.

We knew what we were singing and why and it electrified us. A thrill vibrated upwards from my heart through my throat and out through my lips. The unifying force of music, spirit, and conscience sprang alive when we sang together, lifting me above my previous capabilities. "I woke up this morning with my mind / stayed on freedom," I sang. "We are soldiers in the army / we have to fight, although we have to cry. . . ."

Like virtually every political gathering of the time, meetings ended with "We Shall Overcome," hands joined, bodies swaying, souls aligned. I was grateful to have had the chance to meet and sing with the people of beautiful Mississippi, complimented by the welcome they gave me, and honored by their appreciation of my brief effort. Oddly enough, the trip didn't get a mention in my FBI files, unless those references were blacked out.

I had started hanging out with Toni, one of a succession of Herb's secretaries, a homeless, pretty redhead, conversant with mind-altering drugs before anyone else I knew in 1964. She lived on her wits and taught me a few survival skills.

Toni and I bumped into each other at the Philadelphia airport, and decided to go for coffee. While settling ourselves in a booth, I remembered Herb telling me that she may have been a junkie. The waitress appeared, and I ordered my coffee. Toni ordered coffee, tea, orange juice, tomato juice, and a glass of water. She rustled in her bag and came up with a collection of amphetamine pills. Had I ever tried them? I was still marveling at her beverage order when she pushed some of the pills across the table at me. Okay, I said, and put them in my bag. The following week I took some and hated the effect. Feeling manic and out of control in a cold sweat was not my idea of a good high. Months later, I tried again and still hated it. I was already naturally wired.

Yet I had certainly enjoyed the mescaline I'd taken in Cleveland one time, when for two weeks I stayed at the home of my childhood friend, Ellen from

New Rochelle, who lived in Cleveland Heights with her doctor-researcher husband. One night, he brought an envelope home from his lab containing the pure hallucinogen no one I knew had yet tried, not even Toni.

"You might get nauseous," he warned us, measuring the powder and giving me half. "Many people can't keep it down." He divided the other portion into a quarter each for himself and Ellen. I took my dose with orange juice while they swallowed theirs. We waited. After a short time my cramping stomach settled, but they both vomited and missed the wonder of an undiluted mescaline high.

My lustrous state of mind extended well into the following day. Colors vibrated happily and everything appeared interesting. Nothing escaped my focused attention as I made my way to the Cleveland Museum and examined landscapes, looking at them, it seemed, directly through the painter's eyes.

Back at the apartment, still soaring, I pulled out the Guild to work on a Peggy Seeger tune, "No Sir No," a song I still sing (except instead of "All I want is a handsome man," now it's "All I want is a lesbian"). Every note, every chord of my arrangement made a deep metaphysical statement. It was brilliant. I was brilliant. Mescaline was brilliant. But since another appropriate opportunity never arose, I never tried it again.

When I returned to the city, Toni apprenticed me in the art of panhandling, a practice I'd believed confined to Bowery bums. She was a pro with a line and a story for each man she'd approach. Spotting a likely prospect, she'd size him up, then flash a hot smile or shyly lower her gaze for the pitch and come back with more than subway fare.

Just before dawn, walking barefoot together down MacDougal, she'd show me her route, pointing out the stops and proper timing, which was everything when it came to handouts. She knew the exact right moment to greet the bakers through the screened back door of Zito's Bakery to score a bag of rolls, and when to happen upon the smiling milkman as he hopped off the truck for a delivery to wind up, with a quart. I learned the routine until I could almost manage it myself, but with nowhere near her level of expertise.

My resourceful new friend had heard about a cheap summer sublet, a loft in the warehouse district, so, from the Bedford Street flat, I carted my belongings further downtown to what is now called Tribeca. In that hazy, smoke-filled period, Toni and I club-hopped by night and returned to our loft to sleep, so the dark, unkempt space didn't seem as grim as it really was. When Mom and Pop stopped in for their one visit, disappointment was written all over them. I shrugged it off.

My Cheerios-peanut butter diet had added ten pounds, my heaviest weight in memory. Nothing fit, and I felt uncomfortable and clumsy. In fact, pinching cracker packets and sugar cubes from restaurant tables and rolls of toilet paper from public bathrooms was no way to live. Nor was playing basket houses for ten dollars in tips collected in baskets that were passed around the audience instead of guaranteed fees. Party time was quickly losing its luster, and I was quickly losing my taste for it.

For her part, my housemate had started hooking and spending more and more time on the street. She withdrew and disappeared for long stretches, would come home incoherent, unfit for conversation, then nod out. Toni had run out of miracles and I had run out of patience, not to mention money. Summer was over, the lease was up, and it was time to get myself back on the road so Herb arranged some bookings. Telling Toni to take care of herself, hoping she'd be okay and knowing she wouldn't, I packed my guitar and suitcase, grateful to leave and escape the downward spiral I'd been spinning in. She was back on heroin and there was nothing I could do for her. She didn't even seem to understand that I was leaving. It dawned on me that with Toni, down was the only way to go. Returning to work was my way out.

Songs from the Road

A FEW DISMAL hotel rooms and lackluster engagements later, I was delighted to land in Chicago for a couple of weeks at It's Here. I could relax in the comfort of the solid old apartment Selma shared with her husband, Gordon, a documentary filmmaker, almost as much fun to talk to as Mom's old friend. They lived within walking distance of Jo's place above a storefront on Broadway, a street with quirky, offbeat shopping and good walking in cooler weather.

Most of those blistering July afternoons were passed sitting on Jo's back porch. In this typical working-class Chicago summer scene, everyone tried to beat the heat in the shade of wooden decks connected by stairways zig-zagging to the ground like fire escapes.

People sat and fanned themselves, clinking ice in glasses, and nodding to one another across the small courtyards skirting a back alley. From back porches and opened windows, snatches of a Cubs game wafted through the hot, heavy air. We sat and sweated, and Jo said, "There's a rumor going around that I'm a lesbian. Have you heard it?"

"Hell, no! Where did *that* come from?" I asked her, outraged at the slur.

"That's *ter*-rible!" Shaking my head at the depths to which some people will sink I added, "And a damned lie!"

"Yeah, *you* know I'm not, but a couple of them are spreading it around. They want me," explained Jo.

"Aw, to hell with them!" I snapped. "They're just a bunch of finger-fuckers anyway!" Jo wasn't nearly as hard on lesbians as I was, secretly terrified of being one.

Months earlier in Baltimore, after the Blue Dog Cellar closed for the night, fear of my attraction to women had driven me to a lesbian bar to glory in the obvious difference between me and lesbians. I preened and gloated over the three male friends I had brought along for show. They couldn't even get one man, and I could get three. No one seemed to care.

As always, my weeks in Chicago proved creative as well as restorative. From the art world cliché of the times, I had come up with the phrase, "I Don't Know Very Much About Love (But I Know What I Like)." Clever, but tricky to set to music. I searched through Selma and Gordon's record collection for melodic inspiration and came across Buddy Holly's "Not Fade Away." The Bo Diddly beat of his first lines were a perfect fit for my unwieldy lyric so, starting with his chords and tempo, I re-routed his melody line here and there and made it mine. For lyric ideas, I paged through a book of Russian proverbs, consulted my rhyming dictionary and wrote, "I may be young but I've read the old books / And my recipes come from the tastiest cooks / Don't talk tackle when you just play touch / 'Cause Daddy, I'll find out if you protest too much," and one more saucy, sassy number was born.

Another aggressive genre tune, "Do Your Worst," evolved from a catchy chord progression I had been monkeying with on the guitar and the middle section of a melodic phrase from Hoagy Carmichael's Lazy Bones: "You went and pulled the rug out from under my feet / You gave me your heart and now you want a receipt / Your fantasy balloon's about to burst, so baby, do your worst," I admonished no one in particular.

The Republicans were holding their convention and I tuned in, disgusted by the cheering crowds nominating Barry Goldwater. He was so reactionary that he made Lyndon Johnson look good, if that was possible. I turned off the radio, climbed a ladder in the club's foyer, and started playing with chord progressions. I loved singing from on high, and when I visited Judy, she was always setting up ladders to get me to sing.

A local folkie, my opening act, and I wrote a rock 'n' roll parody called

Air-Conditioning in which my priorities were clear in the refrain of "Don't come unless you bring / Air-conditioning!" No one in Chicago would have disagreed.

Getting Grounded

I RETURNED TO New York with some money in my pocket, determined to rent my own apartment. Back at the loft, Toni was nowhere to be seen, and neither was my banjo, a White Lady five-string I'd come across at the Caffe Lena upstate in Saratoga Springs. White Lady made fine, reliable banjos, and of all my belongings that Toni pawned for drugs, I most lamented that banjo.

With my earnings from the road, I found an affordable first-floor studio at the rear of a little old building with a red front door. It was on Barrow Street, just off Seventh Avenue at Bleecker. Excellent furnishings sat on curbs throughout the city before scheduled early morning trash pickup, and from them I selected chairs, a coffee table, and an end table. Fabric-covered crates made bookshelves, as did a pair of two-by-fours resting on cinder blocks. My single window overlooked a back garden and brightened the back end of a long, narrow room. With Mom's sensibility guiding me all the way, I put together my first kitchen. Painted white shelves on brackets held the Fiesta dishes I grew to admire in the days when they were cheap. Mike's cartoons hung over a couch/daybed on the front wall, along with other framed art. Centered against the long wall, someone's discarded round table served as a desk, dining table, room divider, and site for the radio. On their first visit, Mom and Pop gave the apartment their blessing, clearly encouraged by my attractive, comfortable space.

Everyone was pleased, including the FBI when, at length, they located me. According to a redacted source, during the months I lived with Toni, I ". . . *did not have a permanent residence in New York City*," but when in town, "*'stay(ed) with various friends.'*" A stack of blackened file pages ultimately traces me to 23 Barrow Street.

The Café Espresso in Woodstock booked me for a weekend, where Billy Faier, a soft-spoken Washington Square banjo picker, invited me for some downhill skiing. We drove to Belleayre Mountain, where I learned to stop by falling down. The best part of skiing was the hot chocolate by the fireplace in the ski lodge afterward, like at Schrafts after ice stating. Billy pointed out some of the snow-covered sights around Woodstock, quiet and magical, like a winter fantasy. I slept in the room for visiting performers above the funky, laid-back pub on the Millstream, and hoped I'd return often to the dreamy little hamlet in the Catskills.

One night during a gig at Gerde's, Roger (Jim) McGuinn, a nice fellow and a good singer and guitarist, stopped me to ask if I'd ever heard an English group called The Beatles. I had, the month before in Ann Arbor, when a boy had given me a ride on his motorcycle. As we sped along a dirt road in the moonlight, he told me about The Beatles, turning his head to shout the spelling at me through the wind. "NOT like the BUG, but with an '*A*'!" later I learned that the name was a tribute to Buddy Holly's band, The Crickets.

Since I already knew the choruses to "She Loves You" and "I Wanna Hold Your Hand" when Roger started raving about their music I could agree. He joined me during my last set and sang "She Loves You" with me. He couldn't stop talking about The Beatles. Not long afterward he formed The Byrds, and met his idols in person.

In Pursuit of the Higher Mind

THROUGH MY DETROIT friend, Judy, I met both Rob and his cohort, Mike. Like the Hornet and Green Lantern on the prowl, the pair filled whatever room they entered with masculine entitlement. Their conversations were laced with esoteric references to subjects from ancient code systems to the metaphysics of a pendulum's arc. Along with his rugged, lanky good looks and cryptic manner, Mike's searching mind caught my full attention. There was no keeping track of him and I never knew when he'd be in town or when he'd call. But when the call came, I'd be ready for whatever this restless, rootless Argonaut had in mind.

I, too, sought arcane, hidden information holding the key to life's meaning, and I ached to figure out the puzzle that had first stopped me in my seven-year-old tracks on the steps of Levy Brothers' Toy Store. To satisfy my thirst to understand who and what I and everything else was and why, I consumed Joan Grant's tales of reincarnation and various accounts of lost civilizations like MU and Atlantis. I read Velikovsky's *Worlds in Collision;* explored theosophy, dream interpretation, and the Fibonacci number system; and dabbled in Gurdjieff, Ouspensky, numerology, tarot, and more. Each perspective contributed to a larger, more complex sense of the universe in which I meant to locate myself. Each pursuit interested me, but the old question, "What am I and what *is* this?" overwhelmed all others. Despite a lifetime of longing to understand, what I was experiencing, the mystery remained.

After a profitable summer and autumn on the circuit, I arrived home with hundreds of dollars in my pocket and a load of dirty clothes for my laundry basket. Primed by occult tracts, I decided to test the power of mind over ordinary reality. By casting a psychic barrier around me, I willed myself invisible and it worked! No one showed any sign of recognition, made eye contact, or even moved out of my way when I approached. Mind over matter was a snap! Perfectly aligned with the universe, I was ready to sample the smorgasbord of esoteric wisdom in whatever forms it chose to appear.

Of all the arcane practices I'd sampled, astrology felt comfortable and seemed the most accessible. Graphic and multidimensional, a person's chart was a map as complex as the individual and could provide practical guidelines for self-improvement. Four of my planets were in fiery Leo, meaning that I should embrace my natural generosity but guard against pride and pomposity. With Leos' natural talent for performing, it was important not to slip into arrogance, the lower octave of the lion.

Pulling at me were many questions about where I stood in relation to the invisible forces directing the earth's energies, and Mike seemed like a man with answers. When he was around I avoided Sam, who had no interest in the unseen world and scowled at the mention of his name, unlike the casual attitude he affected toward Bob or other men I dated. Sam regularly asked me to marry him, but there were unseen worlds to explore and metaphysical adventures to undertake first.

Mike introduced me to the *I Ching*. "The first reading is often the best in your whole life," Mike later remarked, and he was right. At my core, I was a wanderer. "Strange lands and separation are the wanderer's lot . . . the fire does not linger in one place, but travels on to new fuel." My sun in fixed essential fire. *That's me!*

Good Trip/Bad Trip

LONG BEFORE LSD hit the streets, it made the rounds of counterculture's more dedicated risk-taking explorers of unknown interior depths. Only a few special people who dealt in certain substances knew about morning glory seeds, and Mike had recently experienced this pre-LSD hallucinogen. The effects he described sounded like those of mescaline, only better, and he promised to let me know when he got of them. The morning glory seeds never materialized and it was not Mike, as I had hoped, but Rob who came into some uncut, lab-quality

LSD. He called to invite me to his Lower East Side pad to sample it with him. My basket of dirty laundry sat on the floor waiting to be taken to the laundromat on Seventh Avenue. I stared at it. It could wait.

My one and only LSD trip seemed to stretch over two weeks, but who knows? Real time was impossible to track, as brain, body, spirit, and sensibility merged and separated, exploded, transmuted, and resettled like flotsam in a tumultuous sea. From the moment I stepped ashore a breathtaking new landscape, my life proceeded in warp-time. For starters, my wristwatch immediately aligned with my inner clock, reflecting not standard time, but my current state. If I was hungry, my watch said mealtime. When I needed a cigarette, it read break time, and when I could no longer keep my eyes open, it displayed the hour for sleep.

Colors blazed, music resonated, conversation sparkled. I could sing, dance, and rejoice with a mind flung open to universes suddenly within my grasp. Powerful recognitions lurked everywhere. On the street, each individual face called forth others, all familiar and somehow related to me, each a multidimensional specimen of my beloved human family. I wanted to stare at every person I saw and figure out each affiliation. Impossible, of course, but in the privacy of my apartment, within the seemingly endless terrain of my own imagination I was free to pursue mysteries wherever they led.

I thought about who I'd seen walking across town from Bob's flat to my apartment and pondered the enormous number of people I knew, both first and second-hand. Between various networks of friends, colleagues, schoolmates, ex-comrades, and family, I figured I was connected to every person on the planet. In fact, I was sure of it.

Epiphanies were coming left and right. From the radio on my table, molecules spewed out in rainbow fireworks swirling and fading into sparks of energy. For hours I lay on my daybed watching the sounds. Radio also brought a succession of stories and characters into my space. I welcomed each one, weighed every word, and identified with all viewpoints. Late night talk shows were better than ever. Jean Shepherd's easygoing style amused me, but he played the news annoyingly safe and too often missed the deeper political significance of the stories.

On one of the afternoons during my trip, a taxi cut the corner and almost clipped me. "Hey!" I yelled and banged my fist on his trunk. He swiveled his head and gave me the finger. With heightened powers, I cursed him and his cab. Within minutes I noticed a crowd gathering a few blocks away in the direction he had sped off to. In answer to my inquiry, I was told that a yellow cab had been in a wreck up there. Yes, that *was* a crunch of metal I had heard moments ago. My curse had worked!

The city was in critical danger. The signs were unmistakable. A catastrophe was about to befall the intersection at Thirty-fourth. Increasingly convinced that a terrible earthquake was about to split Manhattan wide open, I hurried uptown on Sixth in a borrowed car, just making the lights. Disaster, I realized, could only be averted by pure, piercing vibration, by the sound of my voice. I'd yell like a Bulgarian woman on a Balkan mountaintop, full strength, from the center of my being. The vibration would re-align conflicting trajectories and bump them back onto the right track, thus holding the city together. Or not, but either way, it couldn't hurt, I concluded as the epicenter drew near. I rolled up the windows to compress and intensify the sound, and also to avoid unwanted attention, the last thing I needed on this mission. I pulled up to Thirty-fourth Street, shrieking like a banshee. The light had just turned yellow, so I sat at and yelled my head off until it changed, and I crossed over in full voice. The city was saved.

The acquaintance who owned the car was a lesbian, which, in my advanced state of receptivity, interested me even more than usual. I managed to get her to my place by charming her, I believed, with my wit and enthusiastic high spirits as I had seen Toni do so often. Her name was Lois Hart, and to calm her well-founded skepticism of me and my motives, I offered my credentials in the form of the exquisite, hand-made book my ex-girlfriend Nancy had constructed for my twentieth birthday.

The heavy cardboard cover was cut like a bustier corset, its bodice trimmed with dainty white lace doilies. Inside was a set of smart, racy, drawings with inventive satire and lots of cleavage. "Expressly for the pleasure of Alix Dobkin" was inscribed across the title page in Nancy's special flowery Victorian script. The final page was a thick, round, cardboard pie plate with raised concentric rings forming a target around the center button, which Nancy had colored pink. The book was a stunner: simple, brazen, and brilliantly executed. As Louise and Mike had been before her, Lois was properly impressed.

"Take a bite of it," she directed. "What?" I exclaimed. "If you're really separated from her you have to take a bite out of that breast." All I wanted was for Lois to get into bed with me, so I chomped off a small mouthful and chewed awhile. "You've got to swallow it too!" "Sure," I said, remembering years of snacking on envelope corners on the way home from piano lessons. How bad could it be? Being an honorable woman, Lois then came to bed, but every so often I caught her staring my way with a perplexed expression on her face.

Something else besides her strong, dark looks and thoughtful manner drew me. It was a closeness of spirit which, apart from sex, I knew no way to codify or express. I believed that Lois Hart and I would meet again to renew the mystical bond between us, but she left, instructing me to return her car to a garage, and I never saw her again. Years later, the news that she had died of breast cancer deeply shocked and saddened me. My ignorance of feminism and dismissal of things female kept me from recognizing the heroic path Lois traveled. Some years later, she and her mythic peers would usher in the Second Wave of feminism, which would change everything.

Winding Down

MY RECKLESS SENSE of invincibility during my high, and accompanying lack of judgment, had not gone unnoticed. Sam was concerned. I hadn't seen him in a while and I missed him, but he didn't approve of mind-altering drugs, so over the phone I assured him there was nothing to worry about. Tom Paxton was prompted to take a detour from the road to see if I was really acting as wacky as he'd been told. He and Midge sat on my couch while I admitted that I had perhaps acted strangely, but I dismissed their concerns. "Really, I promise I'm all right. There's no need to worry about me," I had insisted in my most reasonable tone. "I'm really okay!" They were skeptical but seemed to take me at my word.

But what *was* I doing? No record label had signed me, and I hadn't even made the Riverside *Newfolks* compilation album of lesser known singers. The fact was that I had hit the wall, and upon returning to solid ground I realized that everything had shifted. But how? Where could I go from here? Looking around my apartment for guidance, I spotted a Bible taken from a hotel room as the Gideons had intended. Picking it up, I flipped the pages and randomly stuck my finger into the book. The verse at my fingertip concerned Samuel from a page loaded with "begats." The message was unmistakable. Sam had been asking me to marry him for months. He really loved me, and I loved him. He would take care of me. We would get married and beget.

PART SIX

1965–1971

Marriage

The first hundred years are the hardest.

—POP

SAM KNELT ON the floor to present me with a marquise-cut diamond ring he'd bought at the jewelry store on MacDougal where my ears had been pierced. His love felt like a blessing. I wrote a song with the refrain, "Oh my / Sweet Sam / Loves me every way I am. . . ." He was all the man I would ever want or need. Everything considered, Sam and I were an excellent match. Like red-hot magnets, we'd rip our clothes off and have sex whenever and wherever we could. Besides sharing the same basic tastes and values, we supported each other's ambitions and had fun together. He made me laugh.

From the depths of my subconscious, Dick and Jane's mom surfaced and with a wave of her apron, cheered me onward toward proper wifedom. But could I pull it off, let alone take my place in the family of charismatic Hood women? Lynn and Mama seemed to think so, as did Robin, the youngest, who came up for the holidays.

In February, Malcolm X was assassinated, a horrifying and senseless murder. Mom and I thought it strange that a rival political faction had done it rather than the FBI, although we guessed that the Feds probably had a hand in it. They usually did. As a rule I didn't believe the papers, yet a sense of impending doom seemed to thicken around us. Soon, however, that and all other news became eclipsed by my thrilling ride into the marriage vortex.

From the moment the wedding was announced, hugs and good wishes flowed my way. I'd hit the jackpot! People smiled and congratulated me as if I'd actually done something. Sam gave me a pearl necklace, a Hood family tradition. "Real pearls," he beamed, and, like Snow White, Rose Red, and the Seven Brides, I willingly surrendered myself to the happily-ever-after I'd both rejected and longed for.

We bought each other matching gold bands and planned a ceremony at Mama and Papa's apartment to be followed by a big party at The Village Gate. But after a meeting with owner Art D'Lugoff, Pop added up the figures, sighed, and shook his head, so we settled for a party at The Domska Polska Nationalna. The Dom, a smaller, seedier club across town on St. Mark's Place, was located opposite Gussie & Becky, where Ruth created my wedding dress of simple white pressed velvet with a high square neck and mid-calf-length jacket. She threw in a matching pillbox hat and veil as a wedding gift.

Alice Ochs, Phil's wife, hosted a shower. "You *must* choose a silver pattern," Lynn and Mama insisted, so I hopped a subway uptown to Tiffany's and leafed through a catalog trying to figure out how I felt about it all, and finally settled on the least pretentious. Among the mountain of our wedding presents was one small Tiffany's box with a single Danish Modern place setting from Lynn and John.

The "M" Word

FOR THE WEDDING, extended family and selected close friends jammed together in Mama and Papa's modest living room overlooking Seventh Avenue South. Presiding over the ceremony was a good progressive guy, Michael Allen, a minister from St. Mark's Church across town on Tenth Street. He'd come highly recommended by Fran, who knew everyone worth knowing in lower Manhattan. The Reverend had been making headlines as a civil rights activist in Mississippi, and when we met with him he impressed us as the best compromise between the mildly Episcopal Hoods and the Conservative Jewish Dobkin relatives, plus my immediate, atheist family. Or so we hoped.

The point of having an Episcopal ceremony was to make Mama happy. "That's fine," she said when we told her the good news, "just as long as you don't get that busybody priest I've been reading about in the newspapers. Anyone but him!" (She and Papa both read or scanned the entire *New York Times* from front to back every morning.) At the mention of his name, the set of her mouth revealed the only sign of disapproval, but nothing more was said.

For their part, my parents and attending relatives held their tongues during the decidedly surreal Christian event, understated as it might have been. In deference to my request, the good reverend had agreed to lower his voice whenever he came to a "Jesus," a solution satisfying no one. Every conspicuous whisper drove me further away from my body as it stood in that Charles Street apartment. Practically everyone I knew crowded around me, including an out-of-place Nancy, the familiar, brittle smile on her face. She didn't know anyone and didn't stay for the party. That chapter was closed and I was glad. We had nothing in common anymore and my future with "Sweet Sam" had no room for that part of my past.

On the way to the Dom after the wedding, Mama and I sat side-by-side in the backseat of a cab. The worst mistake she'd ever made, she confided, was learning how to iron. Too late for me, I said, and we laughed. "Never say 'never,'" my mother-in-law cautioned. The cab turned down Greenwich Avenue and we continued east, united in the bondage of married womanhood.

At the end of the boisterous party at the Dom, some younger guests withdrew to dine at the trendy Top-o'-the-Sixes with the bride and groom. The maître d' called my name, and the solid, all-American sound, "Mrs. Hood," rang proudly through the room. The young Hoods spent the night at the Gramercy Park Hotel, a grand old place Sam had booked to solemnize the occasion. *A bit conservative for my taste, but sweet of him*, I thought, resolving to be a damn fine wife and accept whatever that title implied, for better or worse, forever and ever. Now I had a football hero to love and take care of me. I would join the ranks of Dick and Jane's all-American mom, smile by the back door, wipe my hands on my apron, and "live happily ever after." With Sam I could be a wife and also retain my career and other parts of the life we shared.

At the hotel, exhausted and woozy from the merrymaking and champagne, I couldn't wait to lie down, and just managed to hang my dress in the closet before collapsing into bed. The next morning, groggy and hungover, I realized that in the whirl of the previous day I hadn't thought to bring a change of clothes. How embarrassing to leave the hotel in my wedding dress from the night before. But I couldn't even get my hands on that because the closet door had locked itself shut.

Sam called the desk and paced while management searched for the key. No one on staff could remember a closet door ever locking before. The morning proceeded with a maintenance man fiddling at the keyhole. Wrapped in a towel, I sat on the bed shifting my gaze from the television screen to the top of the mirror on the closet door. The familiar reflection was still framed by droopy hair, the eyes still underscored by dark circles. Marriage had helped my looks about as much as the beauty parlor in Kansas City.

Six days earlier, on April 20, gays and lesbians first publicly asserted their claim to equal rights in front of the White House, but I was too wrapped up in my own drama to notice. And, just as the quiet birth of a movement destined to carry me into the next decade and beyond slipped right by me, my transformation to "Mrs." slipped right by the FBI. Almost a year later, on March 29, 1966, they checked with the Manhattan Bureau of Statistics and uncovered Marriage License #7259 dated April 9, 1965. The report correctly lists both prenuptial residences, the dates and places of Sam's and my births, our father's and mother's names and occupations, but mislocated the ceremony "*in the Rectory of St. Mark's church-in-the-Bowerie* [*sic*]."

Honeymooning

FOR OUR HONEYMOON, we flew down to Florida to see Sam's old stomping grounds. He showed me where he had played defensive end for Edison the year they beat Miami High, and introduced me to his friends in Miami Shores. They were friendly enough, but it became immediately clear that our lives had little in common. I had no interest in them even though they promised to support the club. Although disappointed, he also appreciated evidence of the enormous changes Sam had undergone in a few short years whereas, he said, they hadn't changed a bit.

Grandma had settled in Miami Beach and wouldn't hear of us staying anywhere but with her, so for two weeks she gave us her bed and slept in the living room of her small flat. Now, at age seventy-six, she fussed over us as much as we'd allow. Public relations came naturally to Grandma, our biggest promoter. She pulled strings for a lead story in the May 10, 1965, "Women's World" section of the *Miami News*. A headline, "The Guitar Played a Wedding Song," appears beside the quarter-page photo of me gazing up at my husband, who beams down at me over hands arranged to display matching rings. Sam is quoted saying, "The only way to mix business with pleasure was to marry her." Plans for five children are mentioned, but ". . . not until we learn how to handle ourselves can we start to handle others." And from me, "'We're too happy to devote much time to anything but each other . . . I'm not going to travel anymore unless it's something very special,'" I'm quoted as saying, while "giving a firm squeeze to [my] new spouse's hand."

A constant source of encouragement and support for my work, Sam delighted in the songs I wrote for him. Another tribute, "For the Love of Sammie Leighton":

> *Daisy had a bicycle built for two and Amelia flew her airplane*
> *Pocahontas built herself a birchbark canoe*
> *Anne Boleyn had a hell of a migraine*
> *Salome sported seven of the sheerest veils*
> *And a head to meditate on*
> *But in spite of their renown, when the chips were down*
> *They didn't have Sammie Leighton. . . .*

Generally regarded as Florida's Greenwich Village, Coconut Grove was home to a racial and creative mix of offbeat residents. But unlike Greenwich Village, the Grove resembled a sleepy hamlet. Tall or squat palms overlooked picturesque cottages tucked into a lush sub-tropical landscape along narrow winding lanes and cul-de-sacs. It was the paradise Fred Neil always longed for on the road. His door swung open and we were welcomed inside by his girlfriend, Maggie, who immediately put me at ease. Fred and his sometime singing partner Vince Martin awaited within. Vince's recording of "Cindy, Oh Cindy" had been a huge hit nine years earlier. "You've got to move down to the Grove," the three urged enthusiastically and led us to the intersection of two main roads in a business section consisting of four blocks. Fred pointed out the site he'd been eyeing for months. "Build the 'Gaslight South' right here and it can't miss!" he said, waving toward the last remains of a hardware store at 2990 Grand. "It's the perfect spot."

Everybody would come, they told us. There was nothing in Miami besides The Flick, and that didn't count. Big folk names never came to a town hosting the world's greatest entertainers because The Flick, located in white, affluent Coral Gables, booked only locals and, they said, was too cheap to hire first-rate acts. A converted ice cream parlor, it catered to jocks from the University of Miami and offered none of the quality we could bring to the Grove. The velvet Miami air, the ambience of the Grove and its agreeable racial and class mix, strongly appealed to us. That, compounded with Freddy's insistent, "You can do it!" and promises of support made us believers.

After ten days of honeymoon partying, jai alai games, water skiing—which I took to like a natural in my pink bikini with white polka dots—and dog races where Sam lost the money earmarked for our return tickets, I was forced to turn to the same Flick we'd just finished disparaging for a weekend booking to earn our airfare back to New York. We departed Miami reluctantly, making plans to return as soon as we could.

Eager to escape Papa's sphere and venture out on his own, Sam felt confident that high school friends would back his folk club. From Lake Wales in Central Florida, his old cohort Gary would help out and Ken would come down later. It would be foolish not to move to Coconut Grove and open The Gaslight South, so we decided to do it.

Once back in Manhattan, Sam immediately got on the phone to raise money and I started packing up my perfect apartment.

So Long, Greenwich Village; Howdy, Coconut Grove

LEAVING MY LITTLE flat on Barrow Street wasn't easy. Neither was leaving Lynn and our ever-increasing closeness and good laughs. Like Mama, Lynn was quick to see life's absurdities to the point where a mutual glance could set us off into paralyzing guffaws. I would miss her. But then again, I was excited about the prospect of living with Sam in Coconut Grove and building a club there. My career was going nowhere in particular, and with a steady showcase in the smaller pond of Miami, I'd be a bigger fish. Our performer friends would visit for club bookings. We were ready to build our dream.

The songs on Dylan's LPs *Bringing It All Back Home* and *Highway 61 Revisited* were, we agreed, deep and wonderfully layered, but the breathtaking *Blonde on Blonde* became the music of our days. I couldn't hear enough of "Absolutely Sweet Marie," featuring my favorite harmonica solo of all time. His tunes were so singable! As we made the rounds to say our goodbyes we sang, "Everybody must get stoned!" All of our friends were Dylan fans. People who didn't listen to him weren't worth bothering with. Pop agreed with Mom, who said, "You can't listen to Dylan's songs and not change your life!" That's how we felt too. We wondered how he could remember all the words to so many songs.

The plane taxied onto the tarmac of the Miami airport and we deplaned with sky-high hopes and three hundred dollars in cash. Grandma housed us temporarily and Sam signed a lease on the hardware store.

Gary

THE LAST AND final time Papa went broke, the family had moved north from Miami Shores to the deeper South of Central Florida, where Sam met and bonded with Gary, a Lake Wales native. The cartons were still unpacked in the small house we'd rented when a blue pickup truck pulled into the driveway. Across the truck's rear window was a gunrack. This had to be Gary! Although Sam had told me something about him, I had to think, *Uh-oh!*

Western boots emerged from the cab, and a lean, long-legged man wearing a cowboy hat and blue jeans stood squinting into the bright Florida morning. He slowly surveyed the scene and ambled up to the door. An old white hound with black spots climbed down from the cab and ambled after him. Later he said that this was their first look at Miami, the biggest town either of them had ever been to. As he reached the door, I noticed a toothpick sticking out from the straight line of his mouth and a toothbrush peeking up from the front pocket of his Western-style shirt, complete with mother-of-pearl buttons.

If there was ever a culture clash, this was it. Living proof of our worst Southern white stereotype, Gary would shock my parents and horrify my former comrades. I could hardly believe this guy myself. He chewed Red Man tobacco and poached "'gators" with local boys, parking in the woods to "shine" deer with the car headlights, freezing the deer in its tracks. They'd kill it and gut the carcass with an eye out for the game warden. What could we possibly have in common?

Then again, reflecting on Gary's point of view was somewhat sobering, if not downright alarming. I represented everything his culture hated. A New York, Jewish Commie egghead who had been to Mississippi the year before to help register Negro voters, I'd be condemned in Gary's eyes as surely as racists and poachers were vilified in mine.

Thankfully, he proved to be soft-spoken and unpretentious, appeared to be without malice, and didn't say "nigger" in front of me. Now and then a wry observation or pointed question from Gary's direction would penetrate the conversation. Otherwise, it was hard to know what the silent observer on the sidelines was thinking.

For the first month, the compact cottage with one small and one closet-sized bedroom housed Gary, his dog Chester, Sam, and me. Colorful country expressions abounded, like insults such as "pissant," "fuckwad," and "sorry sack of shit." I grew used to hearing someone declare that he had to "piss worse'n a pestered polecat." I learned that "Plumb-nearly" was short for "plumb outta the county, nearly outta the state," and that a situation could go "from chicken salad to chicken shit."

Despite the kidding and good times, it wasn't long before cleaning up after the two guys and a dog began to rankle. In those days it would never cross a man's mind to pick up his own beer cans. Still, I was determined to maintain cleanliness and order, a habit cultivated on Barrow Street. My passive grumbling could be heard over the roar of the vacuum cleaner. "That Alix," I overheard Gary drawl into the phone one day, "she keeps the house real clean, but she sure don't like it!"

One day, his eyes lowered, Gary approached me in a serious manner, touching off my anxiety that I had somehow offended him. Instead, he complimented my guitar playing and asked me to teach him some chords. Practicing dutifully and doggedly, Gary soon learned to play well enough to write thoughtful, often funny country songs.

Sam, Gary, Chester, and I moved into a two-bedroom stucco house for the better part of 1965-66. Forty years later, when the address had long escaped my memory, I had only to turn to my FBI dossier where, next to the page with an enlarged close-up of the *Miami News* photo, it was: 6789 Sunset Drive.

At the end of the driveway, an expansive yard was fronted by a mysterious metal cross mounted on a cement foundation, the remnants of a long-gone structure. The house was going to seed but a screened-in porch and a pool that nestled amid rich greenery and classic statuary redeemed it. Elegantly tiled, the pool was reputed to be the first one built in Dade County. We tried to remember to warn guests that every so often the handsome palm tree overlooking the deep end released a coconut.

Construction

TRANSFORMING THE REMAINS of a shabby hardware store into a cool nightspot was no small undertaking. Folks stopped by during demolition to kibbitz and lend a hand hacking at the ancient shelves and counters. Soundproofing the ceiling was as unpopular as demolition had been popular, and our crew dwindled down to the dedicated few. Into the looming, booming interior we hauled a half dozen five-gallon cans of gooey, contact cement for sticking large squares of white soundboard onto a ceiling as vast as any cathedral.

Or so it seemed. Early one evening as we dangled our legs off borrowed scaffolding and finished off our subs and sodas, harsh work lights sliced through the darkness and illuminated the smoke wafting off our cigarettes. On the radio, Jackie DeShannon sang "What the World Needs Now," and The Byrds warbled Pete Seeger's "Turn, Turn, Turn." My gaze swept over stacks and tubs of construction material foretelling hard work ahead.

We scraped and painted the walls a gentle blue and glued framed panels of dark brown Portuguese cork in an asymmetrical soundproof grid. I had been obsessed, driven to finish framing the last few pieces of cork. Working hard twelve-hour days and nurturing visions of our inevitable success left little room to miss our Village culture. And when I did, I worked harder.

Late one afternoon, only days before our July 30 opening, with only a few panels left unframed, Sam walked over and took my arms. "We're going for pizza," he said, holding me away from my molding strips. "You need a break as much as we do." But I didn't want a break; I was determined to finish the few framing strips left. Suddenly, the accumulated stress and frustration of the previous months surfaced in the single uncontrollable tantrum of my entire adult life to date. Feeling as powerless as on my first day at preschool when Mom pried my fingers from the doorframe, I wailed in frustration, flung myself to the carpet, and beat it with my fists. The boys stood by, stunned. Then I quieted down, cleaned up, and went for pizza.

To both my relief and dismay, I found myself excluded from business details or decisions. Admittedly, the fantasy of Sam taking care of me had been one of marriage's attractions, but being shut out of matters of consequence hurt my feelings. Business was not my interest, but I had experience and ideas, and not having a say didn't exempt me from equal sweat-investment. Rather than verbalizing my gripes, I grit my teeth, rationalized, and shooed my concerns away.

Peggy Seeger sang, "When I was single, dressed oh so fine / Now I am married, Lord, go ragged all the time," but somehow I managed to disassociate from those words with my deeply held assumption that marriage meant being taken care of. When I was single, I had no money, but no debts either. As Sam told me, I was just being silly. After all, we were only starting out and everyone agreed that when the club opened the money would pour in. We'd need to hire Wells Fargo to take it to the bank.

Between the boys' banter, Grandma's stuffed cabbage, and encouragement from supporters and hangers-on, we managed to finish paneling the ceiling. Or at least that's what we thought until months later when a piece of soundboard came unglued during a show and crashed down onto the cobalt blue wall-to-wall carpeting. Fortunately, no one was under it and we stuck the wayward panel back up where it stayed put between our classy, long-stemmed, eighteen-inch globe light fixtures.

A faithful line rendition of Botticelli's "Venus on the Half-Shell," as we called our elegant, naked goddess, greeted each soul who entered. The image had suddenly appeared before my eyes at the Uffizi in Florence, only to emerge from my brush six years later in Coconut Grove on the wall facing the front door of The Gaslight South Café.

Good Press

GRANDMA WAS OUR biggest booster. Ecstatic about our plans, she took us to meet a crotchety old friend of hers, "a public relations genius," she explained as we waited to see him. "He knows all the big people with the show business connections. He'll help you." He was also dying of emphysema. We were shown into his "Florida room" where he sat in a wheelchair smoking a cigarette, a canister of oxygen at his side. Between coughing fits, he advised us to name the Club "The Kiss" and then told me to get a nose job. "If you follow my advice, you can't miss!" We thanked him and left.

To the upbeat tune of the Scottish "Weel May the Keel Row," I composed a jingle and recorded it for radio ads. "I love The Gaslight / I go there almost every night / Folk music's a delight / At twenty-nine ninety Grand."

Sam and I shared a vision and commitment, but he looked ahead while I looked over my shoulder, eyeing the gathering swarm of expenses overtaking our slim budget. I worried like my mother, silently with brow furrowed. Sam would take care of all that, he assured me, all but patting my pretty little head.

Among extensive press coverage, one story got the name of the club wrong and another wrote, "On the wall hang several mural paintings." A local entertainment weekly noted that "Sam Hood's wife, the former Alix Dobkin . . . will act as house performer when there are no other girls on the show-bill."

Days before we opened, the *Miami News* ran the piece Grandma had strong-armed from a contact there. A photo shows the mural and me, paintbrush in hand, perched on an eight-foot ladder, while Sam lounges against the lower rungs. My ten-foot-high Venus, a rose in her teeth, gazes passively down. "We're not in it for money, but for the love of the art," Sam comments prophetically. "How will it look when completed? 'Beautiful,' sighed Mrs. Hood."

In interviews, Sam always dropped every name he could think of. "Undoubtedly there will be Peter, Paul, and Mary, since they are Gaslight investors," he explained in one. "We know them and they're willing to come, and Phil Ochs, Bud and Travis, and The Highwaymen might be booked in the near future." Of those on his list, Tom Paxton and Ian & Sylvia actually did perform at the club, but Johnny Cash didn't.

After the heavy physical renovation was done, Ken appeared and moved into the screened porch. His specialty was pleasing customers and managing the flow of the crowd. A welcome addition to our little band, he and Gary amused each other, and Ken and Sam's smooth teamwork picked up where it left off, thirteen hundred miles and a lifetime away.

Open for Biz

OPENING NIGHT WAS the payoff. Drawing on energy beyond exhaustion, I assumed my duties with good cheer, the floor-beating episode receding from memory. Congratulatory opening night crowds flowed around me while Ken turned on the charm and Sam beamed, shaking hands and accepting compliments. The club had come together and looked magnificent. Gazing up into the swirl of heavy blue curtain separating the entryway from the interior, the magic of the evening and not having eaten a full meal in days made my head spin. The lights dimmed and from the backstage mic the deep voice of my husband resonated in the dark. "The Gaslight South is proud to welcome to the stage Miss Alix Hood." I slipped on my finger-picks and went up to play my set.

Our opening show featured Tom Paxton and lasted three weeks. Sam showed me how to count the night's receipts by separating the bills into denominations and stacking them cris-crossed by hundreds. Over the first weekend there were enough stacks to cover twelve hundred dollars' worth of floating checks.

Besides counting the receipts, opening the shows, and greeting customers, I helped bus tables and kept the room orderly. Things were looking up for the proprietors of the hottest hip nightspot in Miami and life leveled out into a new, satisfying routine.

Then, two weeks after we opened, riots broke out in Watts, Los Angeles, and white people stopped going to black or racially mixed neighborhoods like Coconut Grove. All we could do was hope that the news would calm down quickly, but it was not to be during that stifling summer, and people stayed away in droves.

Fred Neil's girlfriend, Maggie, waited tables at the club. For my birthday she baked a hefty chocolate cake loaded with crushed marijuana leaves. We were joking with the staff about the tiny green flecks when the beat cop dropped in.

Flashing looks and repressing nervous laughter, we invited him to join us. He finished off his slice with compliments to Maggie and left almost as happy as we were to see him go.

Skating the Margins

SAM HIRED GORDON Lightfoot, a young Canadian songwriter and friend of Ian & Sylvia. Although well written, his cold-hearted "That's What You Get for Lovin' Me" left me vaguely uneasy. Years later feminism would teach me to recognize and name the male concept of "romance" that used and discarded women. Also arriving from Canada was an audition tape from the young duo, Chuck and Joni Mitchell.

Bob Gibson, the charismatic charmer from Chicago, had introduced Joan Baez at the Newport Folk Festival. Like Fred Neil and Tim Hardin, he was a formidable talent whose career was short-circuited by heroin, which later killed him. In a tense performance at the club, we watched Bob sway this way and that, a glassy stare fixed on a far-off spot. His hand hovered over the guitar neck as he attempted to reach a tuning peg in ungainly slow motion. The seconds ticked away. Would he try to adjust each of his twelve strings? Poised at either side of the stage, Sam and Ken stood ready to hop up and lead him off or catch him on the way down. The audience shifted in their seats, and just as Sam gave Ken the signal, Bob snapped awake and launched into the same song he had finished long moments before. We all breathed out.

The awesome Odetta headlined for two weeks and blew everyone away, particularly Gary, who had never met as an equal a big, strong, not to mention brilliant and beautiful, black woman who stepped confidently in the world. The presence of the celebrated female icon both on and off stage swept veils from his eyes and scrambled not a few of his assumptions. "I was eat plumb through with ignorance," he confessed after she had gone.

In an instance of perfect timing, Sam brought Simon and Garfunkel to the club just as "The Sounds of Silence" was topping the charts, and we packed the audience in for their single Gaslight South performance. Papa, visiting with Mama, dubbed them "a one-hit group."

That and our Christmas show with Ian & Sylvia paid some worrisome overdue bills. A sparkling tree at the side of the stage overlooked stacks of gifts and suggested abundance, but the illusion dissolved when the holidays ended.

After a brief holiday boom we'd expected enough Weavers fans to fill the house for Ronnie Gilbert, but the crowds continued to stay away. Night after night, fewer than a dozen diehards trickled in for the fine performances. Sam and I visited Ronnie's motel room and chatted with her and the amazing guitarist Bruce Langhorne. Her warmth, intelligence, and easy laugh relieved the awkwardness of meeting someone whose voice echoed through my formative memories. We talked about how hard it was for artists to make a living and tried to cheer each other up. But the future looked grim.

We couldn't pay the rent, always overdue, and we owed everybody money. Neither Florida's bright sunshine and greenery nor a lovely, inviting pool outside could dispel the gloom of those months. The bills continued to pile up, and early one afternoon I dragged myself out of bed to check the mail to find seventeen returned checks in the box. I fled back to the house, flopped on the bed, and sobbed into a pillow. I had been broke before but never had I been afraid to pick up the mail or answer the phone. Sam reassured me, chuckling that it was silly to be so upset, especially now that the worst was over. "You never pick the right time to worry," he crooned, stroking my head. Checks had been returned before, had been covered before, and would be covered again. He'd take care of everything.

The Dylan Show

IN ADDITION TO running the club and stalling the bill collectors, Sam contracted to produce Bob Dylan at the Miami Convention Center just as "Like a Rolling Stone" exploded all over the airwaves. From Canada, the Hawks, out of which The Band would later form, were traveling with Dylan and bunked with us. We turned the porch into a dorm and borrowed cots, blankets, and bedding from everyone we knew and some we didn't.

In the two years since I'd seen him, Dylan's aura had become magnified beyond recognition. His formidable presence electrified all in his orbit and made each moment extraordinary. Everyone around him, no matter how cool-acting, was on constant alert for a sign from Bob, what he might want, or want to do. Reserved and self-protective, he said little, living inside his own head as always. Teenage girls lurked in the bushes beside the house hoping for a glimpse of him. We had gotten phone calls from someone claiming to be Suze, her voice muffled and faint. I wanted to believe it was her, but Bob said nope, it wasn't.

Inside the house, amid a constant stream of jokes and stories of gigs and tours, Dylan's crew and select locals lounged around, read magazines, drank beer, and visited the bathroom. Uncomplaining, I cleaned up after them all. An ongoing poker game at the dining room table featured variations like "Spit in the Ocean" and "Indian Poker," which made me cringe, but less than "Nigger Aviator." "It don't mean nothin'," Gary said, attempting an explanation about black and red cards, but I didn't listen. In that crowd of raucous, racist, drinking men, my sensibilities counted for little.

Halfway into the week, Pop came to Miami Beach as he did every year to prep for the annual Israel Bond dinner. Compared to the uproar of the Dylan concert week when people were everywhere, coming and going, Pop's previous visits to the house had been uneventful. This time, he sat quietly on the sofa, enjoying the action. At one point some of us sneaked off to smoke pot and play poker. Dylan had just bet "the number of hotel rooms with room service in Cincinnati" when Pop stuck his head around the door of our bedroom where we sat in a circle on the floor. The orbiting joint disappeared and for a moment everyone froze. Bob snatched his private reefer behind him, the line of his mouth wavering as he suppressed a giggle.

"Everybody disappeared and I was wondering where you went," said Pop, who had a poor sense of smell. Reluctantly I arose, padded to the doorway, and escorted him to the living room with some phony explanation or other. It was a shame to have to miss the game, but I was thrilled that Pop could share in the excitement of Dylan's presence.

The entourage abounded with personalities and some legendary names in the subculture, like singer, songwriter, and record producer Bob Neuwirth, who recited a poem about a Yak pissing his initials in the snow. Most memorable though was the road manager, Victor Maimudes. One night a bunch of us arrived home before the car transporting Dylan. Victor had noted the cross at the end of our driveway and devised a gag. "I'm going up there," he said, stripping down to his underwear. Someone wove some fallen branches into a circle while I grabbed a white sheet from the linen closet. Victor donned his wrap and stepped up onto the concrete footing. Arms spread wide, his long, dark hair hanging loose, he made a perfect holy tableau ready for illumination from approaching head-lights. Eventually Dylan's car pulled in and the gaunt, semi-naked figure blazed on the cross.

All was quiet until Dylan reacted. Finally he chuckled, granting the rest of us permission, and we whooped and rolled on the grass, shrieking with hilarity. I peed my pants but no one noticed. Pop stood on the back steps smiling and shaking his head in amazement. Years afterward he'd say in an awed voice,

"Remember that guy on the cross in your backyard in Miami, what was his name? Victor . . . I'll never forget the sight of him all stretched out like Jesus Christ."

Victor was road manager and responsible for the sound equipment and all the gear. The night before the Miami concert he took a truck to the airport to pick it all up. To pass the time while we waited, the guys told stories about Victor on the road, like the time in California when he had parked a semi filled with the instruments and PA systems, then forgot where it was parked. "There he is, walking around with this key to a rental, and he can't fuckin' remember where he fuckin' parked this *huge* truck." They laughed and slapped their knees. "He says he still can't remember where he left it."

"They should have looked at the pawn shop."

Storytelling aside, if Victor didn't get the equipment over to the Convention Center, the show would be in big trouble. Sam called the Miami Airport where it sat waiting to be collected. No Victor. The hours inched along. When the phone finally rang, everyone jumped and Sam picked up. "Where in hell *are* you?" The room watched his eyes glaze and his face relax into astonishment. "Opa Locka? You're in *Opa Locka*?" Six miles north of the Miami airport, crop dusters sat in the hangars of the Opa Locka airport. How did Victor get to Opa Locka? He couldn't remember, but had gotten lost and had driven around in circles for hours until he finally found the airport and had been waiting around for the plane with the stuff to land, but nothing much seemed to be happening. Sam reported, "He said, 'For a big airport it's real quiet out here. Kinda small and spooky.'" Controlling his voice, Sam explained to Victor where he was and where he should go. We laughed and shook our heads at the birth of another Victor story.

Backstage at the Convention Center the following night, in a sectioned-off space that served as a dressing room and resembled an industrial warehouse, a propped-up mirror stood haphazardly next to a few folding chairs, a large metal table, and an ironing board. Smoking what appeared to be the fattest joint I'd ever seen, Dylan, distracted and shifty-eyed, seemed more tightly wound than ever. We'd gotten word that Anthony Quinn would be there and wanted to meet him, so Victor was sent out to search the hall and bring him back. Soon after he left, Quinn appeared and was chatting with Bob when Victor burst back in. "I can't find that son-of-a-bitch anywhere!" The actor stopped mid-sentence, and in a frozen moment turned slowly toward Victor. No one made a sound until Dylan and Quinn cracked up and everyone relaxed and laughed.

Sam also produced John Sebastian and The Lovin' Spoonful at the Convention Center. I have always loved their music, but remember the night only as a flash of hectic activity. Both shows made money, but not enough to save us, and one spring morning we were greeted by a large padlock on the front door of The Gaslight South, putting a final end to its misery. "A damn shame, a goddamn shame!" said Gary.

The Little Black Cloud

WITH THE CLUB gone, Gary and Chester returned to Lake Wales, and Ken got married and moved south to Homestead. For a short time the pressure was off. There was nothing to lose and nothing to do but lounge around the pool in the sun with a smoke and *The Recognitions*, William Gaddis's dense tale of forgery. It took my mind off being too broke to declare bankruptcy and having to cash out the big coin jar to buy gas for the Plymouth that never broke down.

The next week the car was packed and headed to north Miami where we rented a motel "room w/ kitchenette" over which a little black cloud took up residence in my mind. Ken was selling appliances at Sears and Sam ended up peddling sewing machines in the next department. He'd sew wooden rulers onto pieces of cloth to demonstrate how tough the machines were.

The Olsten Agency sent me to many temp jobs including the campaign headquarters of Miami's popular young mayor, Robert King High, who had just won the Democratic primary for governor. Since no one could remember the last Republican governor, King High's victory was a virtual ticket to Tallahassee and a career in politics for me and Grandma, who had been hired part-time. Our confidence was the result of Florida Republicans running a nitwit named Claude Kirk. Sam and I would watch him being interviewed and turn to each other, jaws dropping. He could barely put a sentence together, whereas King High was smart, cute, energetic, exciting, and had a vision and a track record.

But on election night the numbers on the hotel's big board burst our bubble. There would be no gravy train to ride. Disappointment turned to horror when the hotel lobby speakers broadcast the national results and shot a chill through me. The baddies had won everywhere. I clenched my fists at the grim future I knew would result.

That our forward-looking candidate had lost to a numbskull was humiliating enough, but worse, Ronald Reagan had won the race for governor of California. Southern California businessmen, the same crowd who'd subsidized Tricky

Dick Nixon's chin reduction surgery, again pooled their resources. They hired a political public relations firm to train Ronald Reagan to impersonate a governor. The B-movie actor, a notorious quick study, thus commenced his A-level political career. In a vivid moment I realized that I was witnessing a catastrophic historic turn, and never again did I take for granted the common sense of American voters.

Cog in the Bureaucracy

SAM AND I found a sweet little house with an avocado tree in the backyard, and months after receiving my application, the State of Florida Employment Agency hired me to find jobs for truck drivers. My joy at the prospect of steady work with good benefits was soon overshadowed by the sinking in my gut. At first, the work seemed interesting and worthwhile. I enjoyed talking to drivers and matching them up with job openings, surveying 8" × 5" cards, their tatty corners worn away from generations of interviewers thumbing through the same low-paying work with no benefits and no future. We were all going through the motions, caught in the same bureaucratic revolving door.

At home, Sam and I raised our voices to the Beatles' "We Can Work It Out," and "All You Need Is Love," and sang along with the Turtles' "Happy Together," and the Lovin' Spoonful and Motown. On the surface, life seemed to be rolling along, but it felt empty. I began to live for weekends, and grew to hate my job even more than Sam hated sewing balsam rulers. I longed for late Saturday nights to come, to be in bed with my sleeping husband, captive to our little round TV screen and the weekly detective movie from the '30s followed by an equally vintage mummy, wolfman, or Frankenstein film. My favorite was *Dracula*, but in the 1931 original, a large Jewish Star of David hangs around Bela Lugosi's neck. It shocked me, and I wondered who else had noticed and what they had made of it.

Because Sam and I had dropped out of everything we cared about, Big Brother lost track of me, but finally located me at the Florida State Employment Agency. Occasional white islands appear on page after blackened page of my dossier baring phrases such as *"trouble-maker," "dissenter," "non-conformist,"* and *"beatnik,"* but the interviews suggest *"no particular reason to question* [my] *current activities or . . . loyalty to the United States."*

From the financial bottom we had lifted ourselves up into lackluster solvency and traded in our trusty Plymouth for a snappy white Corvair convertible.

But the dark cloud overhead appeared permanent, and my mood sank lower by the week.

Then one day a white dove came to rest above our door and stayed for a month. We took it as an omen, a messenger from the North, and my heart lightened. Nothing was keeping us in Miami, so we made plans to move. In the end, leaving our patch of paradise wasn't totally without regrets. Our landlord hated to lose his pleasant, stable tenants who were never late with the rent, and I hated leaving the charmed country cottage. Worst of all, John, with spectacularly bad timing, had just moved Lynn and the kids down to Key Biscayne.

Still, I felt more buoyant than I had in months. The black cloud disappeared. Sam quit Sears and began peddling slogan buttons which could be sold from anywhere. His catalog included "*Horseshit*" in heavy gothic lettering, "*Where's Lee Harvey Oswald Now That We Need Him?*," "*All Work and No Play Makes Jack*," and "*Nixon*" with a swastika for the "*x*."

We packed a U-Haul, hitched it to the Corvair, and headed up 95.

Return to Manhattan

MY PARENTS HAD moved from Philadelphia to Manhattan and we stayed in their tiny spare bedroom until we found our own apartment. Plants flourished under Mom's green thumb. Their silhouettes framed a gray afternoon sky in the big windows at the end of her living room as she and I sat at the table, our moods equally overcast. In front of our eyes, the entire front page of the *NY Post* proclaimed the murder of Martin Luther King Jr. He had condemned the war in Vietnam and was starting to connect politics, military, and corporate power to poverty. Mom and I reflected on the assassination of Malcom X and the FBI, who had tapped Dr. King's phone and harassed him. Our hearts heavy, we sat at the table sighing, our heads shaking side to side. The world looked much gloomier.

Our old friend Fran tipped us off to a one-bedroom apartment on East Third Street in a building with an elevator, a washer, dryer, and storage in the basement. It bordered the local elementary school complete with the happy sounds of children floating up at recess.

Two years after our wedding, Gussie & Becky's boutique had closed and Ruth was gone. Yet the neighborhood hadn't changed and was still redolent of Old Europe, fading into gray and shot through with color. The Dom remained, and the streets were jumping with people of all description. Old Jewish and Slavic ladies in babushkas gossiped and kept abreast of local doings while young mothers shopped and pushed their kids in strollers to and from Tompkins Square Park. Empty-eyed druggies swayed in slow motion, and ponytailed hippies leaned upon front windows of shops purveying drug paraphernalia and raunchy comic books, buttons, and psychedelic Peter Max posters like the ones Sam sold.

Chester's Children in Florida

GARY DROVE UP to the city with Chester and his friend Bill from Lake Wales, and they camped out in the apartment. Even more important than playing guitar, Bill owned a van. Both Sam and I were more than ready to take another crack at showbiz, and the talk inevitably turned to forming a group like the Beatles, but with a chick. We decided to name ourselves "Chester's Children" in honor of Gary's hound. Sam would manage the group in which I'd sing and play rhythm guitar, Bill would provide solos and vocal backup, and Gary would learn bass and perform his original songs. Chester would travel with us for luck.

A piano bar attached to an obscure central Florida motel was the place to get the act in shape before a triumphant return north. Sam talked the owner of The Candlelight Lounge in Lake Wales into experimenting with live music and booked us there for three weeks, six nights a week. We rehearsed, played out our contract, then cruised though Central Florida and bistros from Vero Beach to Gainesville. Sam booked us at Polk Junior College in Winter Haven and Webber College in Lakeland, where we led a "song-fest" in the school auditorium. But weeks of staying in cheap hotels and entertaining lukewarm audiences began to wear, the music started to feel old, and rehearsals were going lax. Sam juggled logistics while everyone's skins thinned, and I tried to keep the peace. There were still good times when I joked along with the boys, yet over the weeks I grew sadder and more solitary, more bored with the music and impatient with our slow progress, our shoestring budget, my friendless condition.

Tempers snapped and Sam had his hands full managing the group. We each dealt with the tension in our own way. Sam drank with the boys and took two Alka Seltzer tablets before bedtime each night to avoid a hangover in the morning, a trick learned from Papa. Not a drinker myself, I opted out of those sessions and lost myself reading studies of the human brain and *Dr. Strange* comic books. I was living with an alcoholic but that was an unfamiliar notion back then. Drinking was just what he did every night. I longed for intimacy and serious conversation but Sam did not share my interests and we continued to draw apart.

Living so close with men and only men intensified my feelings of confinement and isolation. Keeping centered meant constantly defending and redefining my ground, like wearing a rubber band around my ankle that always snapped me back to the same place. My low opinion of women and their boring conversations about housework and babies led to no female companionship and a brittle existence, a lonely life expressed by constant low-level anxiety and sadness.

Restless, I walked a deserted beach and felt myself ebbing away in the moonlight, wondering how I could go on. *I should leave Sam*, I decided. *But how? What would I do? How would I survive?* Ocean breezes ruffled the palm trees. I put one foot in front of the other and listened for an answer, but the only sounds I heard were rolling surf and rattling leaves.

Driving with the guys on an afternoon, we stopped at the side of the road to change drivers. While the boys walked around and stretched I pulled my arms down into my shirt, squirmed out of my bra, and put it away forever. By age twenty-eight, my twelve-year-old heart's desire had become unbearable, and as far as I could tell I looked no different with or without it.

Newspaper headlines kept us informed of multiplying anti-Vietnam war sit-ins, teach-ins, and student takeovers at universities. My generation was musically independent and had produced a culture that defied authority, rejected war, and distrusted everyone over thirty. Thankfully, I had a few years to go.

Many white citizens of rural Florida hated hippies and flower children, and were very likely to confuse us with them. My husband's hair was just long enough to arouse suspicion, and squares who didn't know better sometimes took us for freaks. I hoped that Sam's charm and Gary's authentic sideburns and good-ol'-boy manner might buffer the rudeness well known by darker-skinned people that only recently had been extended to longhaired anti-war types.

Our best meals were free at venues before and after shows. Otherwise, dinner consisted of many tiny ten-cent burgers and sweet pickles from Royal Castle or its first cousins, White Castle and White Tower. One night, after hours of driving, we pulled up to the only eatery open for miles. Promising Chester a burger, we locked the van and trudged into a silent room of cold stares. The counter woman took our order for coffee, fries, and a couple dozen tiny burgers. Her eyes slid over us and she turned her back. We hunched on counter stools and murmured nervous jokes to one another, our outsider status written all over us.

The notes of Barry Sadler's "The Ballad of the Green Berets" suddenly issued from the jukebox. It spoke for these short-haired patriots as surely as Country Joe MacDonald and the Fish's "I-Feel-Like-I'm-Fixin'-to-Die" spoke for us. Sadler's militaristic homage to the Marine Special Forces was night to the day of Country Joe's brazen, "An' it's one, two, three, what are we fightin' for? / Don't ask me I don't give a damn / The next stop is Vietnam." The rewrite of "Muskrat Ramble" was the last song we'd expect to find in that place of business.

Our business was clearly not welcome, and when we departed, grease-spotted bags in hand, not a single, "Ya'll come back now, y'hear?" followed us out the door. Chester gulped his burgers and I glanced back through the van's window to see a waitress with a rag grimly wiping off the stools we'd vacated.

The Comforts of Home

CHESTER'S CHILDREN DISSOLVED by mutual consent, and life on the Lower East Side resumed. To expand his inventory, Sam found a deal on Nehru jackets, bought a bunch to sell and kept several for himself. He cut a handsome figure conducting his business, now being run without me, in a West Village very different from the one we had left in '65. The folk boom had peaked and the presence of serious drugs seemed to make everything harder and meaner. The Gaslight had gone steadily to seed without Sam, who was now eager for a chance to revive the club without Papa. My brother Carl returned to the city and started working for Sam at what was now called "The Village Gaslight." Now and again I helped out or performed my tired old program but I felt out of place and removed. In addition to negotiating with club owner Howie Solomon to take over the Café Au GoGo, Sam was cooking up various projects with Ed Simon, owner of Café Au GoGo The Fat Black Pussycat, and former owner of the Gaslight.

On the Lower East Side I was close enough to my parents for comfort but separate enough for independence. While Sam went off to wheel and deal across town, I shopped at Key Foods and the neighborhood businesses, some of which Mom frequented. She'd ride downtown, stash her bike in the apartment, and we'd walk to Houston and a tiny storefront for bread. Next door, a little old Jewish guy sliced a pound of butter from one massive block and a slab of succulent, fresh cream cheese from another and wrapped each in sheets of stiff butcher paper for us. Then we'd stroll to Russ & Daughters for cold cuts. Walking these familiar streets on Mom's arm diminished my loneliness and the need to face the increasing alienation of my marriage. I thought about the good parts and allowed the city to distract me.

During this period my mother continued to impart practical universal principles, often using music to make a point the way she had during my brush with the piano when every time I'd speed up she'd yell in from the kitchen to slow down. Because she understood the rule physiology later confirmed that repetition deepens grooves in the brain, she'd often instruct that repeating mistakes will set you back and make them harder to correct later. This time she told me that little differences count in big ways, and that even the smallest degree of a divergent angle will inevitably progress into a wide gap. "Lines can look parallel in the beginning, but even the tiniest degree will take them far apart," she said, bringing the sides of her forefingers together and moving the tips outward in a *V.*

Carl's friends from Madison became friends of the family. Fellow students Carolyn and Jim Hougan later wrote scientific thrillers under their own names and combined their work to pen the "John Case" thriller series. Because Carolyn had recommended *The Morning of the Magicians* (Rollo Myers' translation from Louis Pauwels and Jacques Bergier's French compendium), I bought Mom a copy and we spent happy hours tossing ideas back and forth, from ancient knowledge and ethics to alchemy and science, or natural wonders and higher consciousness. Her notes inside the cover read, "exoteric," "pterodactyls(101)," "Lacunae(132)."

Friends and colleagues dropped by our Third Street apartment to eat and gossip. It wasn't unusual for Sam to appear for dinner with Flip Wilson or Doc Watson, Phil Ochs, Jim and Jean Glover, or Len Chandler and his wife, Nancy. I was happy to see and feed them all. One night after dinner as Doc played guitar, I stood over his shoulder and studied his right hand. He used a constant up-and-down motion and between his thumb and curled first finger, the tiniest tip of the flat pick barely stuck out. *If I ever used a flat pick I'd hold it that way.*

When Lynn and her family moved back to New Jersey, just across the Hudson, the isolation that had laid me low on the Florida beach was history. Equally frustrated by our enforced separation, we sometimes joked that John and Sam had conspired to keep us on opposite ends of the East Coast.

I hadn't lost my taste for a hefty metaphysical discussion, and my sister-in-law hadn't either. I'd missed her wacky perspective and our good laughs. The hours flew by when we parsed the Laws of Correspondence, vibrational transformation of matter, Teilhard de Chardin, Madame Blavatsky, Jung, and Gurdjieff. We investigated our astrological charts, explored the natures of Leo (me) and Scorpio (her). With Lynn I didn't feel crazy or out of step with everything around me. My self-confidence restored, I moved closer to my strongest self.

Our family friend Fran hired me for part-time clerical work at her literary agency. An agreeable walk to the West Village office in a brownstone off Sixth Avenue was topped off by the lift in spirit her company never failed to deliver.

Ass-Ending in Woodstock

IN THE EARLY 1960s, the New York State Thruway opened, sharply cutting driving time from the city up to Orange and Ulster Counties. Ninety miles from Manhattan and eight miles from the New York State Thruway, the town of Woodstock denied Michael Lang a permit for his 1969 festival. But publicity had gone out and it was too late to change the name, so the town became identified forever with the landmark event that happened sixty miles away.

For decades the beauty of Woodstock had drawn creative people and free-thinkers who expanded its horizons far beyond the founders' anti-Semitic inclinations. The vibrant art colony had become home to potheads, freaks, and flower children, some of whom remained to evolve into respectable pillars of the community. Dylan bought a house and was followed by his entourage. Tim Hardin installed his crowd in the big, old, rambling Hellman's Mayonnaise estate where I first heard the brilliant Warren Bernhardt playing on Tim's grand piano. Al Grossman moved up with big plans to build a state-of-the-art studio and was reputed to be working on other enterprises with Dylan.

Woodstock in 1970 was the place to be. At least it was where Sam and I wanted to be. Each time we exited the Thruway we'd swing past "Maggiore's Farm," the name painted in large, white letters on the wooden siding of the farm stand. "Oh, I ain't gonna work on Maggie's farm no more," came immediately to mind, a landmark on the musical map of the world courtesy of Woodstock's most notable citizen.

Dylan sometimes contacted Sam for favors. For example, before we moved back to New York, Sam and I spent one week scouting hideaways for Dylan at the tip of Florida, trekking out to view property after secluded property on behalf of an "anonymous friend." "Money is no object," we told the agents, but it was all for nothing when Bob eventually changed his mind. He and his family had settled into a farmhouse on the outskirts of Woodstock village, and deep into mud season of '69, he invited us to visit.

Shivering in a phone booth on Tinker Street, cradling the phone against my shoulder, I called ahead for the (highly confidential) directions while Sam waited with the car running. I was nervous about talking to Dylan. Since his great rise to fame, I could never think of anything to say to him, or my mind just stopped working altogether.

A few rings and then a scratchy connection to the world-famous voice and it started reciting directions: "You're gonna ascend a hill . . ." it said, "ASS-end . . . that's going up, right? DEE-sending goes down?" My mind blanked. "Yeah, I think so," I said, careening between a desire to impress Bob with my coolness and my fear that he'd think I was a jerk. Scrunched up in the booth, I was also freezing, my scrap of paper was slipping, and the pencil stub wriggled in my fingers.

A giggle in my ear and, "Well (pause) don't DE-scend, just make sure you go on up and ASS-end that hill." We did, turned, and arrived at our destination. It was set back from the road against drab-looking woods. All around, patches of melting snow exposed the remains of last year's autumn with an earthy fragrance.

I was surprised. My expectation for someone with Dylan's success was for grander quarters than the collapsed stone fence and unpretentious farmhouse before me. Inside, tall bare windows threw cold light on sparsely furnished rooms. Dylan sat, his presence less surreal than I remembered. Rising to greet us, he introduced Sara, who emerged from the kitchen looking monumental in a long skirt, the baby Jakob on her hip. Bob was calmer and moved more slowly than the last time I'd seen him, no doubt the result of his motorcycle accident. Within the large shadow of her husband, Sara radiated tranquil authority, and it occurred to me that she would have been involved in his transformation. I was pleased to notice that he treated her with respect and even deference. On the whole, the family scene appeared perfectly normal. Except that it was Bob Dylan.

The sun peeked in and out of clouds as he led us outside and quietly discussed his accident. It had scared him, changed him forever. Coming so close to dying and spending that much time laid up made him think about what was important. He now saw things in a different light, he told Sam as they ambled off together. Sara and I lingered behind to chat and our conversation turned to metaphysical matters. We spoke of *Morning of the Magicians* and our ideas of good and evil. I believed in it. She wasn't so sure. She had been studying spiritual history, and I asked which school of thought she followed. After a moment she answered, "The closest I can describe it would be a kind of primitive Christianity," an intriguing remark, but I wasn't sure what she meant. Perhaps there was more to Christianity than oppressive savagery, fear, and "the opiate of the people."

When the time came to leave, Bob walked us to our car and Sara followed, curly-haired Jakob still perched on her hip and *The History of Magic* in her hand. "I've just finished this," she smiled, handing the thick volume to me. "You'll find it interesting."

Intoxicated, I filled my lungs with the scent of newly thawed earth and pictured myself living in Woodstock. With a family. Maybe someday.

All in a Day

EARLY ONE EVENING, the FBI called and Sam picked up the phone. Did he know that his wife had been a Communist? Would he be willing to talk to them? He told them to go to hell. In my files I was demoted to "housewife," a major step on the road to "inactive."

On May 4, 1970, the Ohio National Guard shot and killed four protesting students on the campus of Kent State University. We were outraged and so was everyone we knew. How low would our government go? To keep up with current events, Sam and I read the *Village Voice* and *RAT*, the wildly irreverent first "alternative" paper I ever saw. "Women's Liberation" was also in the news, but compared to anti-war activism and liberation struggles of third world people, I perceived women's rights as marginal.

One day we drove to Woodstock and as Sam pulled into the Deanie's Restaurant parking lot, our opinionated, hot-headed friend Sean started in on feminists. "They're just a bunch of bitter old dykes taking out their frustrations on men," he sputtered. I was quick to agree. Neither a whiny victim nor a raging "women's libber," I had no need for liberation. I was already free to do what I pleased, thank you!

Besides, the last thing I wanted to do was to disturb the delicate equilibrium of my life, much less blow it to bits with new and unsettling notions.

From time to time I sang at Gerde's and performed or helped out at the Au GoGo or The Village Gaslight. Herb was trying to sell my songs, sending me into dinky little studios to record demo tapes for clients. Sometimes I sang my own tunes and sometimes songwriters or producers hired me to sing their material on "spec," meaning spectacular odds against ever seeing any money. One producer asked me for a breathless, submissive reading of his sex-kittenish lyrics. I did my best to deliver and he complimented my performance. Faking took no effort, all the while wondering who on earth would believe it. I couldn't imagine a woman choosing to be a slave, let alone speaking those ridiculous phrases. It then struck me that most of the songs women recorded were actually self-serving male fantasies written by men for men. The woman's role was to deliver the message. Period.

Singing crap paid crap, and finances were again looking bleak when a vice president of Frank Music Company started showing up at The Gaslight to see Loudon Wainwright III, future father of Rufus, who was performing there regularly. This VP heard a set of mine, liked my songs, and offered me a contract with the company founded by Frank Loesser, the man whose *Guys and Dolls* was arguably the best musical score of all time. *A good omen*, I thought, especially when I had signed the contract and held in my hands an advance check with promises of more to come.

Frank Music suggested collaboration and put me together with a young composer. Without singing the tune I had written, I gave him the lyric of a birthday song for my sister Julie, hoping he'd come up with something better. But his first few measures paralleled my own practically note for note. Did lyrical phrases dictate their own melody? In any case, I decided that, on the whole, my tune was prettier and less predictable than his and that I'd be better off working alone.

Consciousness Raising

NEW YORK WOMEN were on the move. The personal, they declared, was political. Everything women were not permitted to do and everywhere women weren't permitted to go was politics. Actions erupted regularly with sit-ins, takeovers, and demonstrations. Even lesbians were making their presence felt and some women feared a "lavender menace." What was being menaced and how was unclear.

Women artists fed up with the closed doors of the mainstream art world were getting together and finding that the artistic was also political. Outrageous, inventive, public actions by artists and allies made headlines. Front page photos showed them picketing the Museum of Modern Art wheeling a jumbo-sized, pâpier maché purple dinosaur representing the backward, good-ol'-boy art establishment. Demanding to be seen and counted, they demonstrated for legitimate grievances of exclusion with determination, but more fun and grit than spite or hatred. They looked happy. Was this the "feminism" I had railed against so recently?

Louise called. She had been meeting regularly with a group of women and her life had been changed. With the receiver clamped between shoulder and ear, I paced the kitchen and listened to the voice of my friend.

"I can't believe I actually marched in a gay parade as a lesbian out there in public with all those freaks and drag queens. Oh my God!" Considering that once she had been almost locked away for being a lesbian, I thought Louise truly heroic. Clearly, feminism as practiced by the women in her consciousness-raising group had helped her stand up for herself and confront her own well-grounded devils. "You should join a group, Alix," she suggested. "It'll be good for you."

While groundbreaking radical feminist geniuses were slugging it out over the details, consciousness-raising, by 1970, had begun to electrify the world. The time had come to get over my antipathy toward women. Mom approved of my joining a weekly consciousness-raising group, and Sam was positive. When I expressed doubts, he surprised me with enthusiastic support, saying, "You should do it, Ay-lix," which he called me when he was being playful. "It'll be good for you." Lynn expressed an interest, so I told Louise that my sister-in-law and I were ready to sign on. Her group was full, but Amy—sister of Jenny from Louise's group—was forming one. I should call Amy, she said, and I did.

I discovered that, like barn-raising, consciousness-raising is a dedicated group project that produces a total exceeding the sum of its parts. The strict equality and personal storytelling format distinguished CR from therapy, and, unlike barn-raising, CR raised everyone's barn simultaneously. Women in the group agreed on topics such as "popularity," "menstruation," and "mothers." Even the most timid was encouraged, but not compelled, to tell her own truth free from the fear of disapproval or rejection. Sitting in a circle, women passed an object from hand to hand, a "talking stick" that conferred exclusive speaking rights. No one interrupted except for requests for clarification. Each woman was listened to and respected. Focusing on the subject chosen the previous week, women voiced their deep personal experiences and feelings, often for the first time. No two stories were alike, yet each was the "norm," including mine. Each teller was respected, including me.

It felt comfortable and exciting, sort of like Party meetings combined with the easy intimacy of a girls' team venturing inward together, making our way into risky, unfamiliar personal terrain with no map. When my turn came to tell about childhood sexual abuse I told about the man at the Thanksgiving Day parade who tried to put my hand in his pants. Everyone was on my side. We noted that every woman there had at least one similar experience and most had more and worse. When the topic was marriage I described beating my fists on the carpet of the unfinished Gaslight South and everyone understood why I did it. Meetings always left me feeling stronger and more confident of my value in the world. So many problems that I thought were personal were actually faults in patriarchy and its institutions. The personal, we discovered together, is truly political in the deepest sense.

Some of the women had dreaded the onset of menstruation, and one didn't know what was happening to her and thought she was dying, while I had welcomed it as a sign of maturity and its attendant privileges, such as drinking coffee. We compared what we were taught, what name we called it, embarrassing moments, complaints. By so doing, we shared and distilled our understanding of ourselves.

The form of the CR group brought to mind the Red Chinese practice of "Criticism and Self-Criticism." It had been the topic of some discussion at a Party meeting during which we learned about the process in which people sit in a circle and speak personally, honestly, and in turn. But that's where similarities ended. With its judgment and censure, the harsh and controlling Chinese system was designed to cut each individual down. On the other hand, through commonalities and empathy, CR groups supported and strengthened each individual.

The contrast between CR and crit/self-crit illustrated Mom's lesson about trajectories of differing angles that start from the same place but lead to the gap separating creativity from fear and control, "power over" or "under" from "empower." How did this relate to the disparity between men and women? Along with a new way of thinking, my plate was piled high with tantalizing food for thought, a concoction of personal and political.

To run across such strangers in my everyday life would have been highly unlikely and becoming friends with them even more so, I thought, scanning the eight or nine working and middle class white women that made up the group. I was no better or worse than any of these professionals, artists, housewives, and moms from assorted backgrounds, each with her own perspective. Each story, equally valuable, brought everyone into sharper focus and reinforced our solidarity. My contempt for women had taken its last breath.

Pregnancy

NO RECORD CONTRACT was in sight, and the Guild had been resting undisturbed in its case for many months, Chester's Children had gone under, no new project excited me, and I felt a void that having a child would surely fill. Swiftly approaching the mysterious, cloud-covered mountaintop of thirty, finding a worthy direction for my life took on added urgency. It was time to think about a baby, and I pictured Mom and Pop's joy when I presented them with their first grandchild. For me, having children had always been a given. Pregnancy was my final female credential and would complete my womanhood. Reinvigorated, I entered the decade that was to change my life in unimagined ways. A common purpose would draw husband and wife together onto common family ground. Sam was definitely in favor of children and in the first month of 1970 we conceived one. Little did I realize that, possibly in order to preserve the species, women are given no clue about the grittier realities of motherhood. Power struggles with a contrary little upstart never once crossed my mind as I retired the diaphragm to its case for a sabbatical.

Immediately after confirming my pregnancy, a class-three, "pre-cancerous" pap smear put me into the hospital before I had time to think. Cone biopsies—in which a cone-shaped piece of flesh is carved from the cervix—are not nearly as common now, I am told. But that's what I had, and when it was done, in a quick blur, I was still pregnant.

The Park Avenue ob/gyn explained what I could expect, agreed that Lamaze was a fine idea, and steered us to classes at New York's Lying-In Hospital, where our child would be delivered. Episiotomy, he explained, was a simple, routine procedure performed for more than 90 percent of births. It was strongly recommended because during delivery, vaginal tissue might tear and become ragged and messy. On the other hand, episiotomy was a simple, clean "snip," he explained, neglecting to mention that not only tissue of what Gary and Sam referred to as the "taint," but also muscle and highly sensitive nerve endings would be sliced. However I knew nothing and said as much.

"Why do we do it?" he asked rhetorically. "Naturally, giving birth will stretch your vagina," he answered, leaning in confidentially. "This procedure will prevent you from stretching and you'll heal tighter than you were before. In the future your young, virile Sam, here, might not be able to hold his erection as well as he does now." Raising his eyebrow, he nodded to my husband. "It happens as men age. This would take care of that and also spruce up your sex life." He beamed and I nodded, compliant, never suspecting that in the third week of October I would wish him dead with every step I took. In his comfortable office, however, this "minor procedure" seemed hardly worth thinking about, and I didn't.

Exuding good health and good spirits, I knew I could handle anything, no sweat. I was reading up on fitness and nutrition, exercising, eating yogurt, and taking extra supplements. Self-satisfied, even smug when the undeniable evidence began to show visible proof that a man had loved me, I was clueless about how pathetic that was. In my new all-powerful state, I could take on King Kong while crying at the drop of a careless word.

Lynn was ecstatic at the news, and the women in my CR group beamed. At the end of a meeting at Amy's, I retrieved my jacket from the small bedroom where her infant daughter, Ivy, slept peacefully in her crib. Soon, in my apartment, the sleeping baby would be mine.

Abundant congratulations and well wishes wrapped me in a cocoon of approval, similar to what I had enjoyed prior to my wedding. Mom and Pop were pleased, but not as overjoyed as I had imagined. They presented us with *Child Behavior*, a commonsense guide to child-raising. Written by Arnold Gesell from his highly regarded institute at Yale, it was based on studies of young children's developmental stages. Nervous parents could be reassured that the troubling behavior of their child was "normal" for its age. The inscription said, "Read and relax!"

The Gaslight's Big Night

CARL AND SAM were managing audiences at The Village Gaslight where the Simon Sisters, David Blue, Kris Kristofferson, Bonnie Raitt, Danny Kalb, Linda Ronstadt, and Hugh Romney (who would later become Wavy Gravy) rotated through. Teenager Janis Ian generously returned her fee one night to help the Club through a difficult cash-flow period. Van Morrison performed with a small band. Clearly a superb player, he wore a guitar but only picked a phrase or two now and then, mostly hanging onto the mic stand while he sang. His restraint impressed me. *It must be a great luxury*, I thought, *to have enough natural talent to be that casually sparing of it.* But lively business on some nights was offset by too many slow ones, and hard times cast its familiar shadow over us.

Then, in the early spring of 1970, shortly before *Fire and Rain* was released, Sam booked young James Taylor, catching him as he had caught Simon and Garfunkel on their way to the top of the charts. As expected, we had to turn people away from his one-night-only Village Gaslight appearance.

On that night, besides squares who had never before set foot in the Village, folkies, friends, and celebrities flocked to 116 MacDougal where extra staff was on hand to serve the throng. With any luck, the health, building and fire inspectors would stay away. Sam outdid himself engineering the capacity-plus seating to the point where I overheard him negotiating with two customers competing for bench space. Both would get to see the show if one person's leg rested on the lap of the other. They agreed. It was worth it to get close to this outstanding young talent on his meteoric rise. Normally, I loved watching Sam work crowds, friendly, confident, and creative. But there was no time for watching that night.

I volunteered to wait tables but quickly foundered, losing track of who sat where wanting what. The failure was doubly pitiful, seeing as our menu and capacity were quite limited. My regard for overworked, underpaid waitresses soared. I was reassigned a job I could do in the alcove behind the stage keeping track of the checks, making change, counting the money, bundling the bills, and stashing them in the freezer around the bend at the back of the kitchen.

Another admirer of Sweet Baby James, Ethel the counselor from my days at camp threaded her way back through the crowd to my tiny space; her presence doubled the thrill of the occasion, as did the company of Sylvia Fricker, who was in town without Ian. It was impossible to move anywhere, so the three of us stayed put, chatting animatedly about my pregnancy, James and his songs, the excitement of the evening, and the great crush of fans. A corporate-looking fellow dressed in suit and tie appeared. "I represent *The Merv Griffin Show*," he informed us haughtily, and asked for James's manager. "Is Merv Griffin really as big an asshole as he acts on TV?" we asked him. He swiveled his head, straightened his tie, and backed out into the multitudes.

Weeks before, Sam had met a guy his age who wanted to open a restaurant and folk venue in Woodstock. Having no experience in the business, he offered Sam the managing partnership. Everything depended on his father's backing, and he would need to check it all out, so Sam invited the old man to come in from Long Island on James's night. Barely able to squeeze inside the club, he was visibly impressed with Sam and the business. The boys began planning their venture, and we looked forward to a summer in Woodstock.

Both Sam and I wanted to live in the country and had almost bought a house in Bucks County, Pennsylvania. It was as old as America with low ceilings, slanted floors, and a root cellar. I liked it, but when the owner pulled out of the deal I felt hugely relieved, since I had no idea where the money would come from. But with the promised success of the club, Woodstock property now seemed within our grasp.

Sean, who was also a chef, came on board to help remodel and oversee the kitchen. The vacant "Elephant Emporium" was transformed into a restaurant/nightspot half a block from the Village Green in the town where the famous Festival we had missed was never held.

Woodstock, Summer, 1970

AT THE CREST of a hill off Orchard Lane—a road as charming as the name suggests and a road I currently walk on to the post office almost daily—Sam and I rented a three-room summer cabin. Surrounded by woods, it sat across the driveway from the landlord's freshly painted farmhouse where he lived with his pregnant wife and five-year-old son, an angry, disagreeable child. I felt sorry for his mother, but a nodding acquaintance was as close as I cared to get to her. She screamed at the boy many times a day and the sound grated on my ears. How in the world did she expect to handle another? From a comfortable distance, I vowed never to raise my voice to my child, a silly pledge that provokes a shake of the head when I think about the times I screamed my head off at Adrian when she was that same age.

During my pregnancy I was determined to do it right and confident that I would. I didn't smoke, I drank lots of water, and bought fresh fruit and vegetables at one of Woodstock's two health food stores. Every morning I'd sit in the sun, belly exposed, and tackle the pile of magazines and books beside my chair, *The History of Magic* among them. It was impossible to remember when I'd felt so fully realized, so deeply content. My Woodstock doctor told me that with my bones and blood type, I was built for childbirth. "You could get pregnant with any guy in the ballpark," he said. I pictured Ebbets Field and felt oddly proud.

For his part, Sam played the part of pleased, expectant father who, when he wasn't working, pampered me. For a time we both lived the dream that he would take care of the business and me, while I had only to take care of the tiny life I carried. That was my fantasy. Sam was smart and capable. He'd work it out, and rather than worry about The Elephant's nightly receipts, I basked in a simple, country-girl mode, reveling in passivity and rarely giving a thought to my former activist life. My body felt more vital than ever before and glowed with good health. A patch of lawn in the back received good sun, and by tearing handfuls of turf from a six-by-eight foot plot of lawn, I made a garden for tomatoes, snow peas, lettuces, onions, radishes, squash, and parsley, bordered with nasturtiums, cosmos, and marigolds to discourage insect pests.

In Woodstock, as in Coconut Grove, Sam laid out the plans and the budget for his club, secured permits and licenses, hired staff, and oversaw the remodeling of the kitchen to Sean's specs, and this time I was happy to stay out of it. As I studied books and articles on pregnancy, my biggest issue was whether or not to take fluoride tablets (I didn't).

My career was over, yet on my birthday I picked up the guitar and began practicing an hour every day using a flat pick, and, holding it the way I had seen Doc Watson do at our apartment, repeating an unvaried up/down motion with the pick, as he did. I devised left hand exercises for each finger, trying especially to increase the strength of my left pinky and ring finger.

Although I had no thought of performing, there were ways I could contribute to The Elephant, so I got busy designing a logo, then a menu, posters, and handouts. Many a satisfying hour I enjoyed, bent over the kitchen table, creating an original font style, working and re-working the elephant image from the original sign hanging over the door, until it suited me. To advertise our first day of business I'd lettered a special handout: *"With unpardonable pride and utter lack of humility, THE ELEPHANT announces that the kitchen is now open. . . ."* Menu items covered a variety of *"delicious deli-type sandwiches"* as well as *"espresso nonsense,"* and the reminder, *"We have the best entertainment outside of NYC, but you already know that."*

On Friday, April 24, 1970, The Elephant's "Grand Re-Opening" hosted a double bill of Odetta and N.R.B.Q. Through spring, summer, and into mid-August, Sam ran six nights of live music, charging admission only on weekends.

Odetta preceded an uninterrupted succession of males: Ramblin' Jack Elliott, Tim Hardin, and John Hammond Jr. for May, followed in June by Sonny Terry & Brownie McGhee, Dave Van Ronk, Patrick Sky, and Jerry Jeff Walker. July opened with Happy and Artie Traum, featuring Bob Gibson as their special guest. The shows drew crowds, and the place was packed for Fred Neil, who recorded a live album from The Elephant's stage. "This one's for Sam," he laughed, a remark making it onto vinyl.

Dion, Tom Paxton, and John Phillips were the café's August headliners, but because of my pregnancy and alienation from the folk scene, I kept more and more to the cottage. Despite being separated from the operation of the Elephant more than I had been at The Gaslight South in Coconut Grove, the ever-present money anxiety stuck to everything. As always, Sam's assurances were comforting and the business deserved to thrive, but customers stayed away, at least on days when I strolled to the nearly empty restaurant. I liked walking into town, gossiping with Sean or chatting with Annie, a dancer who waited tables, all of us on the lookout for customers.

The shows were outstanding, the food tasty, healthful, and reasonably priced, but as the summer wore on, it became clear that The Elephant's days were numbered. Underfinancing and the cost of renovations took its toll, and attempting to shield myself from the obvious and the depressing, I dropped in less and less. Then, at the end of August, like The Gaslight South had before, the comfortable gathering place and all-star venue closed its doors.

I was eight months pregnant and back in Manhattan.

Birth Pains

MY FINAL WEEKS of pregnancy consisted mainly of final Lamaze classes, breathing practices, guitar exercises, visits with Lynn, shopping, cooking, crying, and flopping exhausted into bed. On a Wednesday morning in late October 1970, I began to cramp, and after a while Sam and I grabbed a cab uptown to New York University's Lying-In Hospital, where after more contractions, not much seemed to be happening.

I lay contracting and relaxing for hours in a room with a curtain around the bed. Sam came and went, while now and then, nurses and doctors arrived and poked around, reporting that I was still not dilated. Finally, my doctor discovered that a dissolving stitch from the biopsy eight months before had failed to dissolve. My cervix was being held together against its will, so he broke the stitch which immediately let loose one unceasing contraction, and without a moment to spare or to breathe, my body tried to make up for lost time with the worst cramps I'd ever experienced.

A huge pit of pain gaped before me. I teetered on the edge of that black void with Lamaze my saving grace and only solid ground. Counting the huffs and puffs the way we had practiced, Sam breathed along with me, offering encouragement and comfort, but there was no comfort to be had short of death. I flung my head from side to side, making the room see-saw. Complications required a spinal tap, monitors, and shots. They clapped an oxygen mask on me when an alert nurse realized that my continuous contraction was depriving the baby of oxygen. They wheeled me into the delivery room where, surrounded by anxious faces, I saw the doctor coming at me with huge forceps, one in each hand. That they were not attached alarmed me even further. I pushed harder. The baby came out. And I heard, "She's a redhead!"

Later, aching, crotch afire, and muscles still cramping, I was unable to absorb it all. But my heart leapt at the sight of the bundle that was laid on my chest. A girl, but not a redhead! A dear, tiny Libra worth every agonizing second. On the second day, I hobbled to the pay phone in the lobby to call the venerable Philadelphia folk maven, Gene Shay, in order to cancel an appearance on his radio show the following night. Shuffling back, I spotted my baby through the glass of the nursery. I recognized her instantly and knew we belonged together. Mine was the best-looking baby in the place and a Jones girl for sure. Clearly in Mama's line, she'd be a beauty! The pouty lip, like her cousin Janie's, gave it away.

"She looks like a peanut when you hold her," I remarked about the little parcel lying in Sam's burly arms, and from then on, she was "the Peanut."

It took three days before I could walk without crying. When I complained to the perpetrator that every move, every drop of pee was torture, he replied that it would heal and I'd soon forget all about it. He was half right.

The hospital presented departing mothers with sanitized advertising packets of sample disposable diapers and antiseptic wipes with admonitions to keep everything sterile at home. I thanked them and never sanitized a thing to give Adrian's young immune system a chance to start working on its own.

Dr. Mitty, a cheerful pediatrician in her sixties, had checked out Adrian's hands, feet, eyes, ears and reflexes, and pronounced her fit. But what about my milk? Where was it? Oh, she assured me, it would come. Why hadn't anyone mentioned that mother's milk does not always come immediately after giving birth? How many more times would I be ambushed by ignorance? No one had ever mentioned anything like the fact that my breasts would turn into painful aliens bearing no relationship to what I used to have. They felt like two socks packed hard with wet sand that had been stuck on my chest, and didn't stop hurting until the day after I was discharged and my milk came in. Then, everything changed. The little peanut and I could rock contentedly to the animated sounds rising up from the playground below.

And in due course, I was able to take a step without thoughts of homicide.

Baby, Baby, Baby!

A HAND-LETTERED CARD announced our six-pound, ten-ounce, and nineteen-inch Adrian. Adrian Leighton Hood. Three syllables, then two, then one. Our infant shined so brilliantly that in her first photographs she appears as a bright patch of white between two cradle ends. I spent hours examining her. I sketched her asleep. Or, her face on my chest, we'd drift off together in that perfect contentment of a sleeping babe-in-arms.

Through my first-hand experience with the miracle that produces human life on earth, every person to meet my eyes appeared miraculous. More important, a woman like me had, I suddenly realized, brought each one into the world. Some woman had cared for each derelict lying in Bowery doorways across Houston Street. Seeing them, I had to wonder about the blows time might deliver to a mother's heart. My own mother, with little in the way of information or acceptable role models, considered herself inadequate, yet had successfully raised three children. My respect for her skyrocketed, and I prayed to do half as well. *Who could have known what this business would be like? Other mothers*, I thought, excited to bond with Mom in fresh comradeship. But I had miscalculated. Responding to a babysitting request, she announced the end of her child-rearing days. Still, she sympathized when I related the ordeal of Adrian's delivery. "It must have been God-awful," she clucked.

Stiff and self-conscious, Mom talked baby talk to her new granddaughter, played baby games, and exercised each tiny limb to improvised little songs. Pop snuggled her and crooned, "Ah, loo, loo, loo, loo, loo, baaay-bee," as he had with each of us, pacing slowly back and forth, his eyes shut tight, his heart open wide. Grandma came up from Florida, Mama and Papa from their new home in New Orleans, my sister Julie from school in Wisconsin, and friends and colleagues all paid their respects: Jim and Jean, Flip, Paul Siebel, Buzzy Linheart, and Kris Kristofferson, who balanced a blasé Adrian on his knee.

Every chance I'd get I'd nuzzle that fat little neck with the magnificent baby aroma. On our nightly trek around the living room, my fingers tapped rhythms on her back in time to Cat Stevens's "Peace Train" spinning on the turntable as I sang along. Backstage at the Au Go Go, before his conversion to Islam, Cat had projected the same coolness and almost hostile disinterest in women that I'd sensed from Tim Hardin. On the other hand, Cat's girlfriend, warm, friendly Rita Coolidge, had chatted with me while Sam and Cat conducted their business.

Those social days were over, and after a few miles around the living room with Cat or the Steve Miller Band singing, "Muh baby's callin' me home . . . ," we'd adjourn to the bedroom rocking chair. Little Adrian Leighton may have looked like the Jones side of the family, but when it came to the fear of missing something, she was a chip off her mother's block, forcing weary eyelids open in mighty battle with the exhaustion weighing them down. I counted my blessings, grateful that disposable diapers had come along not a moment too soon.

My single focus on this daughter—in whose presence all else faded—left little room for Sam, who spent most of his time across town managing his clubs. Although a proud and devoted dad, mostly he kept his distance, leaving the serious one-on-one bonding to mother and child. Utterly connected to her and her alone, I drew away from him to indulge my desire to have her all to myself.

I studied her for hours like I remembered Mom studying me. My entire life until she died, I'd ask what Mom was looking at and she'd say, "Just you," with a look of satisfaction, the way I answer Adrian, who now seems as nonplused as I remember feeling about Mom's peculiar habit back then.

Germaine & the Key of "V"

I'D BECOME ADDICTED to WBAI-FM. In the early 1970s the New York City community station sparkled with radical, innovative programming that included quirky late night shows and Marion Weinstein's weekly *Marion's Cauldron*. Her plain language and jokes, cracked in a high-pitched Bronx accent, made the supernatural seem natural. She was familiar with psychic tools like astrology, the *I Ching*, and Wicca. Since I concurred with every word of her broadcasts, I figured that Sam wouldn't be interested, so I didn't bring them up. He made his disinterest in subjects of concern to me abundantly clear. We were increasingly finding little to say to each other.

Late one night, with Adrian finally asleep in her crib in the living room, we lay in bed and *Electra Rewired* came on the radio. Sam seemed to pay no attention to the late-night feminist call-in show with Nanette Rainone, Ann Snitow, and Liza Cowan, who were interviewing an Australian dynamo named Germaine Greer. Her book *The Female Eunuch* had just been published, and she was saying things about marriage, men, and men and women that I could never have imagined, let alone imagine hearing spoken aloud, anywhere, ever. Everything in our world was geared to support men. Historically, women had been kept out of the mainstream in literature, art, politics, and medicine, business, and trade. We were not respected, our work was not valued, and we weren't either. "Women's work," like child raising and housework, wasn't considered "real" work.

To hear Greer describe women's experience honestly through deep logic and insight made my heart leap and my mind explode into a thousand possible options for myself. Until she spoke the words, her ideas had been unthinkable. The woman was a genius! She damned "conventional political methods" and warned us not to wait for "the revolution" or try to change the world but take a look at our lives as we truly experienced them. In her own words: "Marriage cannot be a job as it has become. Status ought not to be measured for women in terms of attracting and snaring a man. The woman who realizes that she is bound by a million Lilliputian threads in an attitude of impotence and hatred masquerading as tranquility and love has no option but to run away, if she is not to be corrupted and extinguished utterly."

Next to me, Sam studied the sports section of the *New York Post*. From his occasional grunting sounds I knew he was listening, and I was relieved not to have to repeat Germaine's revelations to him. "Well, what did you think?" I asked when it ended. He appeared to ponder my question for a few seconds, then said, "Gobbledy-gook," and turned a page.

His dismissal shook me, but I said nothing and considered the implications. There were options. Change was possible. Mom's lesson sprang immediately to mind and I saw her forefingers tracing a *V*. He had his life, I had mine, and after being aligned for years, our angle had shifted to paths now leading us to worlds apart.

My friend Danny Kalb was playing at the Au GoGo with The Blues Project and I took Adrian in the sling across my chest to see them. Walking homeward on Bleecker Street while she slept, I noticed a small crowd gathered next to a row of motorcycles at the curb. Walking nearer, I could see bikers standing in a semicircle, their attention fixed on a dark-haired woman who looked to be holding court. Closer inspection revealed none other than Germaine Greer herself, clearly running the scene and having a fine time doing it.

I knew it was her because she was wearing the same outfit she'd worn the evening before on *The Tonight Show* that Sam and I had watched together in bed. Noting his grunt each time she scored a point in her attractive Australian accent, I knew better than to ask his opinion. Germaine had held her own with Johnny and was doing the same with the motorcycle gang. In the flesh she looked just the way she had on TV, but more stunning.

Speaking was difficult, and I stepped back to catch my breath. Taking a lung full of air, I approached cautiously. "Excuse me, but are you Germaine Greer?" She turned around and lit up the block with a toothy smile. "Yes, I am," she answered and we shook hands. My mind froze, and the only thing I could think to say was a hearty, "Right on!" with an upraised fist. Her smile widened and she punched the air back at me in sisterhood.

I floated over to the East Side, wishing I'd had my copy of *The Female Eunuch* with me for her to sign. But no matter. We'd made eye contact, and she'd already changed my life. Anticipating his dismissive grunt, I didn't tell Sam.

While he labored to keep his business afloat, I tended our infant. Strung across my back in one sling, or across my chest in another, Adrian's weight was negligible. She was good company and kept me warm in the chill weather. The bald, perfect little head housed a determined mind of her own, and over the months my formerly passive infant was turning into a serious force with which to reckon. According to the Chinese, energies of Dog (her) and Dragon (me) do not mix easily. Sure enough, as compliant infancy gave way to more demanding babyhood, conflicts became more overt. Greer had introduced possibilities less and less possible for me, a contrast generating more and more frustration. In due course, obsession with Adrian narrowed my universe to the point where alienation from both husband and child left me feeling lonely, bored, and increasingly stuck.

Days when exhaustion flattened me and no spark could be located, I'd stand at the changing table Adrian would soon outgrow. Lost in despair, I'd regard the slate sky of late winter outside the window. In my mind I looked up from the bottom of the deep pit I had dug for myself. Layers of cobwebs stretched between me and a tiny, pale circle of daylight far above me, and I'd think, *I'll never get out of this.* During those times it took all I had to put one foot in front of the other.

"Shinin' Thru"

THROUGH IT ALL I was consulting my chart, throwing my *I Ching* coins, studying my palms, analyzing my handwriting, and looking up numerology and dream interpretations. Despite all my efforts, I still hadn't uncovered the secrets of the universe, nor had I answered my age-old question. Yet, in my songs, a serene mysticism began infiltrating the political cynicism of my past. I'd have preferred making pithy political statements but couldn't work out how to avoid repeating myself or sounding trite.

Without forgetting what I knew about injustice, class struggle or the corporate military-industrial-congressional complex, I now turned toward spiritual allegory: "Every seed that you shall sow / You know that it will bloom / And every deed you do will be known / Take care, the love that you bear / For all is returned to the maker. . . ."

Despite having been cautioned against overuse of the *I Ching*, I had been throwing the coins one night, reading and re-reading hexagrams until my head swam and words lost their meaning. I closed the book, picked up my guitar, and began noodling with variations of unresolved intervals based on the E7 chord. After working them into a loping beat, the words, "Put the book back for a while" came to me in a perfect rhythmic fit. To Americans, "The Book" generally means "The Bible," and I figured that people would assume I was writing about Jesus, so I decided to go with the flow:

When the Carpenter came by
He nailed a picture there for everyone to share
He lived and died and tried to help us find
The light that's shinin' thru' all the time. . . .

It was up to me to find my own light and quit trying to please others. I also had to revisit Cynthia Gooding's knockout question. A decade after she asked, I still hadn't decided "what kind of woman" I was. At least now I had Lynn and my weekly CR group meetings to help locate myself. If there was an answer to Cynthia's question, these women could help me find it.

For one thing, my priorities needed re-ordering. What was me and what wasn't? What made me happy? Unhappy? What habits or perspectives felt genuine and which of my familiar ways and beliefs could I give up? Distinguishing my reality from propaganda was hard work, and there was no telling what would be left of me when the phony, man-pleasing attributes were gone. Letting the eyelash curler and bra go had been a snap compared to separating my point of view from a lifetime of cultural programming.

In the attempt to sort myself out, my song "Fantasy Girl" became a trash bin for male-centered female self-images I managed to root out over the eighteen months it took to write. My experience with the fictions of self-absorbed males dovetailed brilliantly with a page of Nancy's birthday book in which a "Fantasy-girl" cartoon depicts the ultimate in glamour and femininity. "L'Oreal ash golden blonde" is scrawled in a triangle to one side of her big hair, and "Lots of body by sun-up" on the other. Arrows for "Smudge eyeliner" point to smoldering, heavily lashed eyes. Leading downward, they dare the beholder to note the two tiny stars pinpointing "rouge tint nipples—plum mauve."

Opening with, "Here she is, and made to order / Spicy and clean and sugar and smiles / She'll caress you and nestle your feathers in style," my "Fantasy Girl" takes the facade apart, topping it off with, "She's the Kewpie doll you've never seen / An Amazon, a Gypsy queen, and boy does she know you! / She's seein' right through the boo, boo bee doo!"

I was also writing reveries in the romantic key of D, with the low E string tuned down for extra depth and resonance like everyone used for "Hangman, Slack Your Rope," "Green Green Rocky Road," and "Old Blue." The shadow of the future beckoned in "Conjugations of Gravity," with "Sweet, sweeter, sweetest love / I just can't keep myself from you . . ." I surrendered to fate, sensing that something very exciting and very good awaited just around a bend.

The fall weather snapped and fired up the trees with color. My heart leapt at the lustrous yellow shot through with scarlet. As Lynn and I kicked our way through leaf piles spilling over curbstones, lonely walks on Florida beaches seemed a universe away. Her sharp eye for incongruity and my mordant world view kept us hooting and cackling the way Joan and I laughed our way through our sophomore year at Tyler. My sister-in-law's marriage was in worse shape than mine. Like me and Sam, she and John were sharing a home and going through the motions while living virtually separate lives.

My sister-in-law and I entertained and commiserated with each other through that winter of 1971, which passed uneventfully, and in June she rented a big old farmhouse in Vermont. There was plenty of extra room and she invited Adrian and me for the summer. The city heat would weigh heavily in hot weather, and in the days before the pooper-scooper law, the city stank to high heaven. Vermont would be healthier, Sam agreed enthusiastically, and my heart buoyed up.

The week before I left, I tuned into *Electra Rewired* on the radio. Liza Cowan, now the sole host, complained that all the new songs she was hearing were written and sung by men. She invited female songwriters to contact her, so I called and introduced myself, saying that I'd be out of town for the summer. She said to ring her when I got back to the city.

Vermont

NESTLED IN THE center of northern Vermont, Hardwick lies five hours northeast of New York. Except for a handful of weekends, business would keep the husbands in the city all summer, a comforting thought as I set off toward my future, John driving and Adrian sleeping on my lap.

A few miles up a dirt road outside of town we pulled into a driveway leading to the weathered building where the summer's pastoral would unfold, and where Lynn, J. K., and Janie awaited us. True, the house was funky and falling down, impossible to keep clean, and walking in certain rooms upstairs was risky, but the safe parts were airy and functional. A fireplace in a brick wall of the large, dark, low-ceilinged kitchen would take the chill off cool, sometimes freezing summer nights.

Lynn led me to the southwest corner bedroom on the first floor that Adrian and I would share, and my heart soared at the first step inside. Vitality seemed to swirl through the floorboards, a magic spell exhaled from the ground. Long windows offered up two sweeping views of meadow and mountain. A single chest of drawers and double mattress on the floor were all the furnishings I'd ever need to lift my spirits here, where I felt anchored yet transported, vibrating along with the organic world.

Tranquility reigned that summer, a world away from the grit and grind wearing me down in the city. When the sun set and the birds' evening songs floated up from the field, I'd lie on the mattress and lean back on the pillows with Adrian at my breast. Out the window, color streaked through the darkening sky to silhouette the black mountaintop. Crisp mountain air flowed through the house, carrying regular whiffs of Lynn's freshly baked bread.

Each morning began with the cackle of a rooster, the feel of a fat, happy baby at my side, and, through the window, a pastoral vision lit by the glow of the rising sun. Our garden yielded fresh, abundant tomatoes for sandwiches and peas for snacks, zucchini for bread, and black raspberries for pies. Chocolate fudge didn't get any better than the heaping trays displayed on the big round oak kitchen table. Harvesting vegetables, collecting and splitting wood, sharing household tasks felt more like unfamiliar luxuries than chores. In return for keeping things orderly in the crumbly old house, my reward was beautifully prepared meals, breads, and treats. Adrian ate what we did, but her favorite, like mine, was yogurt. She crawled and practiced making sounds. Her major value to Lynn's kids was entertainment. A friend, Sharon, visited with her young boys, who loved watching Adrian eat dirt while she continued, oblivious to the children hooting and falling down with laughter around her.

Julie visited and showed us yoga exercises. I had to laugh when Adrian crawled over me during "The Plough," lowering her little milk-nose down to mine. She was a handful, now starting to walk, and my sanity was saved by Lynn's adult company and the gift of uninterrupted bits of time during the day in which to think, practice guitar and work on songs. Deep contentment inspired "Caledonia County," written in the clean, simple key of C. "In the country life, I lie on my back / And stack up the simple fruits of living . . . and the world appears to clear up the dismal ghosts of the city, like a sister, whisper / Come now you'll be / Home in the country with me." From the refrain, the phrase "like a sister" signified the abundance, creativity, and wholeness surrounding me that summer.

Unconsciously voicing a common vision that was dawning for legions of females at that time, "Caledonia County" described women living together, simply and in harmony with the earth. On a weekend when the husbands visited,

Sam praised my new piece, likening it to a new James Taylor song he'd heard. As always, his encouragement was welcomed, a rare connection between the different universes in which we each lived and traveled.

On June 22, 1971, the FBI decided that, *"In view of the fact that HOOD no longer meets the SI* [Security Index] *criteria, it is the recommendation of the NY Division that she be removed from the SI . . . instant case will be closed and HOOD will be placed on the RI* [Reserve Index] *of the NYO* [New York Field Office]," and reviewed on "10-17-80" and "6/3/91."

A World of Women

FEMINISM SATISFIED MY political hunger, filling the void left when I'd quit the Party ten years earlier. Before feminism came along with a rational analysis, the politics of being a woman had remained invisible. Feminism illuminated everything, revealing that just as I had overlooked and undervalued individual women in my recent past, I had simultaneously disregarded general female creative principles and values of the natural world, the same world men paved over while covering women over with restrictions, expectations, and demands. Having managed to miss the inescapable common sense of feminism in the past, I suddenly became galvanized. Feminist analysis made its own case every day, the evidence popping up everywhere I looked. It explained why I could never have played Major League baseball no matter what my skill, and why the privilege of choosing dance partners belonged to boys alone, as did keeping a steady beat, and how being judged a good painter meant painting "like a man."

The Female Eunuch sat on the floor by my mattress. Germaine Greer's elegant reasoning brought my mind fully alive as it dissected patriarchal beliefs and systems that had kept women in virtual slavery. With so many pictures coming into focus, the world looked newer and more exciting each day. Not since my LSD trip had I been so revved up. Whatever force drove both the green fuse and my red blood had to be female.

Feminism answered the argument I'd had with a sociology instructor at Tyler who claimed that no great art had ever been created by a woman, to which I could only name three female cultural icons while he rattled off scores of men. I remembered the "no-two-chick-singers-in-a-row" rule, and being automatically shut out of full partnership in business. I thought about how the terms "housewife" and "mother," obscured the hardest work I had ever undertaken. I thought about my episiotomy.

And that wasn't all. Less than a month earlier, back in New York, in our effort to sell some songs Sam had set up a meeting with Bonnie Raitt. She was looking for material for her upcoming self-titled album, her first, and she was getting a lot of attention. I loved her work and we thought she might be interested in my bluesier tunes, like "Look No Further," and "And Then Some." Sam was absent when she arrived one day just before dinner. Adrian was at her fussiest, and I never made it through a song. Bonnie left, understandably irritated by the constant interruptions. Later, Sam scolded me for being "unprofessional." How disconnected we had become, I thought but didn't say.

Thanks to the CR group I was able to recognize that and other dirty deals for women, most of which had never before occurred to me. Together we continued from the individual to the universal to uncover how women lost out, spanning the obvious "huMAN" nature being about *man's* nature, and that "MANkind" in fact means *men* and their kind according to the institutional structures and history that obliterated women altogether: the "superstructure" of patriarchy, which twisted everything to men's advantage right down to our so-called "mother tongue."

Feminism made sense of the world and my life, which was more and more centered around women. The key was to use a woman's eye and view the world with a conscious woman's perspective. Without feminism and without each other, we didn't stand a chance. It was increasingly clear that living cooperatively with Lynn doing physical work in a beautiful place over extended time strengthened both mind and body. We were always thinking, talking things out, comparing experiences, laughing at the strange ways of people and oddities of life, exploring ideas, helping each other take care of ourselves and our children. We exulted in companionship and lack of self-consciousness, a sharp contrast to the loneliness haunting both our marriages.

Lynn and I decided to leave our husbands. I had not a single doubt that removing herself from a bad marriage was the best thing Lynn could do for herself, and Lynn never wavered in her support of me separating from her brother. In my mind's eye, a tiny woman appeared in the area of my heart. Newly liberated, her miniature arms waving, she danced and punched air in celebration.

I still loved Sam for his humor and brilliance, for being a truly kind and decent man, a "*mensch*," who had always loved my music and supported my work. But that wasn't the issue. Even at his most empathetic, Sam's understanding of me and my feelings would never approach the blood knowledge carried by a life-long female drawing upon a millennia-long line of female ancestors. A sense of preparing myself for different, somehow spiritual work had begun to come over me. I was, I felt, preparing to be a warrior, feathered breastplate and all, and I knew that it was women's business which Sam could neither participate in nor understand. I didn't understand the force pulling at my heart and soul either, or where it might lead, but there was no resisting it.

In a matter of months my world had been transformed, from the empty days and desperately lonely nights pacing the Florida beach when, despite all evidence to the contrary, I believed myself incapable of surviving without Sam. Looking back it seemed absurd because, in fact, I had supported myself since college. The single difference between the Florida beach and Vermont farmhouse was a support system, and mine came through. Over the phone, Amy, from the group, encouraged me. "You can do it, Alix!" We were in it together.

At the zenith of that Vermont summer, Sam and John arrived for their twice-monthly weekend. The next time, Sam would be driving Adrian and me back to the Lower East Side. I could hardly bear to think about resuming life in the city. Lynn and I agreed we'd tell the guys our decision the night before they left.

Sam walked into the bedroom, and it suddenly looked plain and shabby. A universe yawned between us. Conversation was awkward. We were so disconnected. He stared out the window at the mountain while I sat perfectly still on the mattress where Adrian slept. There was no script and no telling what kind of reaction he would have to splitting up. I'd have to play it by ear and improvise. Sam surprised me by listing the reasons it wasn't working and, as usual, was extremely persuasive, as always. We talked about the distance between us, how our interests and lives no longer fit together. His line of reasoning led exactly to what I had in mind, and just as I'd hoped, he spoke the words and I had only to agree.

"Maybe it would be best if we separated for a while," he said.

"Maybe it would."

Tiny Woman pumped the air with her fist. Of course, this was only the first step, but it had been taken, a line had been crossed. A burden lifted from my shoulders. Silent for a while, we considered what had just happened, the great unknown hanging heavy in the air, mingling with the smoke from our cigarettes. Looking down at our sleeping baby, Sam chuckled, "Look at that little peanut," and started making jokes and telling funny stories that kept me laughing for the rest of the night. If I was to be strong it would be in this room while my gut sense of being on the right track held steady, cheered on by Tiny Woman.

Lynn said I'd do fine, and I believed her, while being increasingly aware that this change would leave me even less financially secure. Yet, I would manage somehow, as I had before. And I'd take care of Adrian too. The next day I called Mom from a pay phone in Hardwick. "What will you do for money?" Her voice was tight with concern. "Will you be all right?" "I'm working on it," I said, and told her not to worry, partly relieved that she did.

And Beyond

If you always do what interests you, at least one person is pleased.

—KATHARINE HEPBURN

SAM DROVE ME and Adrian back to Third Street. It was a sad time for us both and I felt terrible for him. But it had to be. While he moved his things out of the apartment, Adrian and I went to stay with Lynn in New Jersey. Sam's situation was unstable and sporadic. He moved to a cheap hotel, and his life was a shambles, but he forked over as much child support as he could, when he could. He was crazy about Adrian and I encouraged their relationship when he showed up to collect her for the afternoon. She loved going with her entertaining dad to Max's Kansas City, the notorious bar and nightclub where he worked and which Andy Warhol and his crowd were putting on the map.

Determined not to dump my money troubles on Pop, I carefully reviewed my options, the best of which amounted to what Mom had steadfastly refused to accept when it was called "Home Relief." I'd apply for welfare, but only temporarily, until Adrian was old enough for school.

Welfare

THOUSANDS OF WOMEN did it, and I could do it too, so early on a drizzly autumn morning, I stuck Adrian in the sling, bundled us up, grabbed an umbrella, and made my way to the Department of Human Services. Hours before the doors opened, mostly black women and their children waited in line. I went to the end and kept a silent, low profile.

Lifetimes of poverty were written on the faces and bodies shuffling through the welfare office doors when at last they opened. The interior seemed designed to suck the spirit out of those unfortunate enough to land there. IDs and various forms handed in, we slumped on uncomfortable benches to gaze at the clerk behind a desk who ignored the masses awaiting a summons. Adrian mostly slept while I observed bored mothers quieting restless babies and managing older siblings. Compared to them, I had it easy.

Women at the front desks labored in underpaid, overworked, gatekeeper positions at the bottom rung of the bureaucracy. Veterans of the process, they were familiar with the standard tricks and scams. But how many clients had ever been interviewers like me in Miami?

Radiators hissed and children fussed. Monotony and the longing to be elsewhere infused the stagnant air. People rose to their name under watchful eyes monitoring proper order. By four o'clock when I was called, the positive attitude I'd assumed along with my umbrella that morning had evaporated like the rain. I was directed to a cubicle where an angel named Hope waited. Many of the DHS Interviewers, she told me, had once been "clients," as we were dubbed. A fellow New York Jew, a progressive, musician, and thinker, she and I instantly hit it off. Better yet, she cut red tape and bypassed weeks of waiting for final approval. Tears flooded my eyes as I thanked her.

With a rent voucher and food stamps in hand, I walked away from the building knowing that at least for the time being Adrian and I would have a roof over our heads and yogurt on the table.

Why Women Only?

THE CR GROUP decided to spend Thanksgiving Day together. No men, only us and our children. *How sad*, I thought, *to have a holiday gathering without men!* However dull, depressing, and senseless it was bound to be, I decided to be a sport and go along with the rest. As it turned out, the evening, fortified by abundant feasting, was lively and frequently hilarious. Shrieks from scampering and crawling kids mingled in the din, and laughter resonated throughout Roseanne's small house in New Jersey. Lacking the usual low-frequency grumbling and demands, the cooperative childcare, cooking, setting out, clearing, and cleaning all proceeded with a light touch. Life with women, I decided, felt altogether agreeable, familiar, and deeply comforting, like coming home.

Louise's tips always seemed to pay off, so when she alerted me to a performance she'd just seen and thought I would like, I took it seriously. A group of six woman had gotten together to write and act out original skits based on their lives. "It's All Right to Be a Woman Theater" was packing them in at the Washington Square Church in the Village. The shows, Louise had cautioned, were for women only. The last rays of sunset splashed gold across blank loft windows as I headed across town with Adrian slung across my chest, wondering about the odd women-only policy. I expected to miss men's presence and the idea seemed untenable.

At the church I handed over the suggested dollar donation and found a seat in the crowded room. All around me, faces beamed and women buzzed, screeched, and hugged one another. This was unlike the picture I had imagined; it felt comfortable and I relaxed immediately. Joyful women swarmed around small groups that broke up and joined the flow and no one minded being jostled. Their excitement was contagious and filled with exciting possibility, like a camp reunion with women I'd never met. Some of the actors were lesbians, Louise had said. More than a few in this crowd surely were, I mused, although it was hard to tell. Senses sharpened and nerve-ends tingling, I closed my eyes and floated on the soothing register of women's voices, relaxing and invigorating, like a spa for hearts and spirits.

Everyone related personally to the scenes dramatized in the "dream plays" and "crankies" where a woman cranked a roll of paper displaying stick figure sequences illustrating narratives that described common experiences like dating, experiencing menstruation, and playing girls' basketball. The entire room laughed, groaned, and sighed together in recognition. In the safety of sisterhood, pretensions and charades appeared thoroughly ridiculous. I was a part of it all, and these women were my people. I walked home on air and floated for days.

Why "women-only"? The evening supplied the answer with an electric intimacy I could see, hear, and feel on every inch of my skin, right through to my core. I knew the heady feeling of unity and sense of shared awareness and purpose, but never before with free, conscious, fun-loving feminist women. I had also experienced an entirely new sense of safety. Normalized on every level, pervasive male violence was, I realized, noticeable only in its absence. That is, in the absence of males.

It was dawning on me that without men in the room, women became superwomen. But the presence of a single male instantly threw every woman I knew, myself included, into a familiar state of guarded tension and reference: a frame of mind in which making him comfortable, pleasing him, and fulfilling his needs took top priority.

One night while Adrian slept, I sprawled on the big brown easy chair, emptied my mind, and picked up my sketchbook, dating the page, "November 10, 1971." Beneath a rough drawing of Adrian's bald head, I printed in caps: "I COMMIT MYSELF TO MYSELF—I DON'T KNOW WHAT IT MEANS—I FEEL DIFFERENT AND I FEEL SADDENED ALMOST—IT'S LIKE BEING COMMITTED TO NOTHING." For a while I sat pondering my interior void and in due course an idea took shape. Except for matters concerning Adrian and basic survival, what would happen if I made decisions based on what made me happy regardless of what others wanted or expected? Without knowing where it might lead, I vowed to follow that path. Then I forgot about it.

It took months before I noticed that men had disappeared from my life, and years before I realized the connection between that development and the vow to please myself. Since separating from Sam, I had dated a man I met at a party, but it was an empty experience and nothing I cared to pursue. My friendship with Danny Kalb quietly faded, and one day the thought came to me that men and my relationships with them had become inconsequential. On the heels of this realization came another: a woman not trying to please others and not caring about what men thought could more easily detect the toxic threads connecting women to men. This X-ray vision required being clearly centered in woman-ness and looking through a "feminist lens," as it would become known.

On a visit with Lynn one afternoon, a neighbor dropped by. Like feminism, the crisp October air invigorated my spirit and sharpened my senses. It blew through the kitchen where we drank coffee and talked girl-talk. As I recall, the subject of most conversations back then consisted of little else besides men, women, men and women, and marriage. When, we wondered, did men get to be in charge of everything, and how had women become so dependent on their goodwill? Men's jobs were simple compared to the hard work of bearing and raising children. Our workday went twenty-four hours nonstop, required dozens of skills to accomplish all sorts of tasks—some in the face of mind-boggling resistance—that exhausted every system and cell of a person's body for little thanks or recognition, let alone pay.

And worst of all was the lack of adult conversation. What man could or would do that for so little? We grabbed the *New York Times* and scanned the staff listing. With the possible exception of one ambiguously named marketing person, they were all men. Hah!

At one point the neighbor asked, "Alix, are you a lesbian?" I thought hard, then heard myself say, "I don't know . . . but deep in my heart I hope I'm a lesbian."

Where before, the sound of "lesbian" had struck me as awkward, harsh, and sharp-edged, I now saw curves and heard strength. Somehow saying the words gave me permission to love women. Naturally, I hoped Lynn would want to be a lesbian too, but she was still living with John and I needed to be true to myself whatever Lynn did or didn't do.

Standing in the center of the darkened living room one night, my guitar in hand and my eyes wide open, a vision took shape. Rows and rows of women's faces looked up at me from an audience composed entirely of women. Nothing like it had ever before entered my mind and the astonishing image soon faded back into the shadows by the crib where Adrian slept.

Besides "Shinin' Thru'," "Every Seed," and "Caledonia County," I had finally completed "Fantasy Girl." It described the self I had shed when I decided to quit trying to please men: "Here she is, and made to order / Spicy and clean and sugar and smiles . . . ." Another, in wistful waltz-time, idealized "My Kind of Girl," specifying who I wanted to become, and that special woman whose path had not yet crossed with mine:

> You're my kind of girl, if you've got a mind to speak of
> You're my kind of girl if you've got to speak your mind . . .
> . . . Time lies inside you, moves as the tides do
> Reflects you and guides you . . . .

Liza

A FULL SEVEN months had passed since Liza Cowan's call for female singer-songwriters to appear on her radio show, so I called her at WBAI and we settled on early December for a guest spot. My new tunes would be showcased on the radio, not in a club scene that no longer drew me. The old Village folk community had changed into something hardened and electrified, and my music no longer fit in there or anywhere else I knew of.

Elektra Rewired opened with Stravinsky, was followed by an eclectic mix from Motown to Moondog, and in the months before I was to go on I didn't miss a show. Besides playing music and posing quirky ruminations or commentaries on the air, sometimes, in the early morning stillness, the liquid rhythm of Liza's voice intoning unintelligible medieval Italian love poetry caressed my senses, transporting me. In addition, she conducted interviews and discussions with friends and family members. Sometimes she booked the witch Marion Weinstein, and the week before my appearance, Liza's guest was her mother. Instantly intrigued by the contrast between the two women's memories and perspectives, I admired Liza's mother's sophistication and frankness and felt oddly acquainted with her. Liza, however, was a complete unknown. In one week she and I would be sitting face-to-face in the same studio with me on the spot.

Then, on the night of Pearl Harbor Day, 1971, with Adrian asleep and the upstairs teen installed for babysitting, I slipped into my second-hand sheepskin coat, gathered my guitar and the folder of new lyrics. Stepping out the door, I was suddenly gripped by nervousness. "It's just energy," I told myself, re-routing my tension away from anxiety toward anticipation.

The WBAI studio was located on an upper floor of a church on East Sixty-second Street. At ten thirty P.M. the street was deserted. I leaned out of the wind into the doorway to look for the buzzer, hair whipping my face. *On such a freezing night would any volunteers be there to ring me in?* After many minutes rocking foot-to-foot, I heard a disembodied voice crackle through the speaker and I was buzzed into a small foyer leading to a long set of narrow stairs.

Applying a tissue to my runny nose, I glanced up to the top of the tall staircase. A beautiful young woman with wild black hair hunkered on her heels and beamed down upon me. Her smile widened between cute dimples and immediately put me at ease. I grinned back at her and climbed up to meet my fate.

The pre-broadcast interview was conducted at a card table in a cramped corridor. Never before had Liza invited a guest unheard. Puzzlement narrowed the shining dark eyes. Chagrined, she confessed to being unfamiliar with my music and apologized for not listening to a tape in the months since we'd first talked. There was no doubt in my mind that my songs would resonate with her. "I can't believe I did that!" she said and explained that putting me on the air would be risky, but my credentials reassured her. I loved that she knew Marion the witch ("Oh, she's one of my best friends!"). She couldn't believe that I knew the legendary Ethel Raim and her group, The Pennywhistlers ("Yeah, I've known her since I was twelve!").

Once we were situated in the studio, the smiles came thick and fast as I sang my songs, even the new ones that only Adrian had heard. She admired them all, saying they were the first songs she was aware of that were specifically by, for, and about women. Here, I realized with a jolt, is a gorgeous, smart woman with compatible interests and tastes.

The next day Liza's mother called her. "What in the world was going on with you two?" she wanted to know. "You sounded like a mutual admiration society!" For my part, aside from several lengthy gaps when we grinned stupidly at each other across the microphones, I thought we'd done a fine show.

Radio Daze

THAT WEEK, LIZA accompanied Adrian and me to nearby Tompkins Square Park playground and invited us to visit her uptown. We could take Adrian to Central Park, an easy walk from the Park Avenue apartment she shared with her best friend, Penny.

What awaited us on the crisp December day, I couldn't imagine. After all my years in Manhattan, this was the first time I had known anyone who lived on the Upper East Side. Beautiful and smart, but was Liza also rich? A bright sun beamed down. Smiling doormen inquired politely how I was as if it really mattered to them. Having help with the stroller was a strange but agreeable experience, I decided, as the elevator man delivered us to the correct floor. Liza's housemate opened the door and ushered us in. Plainspoken and intelligent, Penny held strong opinions and I liked her right away. Both women were sound, articulate thinkers and ardent feminists, well read in the current literature. Liza explained that they regularly examined the issues together. "Penny and I formed our own consciousness-raising group. Who says you need a lot of people to raise consciousness?"

When not at WBAI with Liza, I listened in, relishing the offbeat music, the lefty politics, and especially the improvised, cutting-edge, late-night programs. In those early days of 1972, talk show host Bob Fass, "The hippie guru with the whispery bass voice," as Liza noted, dominated WBAI's insomniac slot. But thanks to no-nonsense station feminists, *Elektra Rewired* held its weekly midnight spot. On Monday nights, Liza covered far wider, more offbeat terrain than did Bob.

A few good guys worked at the station in addition to Steve Post, whom Liza was dating, but, to Liza and me, men increasingly resembled cardboard facades posturing in two dimensions. Nonetheless, Liza and I continued to feign interest in them and go through the motions. With our friend Marion, we even devoted one entire show to a discussion of how feminists could date men. It seemed like a legitimate topic and we encouraged listeners who called to talk on the air. Marion didn't have to fake enthusiasm or pretend to believe that men were worth women's time, but much eye-rolling passed between Liza and me in what would be our farewell to heterosexuality.

The path ahead was intriguing but not clear. The romance I craved was inconceivable and my experience with Nancy offered no guidance. Lynn or Liza? I couldn't imagine what it was I wanted from or with either. My feelings for each woman were strong yet different, and for some reason I felt I had to choose. Scorpio waters run deep and slow, and to fiery Leontine dispositions such as mine, my sister-in-law seemed hopelessly stuck. On the other hand, Liza was independent, lived in the city, and seemed as eager as I to pursue whatever was drawing us together.

Pre-Lesbian Tension

PERCOLATING JUST BELOW consciousness was a sense that lesbians were critical to Women's Liberation, but what was it like to be a lesbian? Wouldn't it be great if a lesbian spoke to our CR group? No one seemed to care as much as I, but, as I told them enthusiastically, we had a chance to find out first-hand. From real lesbians. Supportive yet somehow distant, the group agreed to invite one. What lesbian secrets would be revealed, and why didn't anyone else share my curiosity?

Louise put me in touch with a local couple named Fran Winant and Judy Grepperd, and on the designated evening, a half dozen of the most self-confident in the group showed up at my apartment. Rather than life histories, they said, we would hear about their daily lives as lesbians. The more demure Judy spoke less often than her partner, whose bright intelligence beamed from behind round, wire-framed glasses. "We've never done this before," Fran began after introductions. Caught in a peculiar tension, I hoped that the other women, especially my sister-in-law, would like this pleasant, unassuming duo. At the same time, I was poised to dismiss them in particular and lesbianism in general. On the spot. For any reason.

Strangely, the more we learned about these working-class women, the less they resembled my stereotyped picture generated by the diesel Dykes and daunting butches of Rusty's in Philly. It turned out that their lives were very much like ours. "We have good times and bad, we work and socialize, cook, eat, clean up, and sleep. The difference is that we love women and prioritize them, which changes everything. We share our lives in ways that heteros don't, and maybe can't."

Questions followed, including the predictable, "Don't you miss men?" To which Fran and Judy shot knowing looks at each other. "Nope, we never think about 'em. All men do for us is piss us off when they hurt women." Great sex, they assured us, was possible without a penis. I was skeptical of that but beginning to feel comfortable with the erotic power certain women evoked in me. Historically, isolation and silence had kept women down, but that was all changing. "Before feminism, the only places we could get together were the bars and private homes," they explained. "Lesbians were too scared to come out publicly, but now we have a community." It seemed that tons of lesbian feminists lived in New York and more were coming out every day.

Later, I read Fran's *Dyke Jacket*, and *Eat Rice, Have Faith in Women*, elated that this gifted, modest young poet had brightened my apartment with her gentle smile and twinkling eyes. She and Judy belonged to a loosely knit tribe of fierce and brilliant New York City groundbreakers. Through Louise, I came to know some of the fabled names on her distinguished list of ex-lovers, and over the years I was privileged to meet the dyke visionary and architect Phyllis Birkby, writer Bertha Harris, and cultural anthropologist Esther Newton. These extraordinary women and their peers had declared war on patriarchy and its suffocating institutions, but I had yet to plug into their creative, female-centered powerhouse.

Louise invited me to a party at her East Village studio on Cooper Square. The expansive space was filled with smoking, drinking, flirting, and laughing lesbians including Phyllis and Bertha. My old chum stood, flanked by two exes who kidded each another over Louise's head, "I remember when you stole her away from me!" Arms around each other's waists, the three burst into hilarious laughter. What a change from the drunken pitched battles I'd heard of at Rusty's a decade earlier. This, I decided, was who I should be.

Aside from Adrian and her latest trials and accomplishments like having fits and learning to walk and talk, I recall thinking and talking about little else besides feminism, patriarchy, men, women, and lesbianism. Back then it was possible to contain, on a single bookshelf, every piece of current feminist literature, the ferocious, innovative, uncompromising theory from cutting-edge thinkers and writers. New York City's Radicalesbian manifesto of the time, *The Woman-Identified Woman*, began with the question: "What is a lesbian?" The anonymous pamphlet explained that: "A lesbian is the rage of all women condensed to the point of explosion," which didn't answer the question, but sounded fine to me.

Up, Up, and Away

SWIFTLY APPROACHING OUR own point of explosion, Liza and I were seeing more and more of each other. Many times a day I thought about her and wished we were together. What did this mean? Even as we slowly overcame our timidity and our comfort with each other increased, I still had no idea. I didn't dare. One night she casually mentioned "sexual tension" between us and took my breath away. Yes, I agreed dumbly, there did seem to be something there.

That week, Mom agreed to take Adrian overnight for Liza's show and I arrived at the station carrying the tape of a new song. It was "The Woman in Your Life Is You," which had come to me courtesy of the same spirit that had brought me every good thing in my life. Excited and curious about what the wee hours held for us, after the show Liza and I grabbed a cab back to her apartment.

At her apartment I felt ". . . like a fool in a comedy of errors . . . My parts (didn't) seem to relate to me or each other," as I described the scene later, how we lay down, side by side in her bed, and how, suspended in unfamiliar territory, I felt small and insignificant beside her. We didn't fit, and it was impossible to imagine how we ever would. I put my arm under her neck and she lay her head on it. I wondered, *Now what?* I was supposed to know how this was supposed to go but the only thing I knew for sure was that no heat was being generated. Our kiss, lip on lip, was nothing spectacular. Eventually, feeling self-conscious, I put on my shoes and shuffled to the living room. On my way out I muttered, "I guess that was premature."

"No it wasn't!" Her voice bounded out from the doorway of her room, "Guilty of premature lying in bed together!" I was confused, I explained. There were no floods of recognition. Our bodies and our mouths had revealed only what we already knew about each other.

"What did you expect, divine inspiration?" she said at the elevator (I had).

She drove me home. I talked all the way and she hardly said anything. When we parted, she said, "Don't worry about my not talking." I said, "Don't worry about my talking."

Because she already had an intro for *Elektra Rewired*, Liza used "The Woman in Your Life Is You" as her outro, playing it to sign off each Monday morning at two A.M.

The woman in your life will do what she will do
To comfort you and calm you down, and let you rest, now
The woman in your life she can rest so easily
She knows everything you do because the woman in your life is you

Marion introduced Liza to a remarkable, seven-foot-tall gay astrologer who helped me focus on my future. Cameron turned out to be a kindly, gentle giant with Southern charm. Marion sang his praises, saying that astrology was for him a powerful psychic channel and that he was terrifically accurate. "You could be happy either with men or with women," he said after studying my chart, "but it looks like you would probably be happier with women." *Okay*, I thought. Looking deep into my eyes he declared that this week would be the most crucial turning point of my life. It felt like that to me too. He searched his ephemeris. "Oh, you have a magnificent Venus square Venus going exact this Thursday," he said, his voice rising. "It's *won*-derful." He smiled happily at me, unaware of the date Liza and I had made for that Thursday, Valentine's Day, three days hence. Everything would go smoothly the next time Liza and I lay down together.

I'd known that when she surprised me by calling for another date. Relieved that the disaster of the previous week had not driven us irreparably apart, I could relax and we'd try again. The signs were right, the old confidence kicked in, and this time we fit together perfectly. Somehow, we knew just what to do. Although I hadn't really known what I'd been after, this was the destination I had been seeking ever since Jane Powell sang "It's a Most Unusual Day." Sex with men could be fun, and even exciting, but women were a multidimensional universe apart. Women made me happy and life among them felt right. With women I was free to be my entire self, no holding back what I hadn't even realized was being withheld. Every cell in my body egged me on. And in her final appearance, Tiny Woman danced for joy.

I had been born and raised in the heart of cultural/political activism and I'd been pulled into the heat of fundamental change. Needing to help fix what was wrong with the world now meshed with my vow to take responsibility for my own happiness. Again I found myself at the right juncture at the right time, in perfect alignment with the flow of consciousness and the evolutionary forces of history. The world appeared new, born again with women in general and lesbians in particular. That much had been confirmed by Cameron's reading.

Liza slept, her arm circling my shoulders. I filled my lungs with her exhaled breath, sweeter than fresh air on a sunlit country morning. Destiny would direct us through many adventures in unimaginable worlds of lesbian-feminist community and culture; a universe newly hatched, like me, and big enough for more stories than I could ever have fancied when I was just a girl.

EPILOGUE

In the fall of 1971, when I stood in my Lower East Side apartment envisioning row upon row of female faces looking up at me from an audience of women, such a reality seemed impossible. That my personal identity would connect me to my audience at a profound level was equally far-fetched, yet less than five years later it had all come about, and has lasted to the present day.

With Liza's initial and crucial support, I managed to launch my new career as a lesbian folk singer—a new cultural category that a few other women and I were creating by performing the first concerts exclusively by and for women for two dollars a ticket ("more if you can, less if you can't"), coast to coast. Even early on, in large part thanks to Liza, I was able to earn a marginally adequate living by producing and selling myself and my music.

At the start of my career in women's music I met Kay Gardner, a master student of renowned flutist Jean-Pierre Rampal. We formed a duo, and then found a lesbian willing to learn to play bass. Our engineer and third producer, Marilyn Riese, was located through Liza's radio contacts. The title of our album, *Lavender Jane Loves Women*, honored Jane Powell for obvious reasons, and Jane Alpert for her *Ms. Magazine* article exposing male chauvinism on the left.

My age was exactly 33 1/3 when *Lavender Jane Loves Women* burst onto the burgeoning women's community as the first lesbian record album of all time produced entirely by women. Particularly vivid in my memory is a late fall afternoon in 1973, sitting on the living room sofa holding my finished cover drawing (a sideways heart partly bisected by a horizontal vulva) thinking, "This record will let lesbians all over the world know that they are not alone." And that is exactly what happened. What I didn't know was that the golden age of Women's Music would last for more than twenty years and into the twenty-first century entertaining, educating, and inspiring women throughout the United States, Europe, and around the planet.

Much of my life since 1973 has been documented in song, including my relationship and breakup with Liza, about which I wrote "Separation '78." I continued to clarify my thinking through writing song lyrics until 1990 when songwriting lost interest for me—with one exception, "Earthday 2000," which I wrote for Adrian's wedding.

The phenomenon of women's music blossomed out of the lesbian-feminist movement, along with lesbian publishing and art, creating a rich subculture that defined and sustained an entire generation of women. Before we actually built it, no one could have imagined a world that was safe for characters like Snow White and Rose Red, teenagers like Mickey and Lorraine, or women like Louise, Mike, and me. For those who made, listened to, and supported it, the music was the heart of this new world, and I threw myself into my role as one of the architects of women's music in the late 1970s and '80s. By then, hundreds of lesbians were busily earning their daily tofu in the women's music business— entertaining, producing, booking, publicizing, managing, stage managing, and working lights and sound for live concerts, festivals, and conferences. We engineered, promoted, and distributed records, wrote articles and interviews for the national and local lesbian and women's press, deejayed radio programs, and hosted women on the air.

Once more in sync with history, I found myself working with a host of remarkable women to build a community based on our self-determined best interests to further our well-being. No wonderland could have held more promise for someone whose lifelong essence rested upon being original, unconventional, and radical. To this veteran political warrior, musician, and lyricist advancing an analysis and an agenda, the chance to help create an international lesbian-feminist culture appeared very much like utopia, and in most respects, my experience lived up to my expectations. And then some.

Professional singing, performing, and songwriting skills in hand, I was well prepared to contribute to the groundbreaking political and cultural work of my feminist generation. My payoff was a loyal constituency of peers who appreciated my music enough to shell out money to listen to it, and still do. They make me feel like a star by stopping me for an autograph or a hug, inviting me to their towns, producing personal appearances, and putting me up in their homes.

File folders stored in a cabinet in my back room and at the Schlesinger Archive at Harvard University contain letters thanking me for my work. They tell me how a song, talk, or article has made their lives better, which makes me feel good about my own life. In addition to turning up at my shows, lectures, workshops, panels, readings, keynotes, vocal workouts, potlucks, and a variety of gatherings at which I've appeared, lesbians have supplied me with countless

great laughs, a few lovers and as many breakups both good and bad, many brilliant friends, colleagues, and particular beloved comrades. Most important, like Mom and Pop before them, all these people have allowed and encouraged the creative and personal freedom to be genuinely myself, an attribute far too many communities lack.

On the other hand, the astonishing number and diversity of those of us who love and prioritize women blew some of my early fantasies apart. The thinking of lesbians turned out to be nowhere near as monolithic as I assumed when this memoir ends, and no expectation proved more off the mark than believing that we would all agree with one another (and, of course, that everyone would agree with *me*). And even when personally agreeing with me, one musician on each of my first three albums felt obliged to hide behind a pseudonym because writing and speaking (some of) what was on my mind made me too controversial a figure for them to associate with.

In fact, steadfast commitment and loyalty to women and women-only space has gotten me picketed, boycotted, trashed, and blacklisted by lesbians. Uncharacteristic as they have been, these instances, although hurtful to my feelings and pocketbook, provided excellent song material ("My Lesbian Wars"). They are also the exception that proves the rule of ongoing, resolute support and sustenance from my community.

My folk music career lasted about a decade and I worked over twice that long in women's music, but the parallels are clear. In both instances I was privileged to work, play, and form friendships with the very best in my field. The second time around, instead of Bob Dylan, Bonnie Raitt, and Bill Cosby, it was Melissa Etheridge, Bernice and Toshi Reagan, Holly Near, Linda Tillery, Vicki Randle, Deuce, Karen Williams, Kate Clinton, The Topp Twins, and plenty of other splendid performers too numerous for this list.

My career in women's music sprang from the soil of J. S. Bach, The Red Army Chorus, Louis Armstrong and Broadway shows, with plenty of help from Pete, Woody, and countless old folkies. It has conferred a life rich, challenging, and satisfying beyond my wildest dreams.

ACKNOWLEDGMENTS

In 1993, writer Kay Hagen upgraded and generously passed on to me her old word processor on which this volume was initiated, so I begin my acknowledgments with her. In the same year, it was my good fortune that lesbian novelist Maureen Brady conducted the eight-week women's writing workshop in Woodstock that set me firmly on my book writing path. After the series ended, we continued to meet through several decades and incarnations, during which Tana Miller, Jo Salas, Evelyn Schneider, Kappa Waugh, Lori Wilner, Jan Zlotnik Schmidt, Leclanch Durand, Debra Moscowitz, and Laura Kaplan helped me find and get to my point(s) and took my work seriously. I am especially indebted to them for wise criticisms and knowledgeable guidance through the years, not to mention warm friendships and healthful, satisfying refreshments.

Over the years, I have pondered many a good story and shared many a great laugh with Sarah Schulman, fearless thinker, uncanny observer, standout writer, and repository of wide expertise. I will be eternally grateful to her for staying with this project, showing me the ropes, explaining what a "trope" is, and cheering me on. Deep appreciation also goes to Gail Slotwinski for her long standing friendship and counsel, and my dear friends, Suzanne Bellamy, Susan Wiseheart, and Lynn Hood Peck who served as readers, along with Janet Mason, and the late, brilliant author and friend Carolyn Hougan. These women encouraged and provided me with smart, no-nonsense feedback, all useful.

Len Chandler generously shared his stories, as did Liza Cowan, Jo Mapes, and Mike Miller, who along with River Lightwomoon, Retts Scauzillo, Boo Price, Joan Kosloff, Patricia Hynes, Dorothy Abbott, and Drs. Linda Barufaldi and Ruth Simkin, encouraged and supported my work for decades.

Many thanks to Kate, Sophie, and JoJo, whose generosity, hospitality, and view of the Hudson River are deeply appreciated, and also to Joanne Sackett and the persevering Woodstock Public Library staff, where Amy Raff cheerfully searched out some pretty obscure information. Kathy Jacobs at the Schlesinger Library of the Radcliffe Institute for Advanced Study at Harvard University has provided ongoing positive interest, which I've also received from Krystyna Colburn, and Chicago writers Achy Obejas and Jorjet Harper, as well as Karen Kurzband Hewitt, Mike Lipsky, and Arthur Lazare, from Mrs. Collin's class.

Heaps and mobs of thanks to my publisher, Don Weise, for his creative input, enthusiasm, and vision. It has been a pleasure to work with him and his colleagues at Alyson Books, Paul Florez, Chris Van Cleef, and my gifted and helpful copyeditor, Sarah Van Arsdale.

This memoir could and would not have been written without Frances Goldin, literary agent extraordinaire, whom I've known since before my birth and who appears in these pages. Champion of Manhattan's Lower East Side, her activism, generosity, and fierce integrity are legendary. For my entire life, her magnetic force of character has been a model and inspiration, and when this project came along, Fran's faith in me, her high expectations, and tough critiques carried it from inception through the final years of grueling edits. She's smart, observant, good-hearted, and always thinking. No words suffice! The kind cooperation of her partner at the Frances Goldin Literary Agency, Ellen Geiger, and associate Sarah Bridges have made the work flow smoothly in the proper direction.

Heartfelt appreciation goes out to all branches of my family: to the late Sam Hood, who never quit my fan club through good times and bad, who died decades before his time, and whose loss I and many others feel deeply and regularly. I am grateful to Judy Upjohn for her continuing support, to Carl, Pat, Loren, and Allison for their enthusiasm and trust in me, and to my talented, hardworking kid sister Julie, whose memory of our family often bears little resemblance to mine, yet is, no doubt, equally accurate. Thanks to my beautiful "granddog" Emma for her undiminished joy at seeing me, and my incomparable, awe-inspiring grandchildren: Lucca, Marly, and Sorella, as well as their first-rate father Chris Lofaro and "Grandma Nancy" Lofaro, with whom I happily share grandmother duties.

Most important, I thank my smart, kind, remarkable daughter, the light in my eye even before she delivered such delightful kids for us to love. Adrian's abilities and strengths have been evident ever since her age reached the double digits, but how, I wonder, did she get to be such a top-notch mother? As Pop might ask, "Why is a cow?"

SOURCES AND RESOURCES

In writing this memoir I have drawn on the following resources: *Behind Fascist Lines: A Firsthand Account of Guerrilla Warfare During the Spanish Revolution* by A. K. Starinov (Ballantine Books, New York, 2001), which referred to Uncle Alex as "a brave commander of a sabotage group," and Carl Geiser, who noted Alex's execution in *Prisoner of the Good Fight: The Spanish Civil War, 1936-1939* (Lawrence Hill & CO, Westport, CT, 1986). *Double Cross: The Explosive, Inside Story of the Mobster Who Controlled America* by Sam and Chuck Giancana (Warner Books, New York, 1992) illuminated the relationship between J. Edgar Hoover and the mob, united against the Communist-led unions who were organized crime's biggest competitor on the New York City waterfront at the middle of the last century.

Which leads naturally to recognition of the FBI for their parallel narrative of my life from age thirteen to thirty, and the vigilant note-taking which supplied me with ancient addresses and dates, some right, and some not so much.

I am indebted to Tracy Baim, publisher of *Chicago Outlines*, then *Windy City Times*, who, toward the end of the 1990s urged me to write a bi-weekly column and then published several years worth, a dozen of which were derived from a section of this memoir in serial form. Susie Ehrenrich's comprehensive *Freedom Is a Constant Struggle: An Anthology of the Mississippi Civil Rights Movement* (Cultural Center for Social Change, Washington, D.C., 1999) included an earlier version of a section here, and Julia Penelope provided a brilliant and early lesbian voice and, with Susan J. Wolfe, edited *The Coming Out Stories* (Persephone Press, Watertown, MA, 1980), quoted here in part.

Thanks to *Sinister Wisdom*, *Off Our Backs*, *The OLOC Reporter*, *Maize*, *A Country Lesbian Magazine*, *Lesbian Connection*, and all the publications in whose pages my work has appeared; and to the late Christine Burton, founder of *Golden Threads*, and to Joy and Judy, who carried it on and let me read in public from my work in progress, along with dozens of other producers and venues who helped make this volume possible. An additional salute to OLOC, Old Lesbians Organizing for Change, for their support, enthusiasm, and good work on behalf of Old Lesbians like me.

Discography

Lavender Jane Loves Women (1973)
Living with Lesbians (1976)
XXALIX (1980)
These Women/Never Been Better (1986)
Yahoo Australia (1990)
Love & Politics (1992)
Living with Lavender Jane (1997)
Alix Dobkin's Adventures in Women's Music (More Than a Songbook) (1979)

An Incomplete Beginning List for Lesbian Culture Beginners

BOOKS

Eden Built by Eves: The Culture of Women's Music Festivals by Bonnie J. Morris, PhD; Alyson Publications, New York City, NY, 1999

Are You Girls Traveling Alone?: Adventures in Lesbianic Logic by Marilyn Murphy with Irene Weiss; Clothespin Fever Press, Los Angeles, CA, 1991

Lesbomania: Humor, Commentary, and New Evidence That We Are Everywhere by Jorjet Harper; New Victoria Publishers, Inc., Norwich, VT, 1994

Dykes to Watch Out For by Alison Bechdel (every one in the series); Firebrand Books, Ithaca, NY, 1986

FILM

Radical Harmonies: Woodstock meets women's liberation in a film about a movement that exploded the gender barriers in music, produced by Dee Mosbacher and Boden Sandstrom, PhD ; Woman Vision, San Francisco, CA, 2002

MUSIC

Ladyslipper Music, Durham, NC: for a comprehensive listing of women's music (mine included) and women in music & comedy: www.ladyslipper.org

Hot Wire Journal of Women's Music & Culture: www.hotwirejournal.com